D0762296

The Age of the Child

Children in America, 1890–1920

Twayne's History of American Childhood Series

Series Editors
Joseph M. Hawes, University of Memphis
N. Ray Hiner, University of Kansas

The Age of the Child

Children in America, 1890–1920

David I. Macleod

Twayne Publishers
An Imprint of Simon & Schuster Macmillan
New York

Prentice Hall International
London • Mexico City • New Delhi • Singapore • Sydney • Toronto

The Age of the Child: Children in America, 1890–1920
David I. Macleod

Jacket Art: Sophie Acheson, Charles Spencer, and Elizabeth Spencer playing streetcar in their nursery, June 1902. Photograph by Charles Hart Spencer, courtesy of Elizabeth Ranney.

Twayne Publishers
An Imprint of Simon & Schuster Macmillan
1633 Broadway
New York, NY 10019

Library of Congress Cataloging-in-Publication Data

Macleod, David I.
    The age of the child : children in America, 1890–1912 / David
I. Macleod.
        p.   cm.—(Twayne's history of American childhood series)
    Includes bibliographical references and index.
    ISBN 0-8057-4105-4
    1. Children—United States—History. 2. Children—United States—
Social conditions. 3. Child rearing—United States. I. Title.
II. Series.
HQ792.U5M33   1998
305.23′0973—dc21
                                                            97-49321
                                                            CIP

This paper meets the requirements of ANSI/NISO Z3948–1992 (Permanence of Paper).

10 9 8 7 6 5 4 3 2 1

Printed in the United States of America

To Beth

The new model family: Mr. and Mrs. F. D. Eyerley and their daughter, photographed by Annie Sievers Schildhauer, Madison, Wisconsin, 1897. (Courtesy of the State Historical Society of Wisconsin: WHi [X3] 43893)

Contents

Series Editors' Note

The history of children is coming of age. What began in the 1960s as a spontaneous response by some historians to the highly visible and sometimes unsettling effects of the baby boom, has emerged as a vigorous and broad-based inquiry into the lives of American children in all generations. As this series on American Childhood attests, this new field is robust and includes the work of scholars from a variety of disciplines.

Our goal for this series is to introduce this rich and expanding field to academics and to general readers interested in children and their place in history. All of the books provide important insight into the changing shape and character of children's lives in America. Finally, this series demonstrates very clearly that children are and always have been influential historical actors in their own right. Children play an essential role in the American story that this series is designed to illuminate.

The Age of the Child provides a superb, highly readable summary and analysis of the vast literature on children during the critical period in American history from 1890 to 1920. Professor Macleod's concept of "sheltered childhood" as a social construct constitutes an important model for conceptualizing of the origins of modern American childhood. It is noteworthy as well that the book gives appropriate attention to southern and middle-western children, indeed to the majority of American children who lived on farms and small towns before 1920, as well as to the immigrant and urban children who are the focus of most works on children during this period. The author also presents a critical but balanced assessment of the striking efforts of urban, professional reformers to structure the lives of American children. Because so many of our current attitudes and practices affecting children had their origin during this period, readers of this book will gain important background for understanding the current discussion of children and their place in modern society.

Joseph M. Hawes
University of Memphis

N. Ray Hiner
University of Kansas

Preface

No brief account can trace the development of tens of millions of individuals in diverse circumstances across three decades. What this book attempts instead is to describe major constraints and opportunities that confronted large numbers of children at different ages. In broad outline, the book sketches the changing social and cultural ecology of childhood around the turn of the twentieth century. This task demands attention to myriad differentiations by gender, race, ethnicity, social class, region, and place of residence that shaped children's life chances. Besides explaining patterns of birth and death—the ultimate life chances—excursions into the demography of childhood provide a check on which experiences were most typical. Since histories of the progressive era have focused primarily on immigrant children in the urban North, I have given equal attention to the more numerous rural children of the South and Middle West.

Inevitably, the history of childhood tells more of things done *to* and *for* than *by* children. This imbalance is compounded by the fascination of historians with reformers and reforms. During the decades covered by this book, conventionally called the progressive era, schemes proliferated for the benefit of children. Optimists were ready to proclaim theirs the age of the child and the twentieth the century of the child. Without ignoring the hopeful excitement of reformers, I have remained somewhat skeptical and have emphasized the power of established ideas and practices. At the risk of oversimplifying, this book subsumes the possibilities of progressive-era childhood within two ideal types. In the family economy, characteristic of farmers and much of the urban working class, children were integrated as rapidly as possible into family activities and socialized to be helpful and economically productive while still young. Under the sheltered childhood, most characteristic of the urban upper middle class, children were set apart, protected from adult concerns, their activities carefully age graded. Their nurture became an end in itself, with their energies channeled toward self-development rather than immediately useful work. Although social and cultural changes were drawing more and more parents to favor the sheltered childhood, reformers tried to force the pace. Broad programs to improve public health and extend education proved reasonably successful. But insofar as reformers' plans required coercion and imposed restrictions by race, age, gender, and class, they sometimes provoked open resistance and often met with noncompliance. Progressives could and sometimes did restrict certain children's options, but they lacked the resources to compel positive action and had trouble changing existing practices. Rising incomes, declining birthrates, urbanization, increasing demand for education, and growing awareness of the needs of children did more to spread the sheltered childhood and expand young people's opportunities than reformers could do directly.

Acknowledgments

For their invaluable assistance, I want to thank colleagues in the history faculty seminar at Central Michigan University, students in my courses on the history of childhood, and the helpful staff in Document Access (formerly interlibrary loan) at the Central Michigan University Library. Central Michigan University provided a one-semester sabbatical leave and a one-semester research professorship during which I researched and wrote the first half of the book. Joseph Hawes and especially Ray Hiner were patient and supportive editors. For help in securing illustrations, I owe particular thanks to Tom Beck at the Albin O. Kuhn Library of the University of Maryland Baltimore County, Gail Stanislow of the Winterthur Museum, several staff members at the Research Division of the Ford Museum, and Elizabeth Ranney. By their example, Ian and Jamie Macleod encouraged my skepticism about expert opinion and overly broad generalizations concerning children. Beth listened, commented, advised, encouraged, and was just wonderful.

1

Childhood: Settings and Contexts

American children of the 1890s and early 1900s grew up amid massive economic and social changes. Industrialization, migration from countryside to city, rising average incomes, and shrinking family sizes altered the settings of children's lives and created new opportunities for Americans, individually and collectively, to invest resources in childhood.

The ways in which resources flowed through families to children shifted. Most farms and some small businesses operated as family enterprises. Individual family members performed different tasks and sometimes generated separate pools of earnings, but basically the family worked as a unit for subsistence and profit. In the growing industrial and commercial centers, by contrast, workers mainly earned wages *as individuals*. Among the working class, a modified form of family economy persisted, as low-wage workers pooled their earnings. Keeping boarders sometimes generated cash income, but housekeeping and child care mostly stood apart as unpaid women's work. In the family economy, children were closely integrated but subordinate members who generally contributed at a fairly early age—providing labor on the farm and pay packets in town. Among the urban middle class and increasingly within skilled workers' families, a different ideal prevailed: the sheltered childhood. According to this model of parent-child relations, children were radically different from adults, to be separated and protected. In respectable families, the mother would rear the children, the father would provide the income, and the children themselves would play, attend school, and remain fully dependent.

Alarmed by immigrant, working-class children, progressive reformers proposed a host of schemes to foster child welfare. They were particularly troubled by immigrants' attachment to the family economy. In its place, child welfare advocates sought to institute or impose their version of the sheltered childhood, sometimes bolstering but often challenging lower-class parenting. Meanwhile, progressives mostly ignored rural children, especially those outside the South, and tacitly endorsed the farm family economy. Reform concern for farm children arose belatedly, mainly in the 1910s, and proved ineffective. Even urban child welfare, however, mattered less to the lives of children than did the broad changes that were reshaping American society.

Town and Country

These changes came unevenly, creating varied settings for childhood. Through 1920, industrial production concentrated in the mill towns and cities of the northeastern and Great Lakes states. In those states, the countryside had deindustrialized by the 1890s, sharpening the division between town and country. Where crossroads villages had once boasted little shops and mills employing rural young people, only farming and retail services remained. Elsewhere, though, agriculture continued to expand. As farmers poured westward, the U.S. government forced Native Americans onto reservations and then alienated portions of those reservations. Both the number of farms and the acreage farmed more than doubled between 1870 and 1900 and continued to increase—though much more slowly—until 1920. Comprising almost one-third of the country's population, the South remained heavily rural. The small stream of African Americans who left the region permanently would not become a flood until the late 1910s, and even then the majority of African Americans remained on the land as laborers, sharecroppers, and small landholders.[1]

For contemporary social critics, the most striking changes occurred within the mushrooming cities. European immigrants settled disproportionately in urban centers. In the minds of progressive reformers, the crowded city districts settled by these foreigners—"the other half," in Jacob Riis's telling phrase—bred the nation's most pressing social problems. Almost as striking to middle-class opinion was the depopulation of farm communities in the influential Northeast. Describing a run-down New England township, Alvan Sanborn told readers of the *Atlantic Monthly* in 1897 that "as soon as a boy has become able to walk, he has walked away from Dickerman."[2]

Yet one can easily exaggerate the decline of rural and small-town America. Even by the Census Bureau's expansive 1920 definition of "urban" residents—everyone living in an incorporated place that had 2,500 or more inhabitants—urbanites formed a minority of the U.S. population until almost 1920: 35 percent in 1890, 40 percent in 1900, 46 percent in 1910, and 51 percent in 1920. If we adopt a more restrictive definition of city dwellers, such as those in places with 25,000 or more inhabitants, only 36 percent of the population lived in cities as late as 1920. Meanwhile, the proportion of Americans living on farms remained stubbornly large: about 42 percent in

1900 and 30 percent in 1920.[3] No one setting predominated: cities large and small, towns and villages, and the open countryside all were home to large numbers of people.

Shifting Age Ratios and the Distribution of the Youthful Population

One overall trend was clear. Although total U.S. population continued to increase, the *rate* of growth was declining. Mass immigration only partially counterbalanced a falling birthrate. Among whites, annual births per 1,000 population fell from approximately 55 in 1800 to 31 in 1890 and 25 in 1920. White fertility rates (the number of children born to an average woman during her entire span of childbearing years) declined at a similar pace, from 7 in 1800 to 3.9 in 1890 and 3.2 by 1920. The fertility rate of African-American women was still 6.3 from 1890 to 1894 but then plunged to 3.8 from 1915 to 1919.[4] Rural birthrates remained higher than urban ones, but the overall trend was downward.

Declining birthrates wrought a momentous shift in the balance between children and teenagers on the one hand and adults on the other. Early in the nineteenth century, young people clearly outnumbered adults. If we define adults as all people age 20 and older and the young as those 19 and younger, there were 128 white young people for every 100 white adults in 1830. But there were only 79 white young people for every 100 white adults by 1890 and just 66 in 1920. The proportion of young people among African Americans was considerably higher but declined sharply, from approximately 117 for every 100 adults in 1890 to only 86 by 1920.[5] By the progressive era, in short, children and adolescents formed a dramatically smaller share of the population than they had just two or three generations earlier.

Not only did children come to seem more precious as their relative population declined; demographic and economic changes also permitted new strategies for socializing the young. In combination with rising income levels (which will be discussed in more detail later), the relative decline in numbers of children gave adults more breathing space, time, and money per child with which to adopt a less ad hoc approach to rearing children. Both at the level of parenthood and at the level of social policy, declining ratios of children to adults facilitated the devising of more considered strategies for socializing children and teenagers. This increase in resources potentially available per child did not guarantee that adults would actually invest added time or money, but it made such investment more feasible. And it did not determine what strategies adults would pursue. But in regions where ratios were lowest, reformers were nerved to propose ambitious programs. In particular, declining numbers of children relative to adults facilitated extension of the period of dependence, when children remained beholden to adults for life's necessities and had time for education and some play. In a society in which young people outnumbered adults and most families were relatively poor, children would have proved impossibly burdensome unless they contributed economically from a fairly young age. But as numbers of children relative to adults declined, parents were better able to support those children until they were somewhat older. By 1900 a relatively sheltered childhood for preteens was common. Child labor reformers tried to make dependence universal for nonfarm children under age 14. And for the middle class, youth workers and educators tried to extend a sheltered adolescence as far as possible into the teens.

The shift toward relatively fewer children occurred unevenly, reinforcing other forms of differentiation, since the poorest regions had the highest ratios of children to adults and the wealthiest, the lowest. Regional differences diminished only moderately between 1890 and 1920 (see table 1). The Pacific coast, New England, and the Middle Atlantic states had achieved relative prosperity early and a low ratio of young people to adults. By 1920 the heavily industrialized Great Lakes states came to resemble the Northeast, but the South remained much poorer, and its population was still weighted much more heavily toward children.

Table 1.   Age Ratios and Per Capita Income by Regions

Region	Population Age 19 and Younger Per 100 Age 20 and Older		Ratio of Per Capita Income to U.S. Per Capita (=100)	
	1890	1920	1880	1920
New England	58	57	141	124
Middle Atlantic[a]	69	61	141	134
East North Central	80	61	102	108
West North Central	92	68	90	87
South Atlantic	109	88	45	59
East South Central	114	90	51	52
West South Central	120	89	60	72
Mountain	68	72	168	100
Pacific	61	49	204	135
U.S. Total	86	69	100	100

Sources: See note 8.

[a] For age ratios: New York, New Jersey, Pennsylvania; for income: add Delaware, Maryland, District of Columbia.

The proportion of children was much higher outside cities, especially on farms. In 1920, the "urban" population nationwide included only 56 young people for every 100 adults. Villages with fewer than 2,500 residents had 71. And farms still had 95 young people for every 100 age 20 or older.[6]

As we have seen, the heavily rural and southern African-American population had substantially more children relative to adults than did European Americans. Smaller ethnic groups varied. According to the Census Bureau, Native American populations were on average quite young, with 103 people 19 or younger for every 100 older persons in 1900 and 102 children per 100 adults in 1920. But enumeration of Native Americans was extraordinarily imprecise, and reported age ratios varied so widely from tribe to tribe that generalization is almost meaningless. Chinese and Japanese residents of the U.S. had few children living with them. Exclusion laws had made the Chinese community a society of aging men, with only 20 young people for every 100 adults in 1920. Since Japanese men living in the United States were allowed to bring over young brides, by 1920 there were 44 young people, mostly American born, for every 100 Japanese residents 20 and older. Still, these children formed only a tiny portion of the country's youth. Nor were Native American children numerous, since American Indians around 1900 were at the low point of a demographic disaster. The Census Bureau reported a population of approximately 250,000 for 1900, although inclusion of everyone who had at least one Native American grandparent might have raised the total to one million.[7]

Compared with adults, American children were significantly more likely to be southern, rural, and African American or native-born white. In both 1890 and 1920, 36 percent of the population under age 20 lived in the South, but just 28 percent of those 20 and older lived there. In 1920, only 45 percent of the young were urban by census definition, compared with 55 percent of adults. Conversely, 36 percent of young people still lived on farms, but just 26 percent of adults did. In 1890, African Americans comprised 15 percent of the population below age 20 but fewer than 11 percent of adults. By 1920, after large-scale European immigration, African Americans still constituted more than 12 percent of youths but less than 10 percent of adults. Since most immigrants were somewhat older, immigrant children formed only a tiny fraction of the country's young people (4 percent in 1890 and 3 percent in 1920). But the American-born children of European immigrants comprised 21 percent of the population under age 20 in 1890 and 25 percent in 1920. Meanwhile, 57 percent of the young in 1890 and 61 percent in 1920 were native white of native parents, compared with 53 and 51 percent respectively of those 20 and older.[8]

In a limited way, adults who recall childhood during this period as centered in a more rural America are right. To be sure, many progressive-era children grew up in settings where the new demography was reshaping age relations and in which reforms building upon those changes were most effective. But large numbers also lived in rural areas and in the South, where ratios of children to adults remained high and progressive reforms came slowly, if at all. Moreover, as we shall see, children were concentrated in poorer-than-average families—a fact that made children targets of reform concern but also impeded acceptance of the new styles of family life and socialization that middle-class reformers favored.

Incomes, the Family Economy, and the Model Middle-Class Family

On average, Americans were growing more prosperous, accumulating resources essential if parents and reformers were to invest more in children. In 1900 dollars, Gross National Product per capita stood at $203 in 1890, $246 in 1900, $316 in 1910, and $320 in 1920.[9] These average incomes looked large, both by world standards and by those of the American past.

Money was quite unequally distributed, however. Regional differences remained huge, and individual inequality increased. The share of the nation's wealth owned by the richest one percent of Americans rose between 1870 and 1920. Individual incomes were highly unequal by 1900, and inequality in wages grew even more pronounced until 1916, when "the widest gaps in American history" separated "high-paid and low-paid jobs."[10] Wartime inflation effected a dramatic, though temporary, leveling of real wages between 1916 and 1920; but until then the rich, the urban middle class, and skilled workers reaped the main benefits from rising per capita incomes.

Prominent among the beneficiaries were the old middle class of business-people and the expanding new middle class of professionals and white-collar employees. Not all members of the new middle class were highly paid, especially young women teaching and doing clerical work. Nationwide, however, clerical workers employed by manufacturing firms and railroads earned average annual salaries in 1912 of $1,209, roughly twice the average pay of wage workers in those industries. Many of the young male clerks would rise to solidly middle-class incomes—described by observers around 1910 as ranging from $1,000 or $1,200 to $3,600 or $5,000 (about $14,300 or $17,100 to $51,400 or $71,400 in 1991 dollars).[11] Although the comfortable middle class formed only a small minority of the country's households, its example and standards were influential in efforts to reshape childhood.

Despite the general superiority of white-collar salaries, many skilled workers' incomes overlapped the low end of the white-collar range. In their work-related identities, most skilled workers remained working class, but as consumers and parents, increasing numbers behaved as members of the lower middle class.[12] The gulf that appalled contemporaries lay between skilled and unskilled work. Between 1890 and 1909, while contemporary estimates of the poverty line for a family of four rose from $550 to $647, average annual wages in manufacturing increased from $439 to only $518. Any family supported by one unskilled wage earner was poor.[13] And discrimination exacerbated the disadvantage for African Americans and families dependent on female wage earners.

Farm incomes were hard even for farmers to calculate but were consistently low by urban standards—as shown by the steady migration of young people off the land. In the South, the top 2 or 3 percent of planters and farmers lived comfortably. Elsewhere prosperous farmers' incomes reached several thousand dollars. But these were untypical. A 1916 study estimated that "the average farm family makes approximately as much for its labor as the average industrial family," though land ownership and lower living costs gave many farm families an advantage in security. The rural poor were poor indeed. Confined to small parcels of land they could own or rent, half the South's black farmers in 1899 produced less than $250 worth of crops— about $4,100 in 1991 prices. Because they owed a share to the landlord and double-digit interest to the furnishing merchant, many received less than half the value of their output. Black or white, the rural South was a land of small farms and poor people.[14]

Most families still needed more income than one person could produce. Accordingly, the majority of working-class and farm families pooled the labor and/or earnings of more than one family member. This was standard among farmers. Townsfolk with a different model of childhood were sometimes troubled: "Many a time a shudder has passed through the mother heart of me," wrote one townswoman, "at the sight of some little fellow struggling with the handles of a plow, jerking and stumbling over cloddy ground from daylight till dark. Boys 'making a full hand,' 'helping Pa.' " But even foes of child labor mostly tolerated the farm family economy. When not harnessed too closely to a labor-intensive cash crop like cotton, children could work around a fairly long school year.[15]

The urban family economy pooled earnings more than it did labor. With blue-collar workers facing both low pay and frequent unemployment, working-class families needed the security of multiple incomes. Sometimes wives worked for pay outside the home; more often they took in boarders. But the largest income supplement came from children's earnings at outside jobs. Indeed, a widely believed theory—formulated by Seebohm Rowntree in studies of York, England, and repeated for Americans by the social worker Robert Hunter—held that only children's wages could lift many poor families above the poverty line.[16] Though recent historians have emphasized the adaptive strengths of the family economy, to reformers like Hunter it was a desperate makeshift that should be replaced with something closer to the middle-class model.

Immigrant children typically grew up with a powerful ethos of family mutuality and expected as teenagers to give their pay to their parents. And if ideology failed, necessity would prevail, for few boys or girls in their middle teens could earn enough to strike out on their own. Ideally pay packets came home unopened, but because the urban family economy pooled money earned individually, mutuality was less automatic than on the farm. Native-stock children, black or white, attended school longer than immigrants, less often worked in their early teens, and were less likely to turn over their whole pay envelope if they did. Immigrant daughters were especially dutiful, surrendering 95 percent of their pay in New England textile towns around 1920, compared with 83 percent for immigrant sons. Yet consumerism could erode even girls' conscientiousness; in Chicago's Packingtown, working girls sported lavishly trimmed hats as tokens that they too had spending money.[17]

A standard interpretation of the family economy emphasizes patriarchal authority. Rose Cohen recalled that her father beat her when she sulked after he begrudged her a penny. At stake was not just income maximization but also maintenance of ethnic traditions of masculine authority. Italian fathers particularly resisted letting wives or daughters go off alone to work outside the home, though they might hire on in canneries or other places where the family could labor as a unit. Yet the family economy was not pure patriarchy. Most households headed by women also operated as family economies, and many women shared authority in other families. Nor should we overstress the parents' commitment to a family economy, for it was also a response to dire necessity, often under compulsion. Low wages drove Italian mothers to bring their children into canneries to snip beans while they packed. In sharecropping districts, recalled a future NAACP official, "the landlord would not tolerate a tenant who put his children to school in the farming seasons." And South Carolina mill owners were explicit: "We want whole families with at least three workers for the mill in each family."[18]

During the progressive era, this form of family would be contested—more in the urban North than in the South—by a newer model that mandated different economic and gender relations and a different style of child rearing. Child welfare advocates, writes historian Linda Gordon, sought to replace "the old patriarchy . . . with a modern version of male supremacy." Fathers "were to have single-handed responsibility for economic support of their families but little direct participation in family life. Women and children were not to contribute to the family economy, at least not monetarily. Children instead were to spend full time in learning—cognitive lessons from professional teachers, psychological and moral lessons from the full-time attention of a mother." This new model had emerged by the 1830s and gained strength with the expansion of the British-stock middle class. By 1890 it was mandatory for respectable white-collar families, though some small businesses still employed children in the family shop.[19]

Maternal nurture: " 'If Moses supposes his toeses are roses' brings forth peals of laughter."
Anna Noyes and her son Leonard, age four and a half months. (Anna G. Noyes, *How I Kept My Baby Well* [Baltimore: Warwick & York, 1913], 37)

The new model of family life was closely linked to ideals prescribing separate spheres for women and men. Mothers, judged superior in morality, culture, and nurturing love, were to make the home a domestic shelter furnishing emotional support for husband and children, child rearing and character formation, and processing and consumption rather than production of goods. The father, meanwhile, would spend long hours in the manly world of work, earning the salary that supported this domestic nest. Ostensibly neat, this division of labor put heavy demands for role perfection on the loving mother and the good provider. And to complicate matters, by the turn of the century each parent faced demands for domestic competence that overlapped the other's realm. As price inflation replaced the long deflation of the late nineteenth century, wives had to become efficient managers of the family budget. Those with large families and incomes at the low end of the middle-class range were hard pressed. At the same time, suburban fathers faced increasing demands that they come home early enough to play with their children and serve as loving parents during the evening. The closeness of mothers and children created emotional expectations to which many fathers never quite measured up.[20]

By 1900, the new family model was just beginning to spread beyond the native-born middle class. Throughout the progressive era, the middle-class family ideal would remain in conflict with the family economy, which was still solidly entrenched in working-class and farm communities. Too often reformers prescribed the new ideal without recognizing or providing the economic resources needed. And widespread realization of the sheltered childhood they advocated required reduced fertility as well as larger incomes.

Fertility Rates and the Value of Children

As we have seen, overall fertility rates declined between 1890 and 1920. But large differences remained. Urban wives averaged fewer children than rural wives, sometimes markedly so: Between 1905 and 1910, the total fertility rate for African-American farm women was 6.9; for urban black women it was only 2.2. On the whole, higher family incomes were associated with lower fertility. Women with husbands in professional and white-collar occupations began having fewer children, and wives from the older business class soon followed. Skilled workers' wives then lowered their fertility, especially after 1900. Thus a 1910 sampling of northern white women in their early forties found that wives of professionals had borne an average of just 2.1 children, wives of businessmen 2.2, wives of skilled workers 2.8, wives of unskilled workers 3.3, and farm wives 3.8.[21] Immigrant women appeared to have more children than women whose families had lived in America for generations.

Of all the differences in fertility around 1900, none so riveted the attention of northern elites as this: immigrants were outbreeding their self-defined superiors, especially in the Northeast. Theodore Roosevelt charged "the descendants of the Puritans" with "the unpardonable crime" of "race suicide." Meanwhile, Jacob Riis told genteel readers, the children of the tenements were growing up in "swarms. . . . Their very number makes one stand aghast." If one looks beyond the Northeast, as alarmists did not, one finds that in 1900 the fertility of foreign-born women nationwide was less than 5 percent higher than that of women born to native parents—largely because it was substantially below that of native-stock women living in the South. Furthermore, immigrant fertility fell dramatically in the second generation, partly because dutiful daughters often delayed marriage in order to work and help their parents. Thus the grandchildren of immigrants were not about to eclipse other elements in the population. But contemporary alarm centered on the great cities of the North, where children of foreign parentage indeed predominated.[22] As a result, concern about burgeoning immigrant fertility combined with progressive reformers' urban focus to win immigrant children of the cities attention out of all proportion to their share of the country's juvenile population. They became the main objects of progressive-era child reform.

Demographic historians recognize that declining fertility was a broad trend, not just a Yankee failing, as Roosevelt thought. But how and why it took hold are less clear.

Technique is uncertain. Rubber condoms and some pessaries were fairly effective and widely sold by 1900. But other forms of birth control, such as douching, efforts to time intercourse away from fertile periods, and withdrawal, probably played large roles. Though these methods were comparatively ineffective, by combining them with less frequent intercourse, middle-class couples of the 1880s and 1890s were able to achieve the lower birthrates observed by demographers.[23]

But why have fewer children even if parents could? Unlike much of Europe's fertility decline, America's was not triggered by decreasing child mortality making fewer children a safer bet.[24] American child mortality did not decrease until long after fertility began to fall, and mortality rates do not explain group differences in fertility.

Explanation of trends in farm family sizes commonly begins with the observation that just behind the frontier, where birthrates were highest, land was widely available, whereas in long-settled regions, where fertility was lower, land was more expensive. Farmers in long-settled areas who wanted to establish sons on nearby farms had to have fewer children.[25] Unfortunately, this model explains northern patterns but fails to account for continued high fertility across the rural South.

Another interpretation is that smaller families offered women more opportunities. As many women gained more education and developed active associational lives outside the home, large families grew burdensome. Mother's Day, proclaimed by President Wilson in 1914, originated as a regretful daughter's tribute to her mother, who had renounced hopes of college education, married, and borne 11 children. A study of late-nineteenth-century Illinois suggests that Protestant women spaced their childbearing in order to leave time for church and reform activities and to nurture each child more intensively. Going further, the college-educated "new woman" of the 1890s and 1900s commonly remained single, or childless if married, in order to pursue a career.[26]

A model of fertility decline based more directly on the costs of children suggests that when children became a major drain upon the family economy, parents began having fewer. Where children's schooling was brief and they worked at an early age, fertility rates were high; where children contributed less and attended school longer, rates were low. Thus sociologists have argued that African-American farm women had high fertility in 1900 because their children could spend little time in school and commonly worked well before their teens. Their urban counterparts had far fewer children because the children could stay in school longer and even in their teens worked less than rural youths. Urban children, in short, cost more. White farm children had access to more schooling, but they too contributed prolonged labor to the family economy. On the other hand, the term *family economy* may hide gender differences that skewed fertility planning, since farm mothers paid a heavy price in childbearing and care for young children, whereas husbands gained future labor at relatively low personal cost.[27]

In urban settings, high fertility may never have made economic sense. Although some immigrants worked their children in order to buy a house, having more children in anticipation of their pay was probably a miscalculation. Despite children's wages, budgets of reasonably prosperous urban workers' families in 1902 showed that those with fewer children could spend much more per person than larger families. By the 1910s, moreover, jobs for urban children were drying up, and children came under pressure orchestrated by reformers to stay in school.[28] As the costs of city children rose, large families more and more clearly did not pay.

For the history of childhood, a vital question is to what extent smaller families resulted not merely from cost pressures but from the spread of new strategies for child rearing. How many parents were intentionally "trading quantity for quality"? According to historian Mary Ryan, some middle-class parents recognized as early as the 1830s that their sons would need careful socialization if they were to become professionals and white-collar employees. Couples began to limit their family size, concentrating financial and emotional resources on fewer children. With rising prosperity, more urban parents could seek opportunities for their children. Recent studies find by the 1910s a strong inverse relationship between family size and children's education. Mark Stern reports that in Buffalo, New York, "skilled-worker children's high school attendance exploded between 1900 and 1915 at the same time that their parents' fertility tumbled."[29]

By itself, the correlation cannot establish whether parents with fewer children simply took advantage of their lowered costs to keep the children in school or whether they intentionally had fewer in order to invest in education. But the latter strategy was well enough known in 1904 for an ambitious young man from a family of nine to feel aggrieved. Struggling to acquire education, he complained, "I was turned out to shift for myself half-equipped. . . . Had there been only two or three children in the family everything would have been different. I am one of the younger ones and I can truthfully say I'd have been willing to be left out for the general good." Prosperous working-class parents voiced the new strategy. A fireman earning $150 a month said he and his wife thought three enough: "My youngsters are going to have a good time and lots of schooling. They must have book learning to get up in the world." A carpenter's wife wanted her girls raised "so they'll be smart women. . . . I think two well brought up are better than six or seven that have to go to work before they know anything."[30]

Such comments suggest a shift in values that census-based studies cannot capture. According to sociologist Viviana Zelizer, urban Americans gradually abandoned the ideal of the useful child between the 1870s and the 1930s. In its place, the ideal of the "economically 'worthless' but emotionally 'priceless' child," already integral to the new model middle-class family, came to pervade urban culture. Despite high child mortality, middle-class parents of the mid-1800s sentimentalized "the empty crib" and grieved elaborately. By the early 1900s the "middle-class cult of child mourning," financed by burial insurance, had spread to the urban poor—a costly casket, cortege with carriages, and individualized gravestone. Adoptive parents began to scorn the useful teenager in favor of the sentimentally appealing baby. And when the courts, which had long appraised children by their earning power, awarded nominal damages for wrongful deaths of schoolchildren, turn-of-the-century editorialists condemned the affront to the value of "the new sacred child."[31] Though Zelizer draws no demographic conclusions, the implications are apparent: as long as children are useful, parents should have plenty; but once children become *individually* priceless, parents cheapen them by having too many. Paradoxically, a child-centered family meant fewer children.

Originating with the urban middle class, a new model childhood—intensive parental nurture plus prolonged dependency and education—became normative among progressive-era reformers and spread among the upper working class. Not only was the new childhood more feasible with fewer children, but as an ideal it probably influenced parents to curb fertility.

Yet the pace and scope of these changes can be exaggerated, for a large share of American children continued to grow up in relatively large families. Rising rates of childlessness toward 1900 and highly skewed fertility made averages poor indicators of the size of families in which typical children grew up. Among white women who came of childbearing age around 1890, only a little more than two-thirds had two or more children, but those who did have more averaged more than five apiece. Consequently, many children had numerous siblings. Of white children born around 1890, approximately 69 percent were born to mothers who bore five or more children during their lives, and 47 percent were born to mothers who had seven or more. In 1910, despite declining birthrates, about 54 percent of white children were born to mothers who bore five or more children and 31.5 percent to mothers who had seven or more. Even within the middle class, which led the trend toward lower fertility, many children grew up in fairly large families. Thus a 1910 sample of middle-class wives in their forties had borne an average of only 2.2 children. Yet 69 percent of those children were born to mothers who had three or more and 45 percent to mothers who had four or more. Admittedly, these figures overstate the extent to which children had to share parental attention, since the oldest and probably the youngest spent part of their childhood without siblings in the household. Child mortality also reduced average family size—by between one and two children for an average white family of seven born around 1890.[32] Still, the improving survival rate partly counterbalanced declining birthrates and kept family sizes up. Although significant numbers of turn-of-the-century children grew up in families that were by historical standards small, the intense nurture that came with being an only child or one of two or even three was still the privilege of a minority.

Two Parents, One, or None

Children's chances of a secure childhood depended heavily upon the stability of their families. Though the progressive era saw tentative experiments in support for mothers on their own, the risks to children from family disruption remained high.

In 1900, more than 86 percent of U.S. children age 14 and younger lived with two parents. Just under 9 percent lived with one parent, almost three-quarters of those with their mothers. Another 3 percent lived with relatives. Only one child in 200 lived in an institution. Thus most children lived with two parents, but nearly one in seven had some other arrangement. Childhood situations of African-American children varied substantially more than those of European Americans, whose patterns dominated the national averages. Whereas 75 percent of rural black children lived with two parents, only 59 percent of children in the small black population then living in cities did so. Cruelly high death rates among black parents, exacerbated by poverty, a weak urban family economy, and some illegitimacy, led to heavy reliance on stepparents, kin, and the community to help rear African-American children, especially in cities.[33]

Cross-sectional statistics gathered in a single year exaggerate the stability of children's lives, however, by missing changes over the many years of childhood. Census-based studies also obscure the frequency of stepparentage and adoption. These arrangements must have been common, since in 1910 11.5 percent of native-born European American children ages 10 through 14 and 22 percent of African Americans lived apart from their natural mothers. Unlike today, a parent's death posed the greatest threat of separation. Though the chances of both parents dying were low, a white child born in 1900 faced a 24 percent risk of losing one parent before the child reached age 15. The risk was more than half again as high for black children. Family stability improved markedly by 1920, as adult life expectancy rose. Divorces were increasing; perhaps one marriage in 10 contracted in the early 1890s would end in divorce and one in 6 by the later 1910s. But the number of children affected was modest, as about half the couples divorcing were childless. Desertion, "the poor man's divorce," affected more children and certainly plunged more into destitution.[34]

Whatever the family disruption, children faced jarring readjustments. Widowed fathers commonly panicked at managing a household. Traumatized by their mother's death, the children found themselves parceled out among relatives or institutions. Then if the father remarried, further readjustment followed, as he and the stepmother might reclaim the children. If fathers chose to keep their children, the eldest daughter often paid the price, withdrawing from school to take over housekeeping and child rearing until he remarried—or permanently.[35]

Many mothers who raised children alone faced intense poverty. On average, women earned slightly less than half what men did in similar occupations. Difficulties arranging care for their children also forced many to take part-time work or do ill-paid piecework at home. Other income sources were limited. Outside the middle class, life insurance offered little beyond burial money. Hence single mothers depended heavily upon family, friends, and neighbors for supplementary income and child care.[36] And the children commonly had to work as soon as possible.

Both public and private charity were miserly, averaging $18.50 per recipient in 1913. Late-nineteenth-century public relief centered on providing poorhouses, mainly for the elderly. For families living on their own, the main providers were private charities, which sought to deter pauperism and chivy the poor toward self-support. Typically, attention focused on the faults of parents rather than on the needs of children. Deserted wives or unwed mothers were often denied aid unless they sued the fathers, and if the suit failed they got little beyond advice to work. At best, aid was carefully calibrated to the family economy, as witness the first case in a 1913 study of widows: the Charity Organization Society provided "$2 a week (later increased to $3) with extra relief in emergencies; the church gave $1 a week. Mrs. A. took as lodgers her brother and cousin; this, with sewing at home, brought her weekly total up to $6 or $7, exclusive of relief." The story ended happily, with three of the children past age 14 and together earning $24 a week. Not all stories ended so well, however. The next case was a widow with six children who received a similar aid package, took in lodgers, and did office cleaning. But her health gave way "and the children were all placed in an institution." Widowed families had little margin for misfortune, and unwed mothers commonly lost custody to institutions because they could not support their children.[37]

In 1911 women's clubs and the National Congress of Mothers began a campaign to authorize local governments to pay regular pensions to mothers of dependent children. Forty states enacted mothers' pension laws by 1920, and some 46,000 families nationwide, with perhaps 120,000 children, were receiving aid by 1921 to 1922. These represented only a fraction of all poor children, however. With caseworkers screening recipients for moral fitness and approved child-rearing methods, the authorities seldom pensioned deserted, divorced, or single mothers. Pensions were unknown or virtually unfunded in rural counties and the deep South. Even big-city stipends were so meager that many recipients worked part- or full-time, and their older children usually did as well. Like much progressive-era social legislation, state laws typically let local officials decide whether to institute a program and how well to fund it. Women's groups, which could draw on sentiment favoring the new model family to secure state legislation, were less successful in battles for local funding. As a result, many children probably grew up like Irma, whose widowed mother received $11 a month, took in laundry, and baked at home. Irma and her sisters hauled water and delivered washing and baked goods with their wagons. African-American families got even less. Child welfare agencies serving whites commonly underserved or excluded African Americans, and mothers' pensions continued this racist tradition. Beyond kin and neighbors, help for black children came chiefly from separate, precariously funded institutions, frequently supported by black women's clubs and fraternal orders.[38]

The least noticed and yet most common source of outside help was the stepparent. Legal remarriages were fairly common, along with less formal relationships among the poor. A stepfather could markedly boost family income, and remarriage sometimes emboldened a father to reclaim children from their grandparents or the orphanage. Yet stepparentage often created strains. Modern researchers suggest that stepchildren are particularly susceptible to abuse. Some former stepchildren report great generosity: "If [my stepfather] had the last penny he would spend it on us kids." But others recall bitter conflict with stepparents or new siblings. One girl's new stepmother denied the children books and broke the chamber pot, declaring it unsanitary. The children, whose late mother had passed on her fear of the dark, now "had to go out in the dark in the night to go to the toilet. We were scared. Whoever woke up we woke the other guy to go along with us." William Owens remembers battling new and slightly older siblings during his mother's brief second marriage: "I fought, cried, tattled to keep my place and when they called me crybaby or sugar-tit I scratched and clawed anybody in my way."[39] On balance, widespread stepparentage was not conducive to sheltered childhood.

When all else failed, children ended up in orphanages. Despite their name, these institutions typically housed fewer than 20 percent full orphans; the rest had one living parent or were children of impoverished parents and deserted or unwed mothers. Contrary to stereotype, for many children the orphanage was not a permanent residence but rather a way station on a disrupted journey through childhood. The average resident in New York City's Catholic institutions around 1908 stayed less than 18 months, and three-quarters returned to parents or other relatives.[40] Although only a tiny minority of children grew up entirely in orphanages, high turnover meant that several percent of turn-of-the-century children had the shock of being relegated to an institution at some point in their lives.

In the 1890s many large orphanages still ran by the rigid rules of nineteenth-century correctional institutions. Uniformed children marched and ate meals in silence, received limited education, and labored in laundries and workshops. At the Hebrew Orphan Asylum of New York, life was regimented to the point that boys who failed to fall asleep by the count of 300 could be beaten by monitors. Under such stress, roughly one boy in 10 wet his bed each night. Increasingly, reformers attacked large orphanages for regimentation and exploitation. In response, some institutions loosened their rules after 1900. A smaller number tried to simulate rural family life by moving to the country and housing children in group cottages. In addition, the years between 1890 and World War I saw a remarkable flowering of new farm schools and junior republics for delinquent and dependent youths, based on the belief that rural life would redeem city youth. The most famous, William George's George Junior Republic in upstate New York, featured self-government and an economy in which enterprising boys lived in comfort while the improvident ate at the "Beanery" and slept in a garret. Established institutions had less incentive to change, however, and often resisted progressive innovations or accepted them only piecemeal. Arguing that temporary sojourners were unharmed by congregate living, numerous orphanages continued mass methods through the 1910s.[41]

The remedy preferred by leading reformers such as Homer Folks was to place children in foster homes. Since the 1850s, Charles Loring Brace's Children's Aid Society had sent some 2,000 children yearly from New York slums to western farms. But Brace had relied on the family economy, promising that boys and girls would gladly work in exchange for a home. While some loved their new homes, others merely furnished farmers cheap labor. Reformers such as Folks wanted in-state placement with parents who would provide the new-style sheltered childhood. The Children's Home Society urged prospective parents in 1897 not to take a child "for what you can get out of him, but, rather, for what you can put into him." The crusade culminated in a 1909 White House Conference on the Care of Dependent Children, which enunciated a consensus that children should live with their mothers whenever possible. If not, a foster home was next best.[42]

But foster children did not all conveniently become orphans in infancy, when couples most eagerly took them as emotional rather than practical investments. Older children were hard to place except as contributors to the family economy. The Children's Aid Society kept operating past 1920, shifting to younger children and going further south and west, where useful children were still appreciated. Other arrangements still isolated and exploited children. A girl placed in 1917 by Boston's Home for Destitute Catholic Children recalled, "I had no idea where my mother and father and sisters were. . . . Those people (in the foster home) worked me to death and the nuns and social workers didn't believe anything I said." Perhaps it was fortunate that in 1923, 64 percent of "dependent and neglected children under care" still lived in institutions. Indeed, the number of institutionalized children had grown faster than the population, from 61,000 in 1890 to 205,000 in 1923.[43] As often happened, reform ideals had outrun resources.

Food, Clothing, Housing, and Extras: Children's Standards of Living

"[We] children were well fed, poorly clothed, and poorly housed," recalled Dr. Hildrus Poindexter, summing up his childhood on tenant farms in Tennessee. Similar priorities shaped most children's living standards. Food took primacy, typically consuming half a working-class family's budget and more among the poor. Clothes and housing came next. Extras depended on the family's size and income; only among the middle and upper classes did such further expenditures loom large.[44]

Historians have recently discerned a major shift between 1880 and 1930 from a producer to a consumer culture, as department stores, mail-order houses, and mass advertising made consumption "a hegemonic 'way of seeing,' " offering "therapeutic release" and "self-realization" for a price.[45] In the most literal sense, prolonged dependency was making more children become consumers rather than producers. But insofar as the new consumer ethic mandated avid pursuit of self-fulfillment through consumption of mass-marketed goods and services, the evidence is mixed. While children's socialization to consumerism increased between 1890 and 1920, for most, the ability to participate actively remained limited.

Though children seldom lacked calories to the point of starvation, class differences shaped their diets. The daughter of a Pittsburgh executive, Ethel Spencer, described a bounteous kitchen: "steaks of incredible thickness and juiciness, for breakfast as well as for dinner in our early years; a whole school of jack salmon, crisp and succulent, on Sunday mornings." Families lower in the middle class ate less lavishly; mothers economized in order to afford refinements that went with respectability. A good roast was an event, and winter fruit was stretched with tapioca or pudding. Households of skilled workers and most northern farmers ate solid fare. After studying skilled steel-workers' families, Margaret Byington's only criticisms of their diets were that children ate the same food as adults and snacked freely between meals. Below these levels uncertainties multiply. Social workers decried the pungent cooking of new immigrants and the custom of sending children to school on breakfasts of bread and coffee. Yet we should avoid romanticizing immigrant kitchens; children could tire of pasta and cabbage soup. Children of unskilled laborers or marginal farmers often remember monotonous, starchy fare, heavy with flour-based items such as pancakes and hasty pudding. While fortunate children began to get peanut butter, the new child's favorite, in their school lunches, a few made do with pickle or even lard sandwiches. Many southern farm children ate well, but a belt of malnutrition crossed the lower South. Frequent moves discouraged sharecroppers from developing gardens, let alone orchards, and landlords' demands that they concentrate on cotton tied them to a miserable store-bought diet of cornmeal or biscuit flour, fatty salt pork, and syrup, that supplied calories but little else. The shortage of dairy products and the consumption of heavily milled meal and flour left many southern farm children subject to rickets and pellagra.[46]

These exceptions notwithstanding, child nutrition on the average seems to have improved over time. Long-term declines in food prices and family sizes, combined with improved distribution by rail, enabled nonfarm families to enjoy more fresh meat and varied foods, though children of the early 1900s remember eating much less fruit and vegetables than in later decades—and often contesting the vegetables.[47] These improvements might explain the trend toward earlier physical maturation that we will see in later chapters.

Clothing offered prosperous parents scope for extravagance, but it more commonly furnished children training in frugality. Because girls' clothing was mostly made and refurbished at home, even some well-to-do girls wore hand-me-downs. Thus a misconceived dress made in red and yellow (Spain's national colors) the year of the Spanish-American War exposed Ethel Spencer to teasing; the dress then passed to her two younger sisters, "carrying with it a heavy load of built-in hatred. I don't think my little sisters had the faintest idea why it was hateful, but they loyally hated it anyway." Poorer children often wore clothes made from adult castoffs. Though tradition holds that Sears Roebuck spread consumerism through the hinterland, ready-made clothing often offered less than instant delight, since cautious mothers ordered items a good bit large. The lesson was one of thrift, not fashion. In respectable families, a hierarchy of clothing taught careful habits. Each day one changed: out of one's best suit right after church, out of one's next-best outfit after school, and into older, worn clothes for work or play.[48]

Children's shoes were a nagging expense that plagued the poor. To many children, shoes and boots were unfortunate necessities, especially those made of unyielding "gun metal" leather and sold in country stores. Therapeutic release came from shedding them in summer. But without shoes, town residents got splinters from boardwalks, and poor children missed school in winter. The habit of going barefoot made debilitating hookworm infections endemic among poor children in the South.[49]

Progressive reformers worried more about housing than about clothing or shoes, since most believed that housing affected both children's health and the moral tone of family life. Reformers decried crowded tenements and condemned the "lodger evil" as a menace to children, especially girls. In fact, only 15 to 20 percent of urban households had boarders, but first-generation immigrant families were large. In the New York tenement where Esther Ginsberg lived as a teenager, three brothers slept in one room, she slept with her mother in another room, and her father slept with her youngest brother on a cot in the dining room. One night she had an experience that would have horrified reformers trying to establish a sheltered childhood. En route to the toilet, she came upon her parents making love on the kitchen floor: "They never said anything to me, and I never said anything to them."[50] Silence had to substitute for privacy.

Flush to the street and five or six stories high, New York's tenements were almost unique in scale. Elsewhere, the half century before World War I saw a boom in construction of separate two- or three-story houses. Often subdivided for rent to unskilled workers, these could be very cramped. A Detroit girl remembers taking baths behind a curtain in the "kitchen-bedroom."[51] Still, children began to gain space as family sizes declined.

Shared space that had multiple functions reinforced the relatively undifferentiated togetherness of the family economy. By the late nineteenth century, however, the urban middle class and small numbers of self-consciously progressive farmers were arranging rooms to separate children from adults and to underline differences *within* childhood. The first separate space was often a nursery for little ones. The attic was also ceded to the young for play. These places were sparsely furnished until the decades around 1900, when parents began equipping nurseries with child-size furniture and decorating them with motifs of clowns and baby animals that underlined the distinctiveness of early childhood. Single bedrooms were feasible only for small or well-off families. But as early as the 1870s, favored daughters of prosperous farmers had private rooms. By the 1900s, it was commonplace for urban middle-class girls entering their teens to gain their own rooms. Farmers still thought any space was good enough for boys, but adolescent town boys began to get separate rooms. Even the compressed bungalow plans of the 1910s proposed at most a pair of boys or girls per room. Especially after 1900, decorators advised middle-class parents to furnish children's bedrooms in ways that underlined gender distinctions: dressing tables and muslin flounces for girls, cowboy and Indian motifs for boys.[52] As in other contexts, the progressive-era middle class used resources to differentiate life stages and gender roles among the young.

Meanwhile, barrackslike arrangements remained common on farms. Many farmers could not build large or would not: "The house doesn't pay for the barn," went an old adage. Even where bedrooms were uncrowded, the absence of central heating and gas lighting led farm children to congregate on winter evenings in the kitchen or sometimes in a sitting room. Large families and low incomes made congestion acute among the rural poor. Across the southern cotton belt, investigators found startling squalor. In a black-belt county around 1908, 83 percent of families lived in one- or two-room cabins, practically unfurnished, chilled by drafts in winter, beset by insects swarming through unglazed windows in summer and yet choked by smoke and "stale sickly odors" if they closed the shutters. "As a result many families entirely outgrow the physical home and use it only for sleeping and huddling in time of storm."[53]

Sanitary facilities varied widely. In the South around 1900 few farm families boasted even an outhouse. Children learned to go "behind the smoke-house, in the underbrush . . . , or out in the cultivated fields." Since parasites passed from feces to bare feet, these practices spread hookworms that debilitated southern children. Most middle-class urban families had indoor toilets by the early 1900s, but only a minority of the working class could afford them. By 1919, however, nearly three-quarters of the households of urban white "wage earners and small-salaried men" had indoor water closets.[54]

By then, middle-class standards made cleanliness and absence of body odor a child's ticket to respectability. The New York State Department of Health advised mothers in 1914 that "every child should have one tub bath daily." Such advice was visionary for much of the working class and even for large middle-class families with a single bathroom. By 1919, about half the urban families of modest means had a full bathroom, but relatively few farmers did. Instead, on Saturday night many farm children followed their siblings into a tub of stove-heated water on the kitchen floor. Others bathed monthly or made do with sponge baths once they outgrew the toddlers' tub; one Michigan farm boy claimed to have had no baths at all after age three.[55] Middle-class standards were far from universal.

Compared with poorer parents, the middle class spent more on extras beyond food, clothing, and shelter; model budgets justified such additions as "advancement." Daughters of the urban middle class and the most prosperous farmers remember ready access to books, magazines, and pianos. Beyond a day's excursion to an amusement park or a nearby lake, however, vacations were confined to nonfarm families with upper-middle-class incomes. Most children traveled little.[56]

Ironically, large expenditures for advancement did not necessarily increase a child's own discretionary spending, for the sheltered childhood reduced some children of the middle and upper classes to beggary, wheedling coins from parents and visiting grown-ups. The youngsters who flocked to early nickelodeons were mainly working-class children who shaved (or were given) a little money from their contribution to the family economy. Farm children had far less access to cash, though a nickel on the Saturday trip to town was common. The money sometimes purchased some small toy but most often ice cream. When asked her most memorable childhood experience, a former Michigan farm girl recalled her first cone; thriftily, she ate the ice cream and tried to return the cone.[57]

Toys introduced children to the delights of consumerism, but those of consequence were mostly gifts rather than purchases. Toy advertising initially addressed adults. Around 1910, as advertisers began appealing directly to children, and department stores shelved toys within easy reach of children, middle-class children still had to importune their parents. Dime stores like Woolworth's extended consumerism more directly to working-class youths by stocking cheap items that they themselves could buy. But we should not exaggerate the significance of possessions. When children of the period were asked their favorite forms of play, dolls were the only toys mentioned consistently. Children seemed more interested in activities.[58]

Christmas highlighted the uneven spread of consumerism for the young. Middle-class children could expect at least one significant gift. In 1899 a struggling small-town lawyer who had not had a client all month noted the approach of Christmas: "I have not the money to spare, but we feel that we must get a doll-carriage for Margaret and a doll for Rachel and we ought to get some simple thing for the Boy." Yet many children of unskilled workers or rural parents received only stocking treats: fruit, candy, nuts, even pickles and bologna. Many turn-of-the-century children remembered the Christmas orange with delight. In some families, a new era dawned when an older child got a job and celebrated her paycheck with lavish presents.[59] The next generation would be more at home in the consumer culture.

Concepts of Childhood

As middle-class parents focused resources on smaller numbers of intensively raised children, each child carried great hopes for the future. And collectively, in the evolutionary terms then popular, children seemed the key to the advancement of the race. Yet native-stock opinion leaders feared that the swarming children of the slums were growing up in poverty and disaffection. This dual sense of the child as promise and problem underlay declarations that the new century must be "the century of the child."[60] What, then, was the nature of these children upon whom so much depended? No one view prevailed entirely.

Middle- and upper-class parents generally regarded their own children as creatures of small foibles and great promise. By the 1890s their clergy had abandoned the doctrine of infant depravity and stressed instead children's capacity for moral growth. Literary descriptions of the priceless child echoed the romantic poet William Wordsworth's exaltation of infants as messengers from the divine: "Not in entire forgetfulness, / And not in utter nakedness, / But trailing clouds of glory do we come / From God, who is our home." A heartrending example was W. E. B. Du Bois's lament for his son, dead before his second birthday: "So sturdy and masterful he grew, . . . so tremulous with the unspoken wisdom of a life but eighteen months distant from the All-life,—we were not far from worshipping this revelation of the divine, my wife and I." Under happier circumstances, some turn-of-the-century Americans looked to children for the serene vitality and innocent intensity that seemed missing in contemporary adulthood.[61]

The middle class did not require moral perfection of its children. In fiction, minor misbehavior had become proof that young heroes and heroines had spunk. Kate Douglas Wiggin, the author of *Rebecca of Sunnybrook Farm*, expressed the growing suspicion of moral precocity: "We must not expect children to be too good. . . . Beware of hothouse virtue."[62]

Such indulgence required a sheltered childhood. By the 1890s, respectable opinion assumed the necessity of play for proper development. Even in the South, a religious journal told readers in 1896 to protect their children: "Let them grow gradually and there will be more sturdiness in their maturity. . . . Don't rob your children of childhood." Booker T. Washington expected sympathy when he told readers of his autobiography, *Up from Slavery*, that work had consumed his whole childhood: "I think I would now be a more useful man if I had had time for sports."[63]

Regarding children of the lower orders, child welfare experts had mixed views. Many who specialized in troubled or delinquent children were ready to pronounce them subnormal; repeated studies attributed juvenile delinquency to "degeneracy" and "faulty stock." Progressive-era social scientists often sorted individuals into hierarchies of "rigidly defined groups or races or types." In their eagerness to differentiate, some child welfare practitioners mixed social scientific catchwords with moralism and ethnocentric scorn. Thus psychiatric social workers at Boston's Judge Baker Guidance Center described their immigrant clients in the late 1910s as "low-grade, of weak character, ignorant type, degenerate, of low mentality."[64] In progressive-era

America, racism was respectable; and eugenicists proclaimed that the wrong people were having too many children.

Yet many reformers believed that environmental influences outweighed heredity. Writers in this vein often portrayed children in romantic terms as victims of a cruel world. John Spargo's 1906 exposé of poverty, *The Bitter Cry of the Children*, closed with a story that epitomized the theme: some "leisured ladies" distributed potted plants to 10,000 tenement children, promising ribbons for those whose plants were "in the most flourishing condition" one year later. But when the hopeful ladies returned, most of the flowers were withered or dead—and so too were many of the children, "like flowers in parched ground." An uncompromising environmentalist, Spargo insisted that "Nature starts all her children, rich and poor, physically equal"; malnutrition withered them. Since parents shaped a child's environment, Americanizing child savers sometimes turned similar tales of children's blighted promise against immigrant parents. Florence Kelley, a leading opponent of child labor, told how a settlement house music teacher bought off the parents of a gifted Italian boy to let him take singing lessons instead of hawking newspapers. But when the presidential election promised a lucrative trade in extra editions, his parents sent him out into the sleet again—"the greedy peasant family had not withstood the temptation to get both the music teacher's gift and the newsboy's earnings. Weariness, cold and wet did their work; pneumonia followed the election night and Angelo never sang again."[65] On the whole, environmental arguments prevailed among reformers, providing a rationale for action to improve living conditions and legislation to limit the family economy.

The era's main effort to develop a comprehensive description of children's instincts and activities, the child study movement, gave a scientific veneer to romantic faith in children's potential and bolstered the necessity of a sheltered childhood. Between about 1891 and 1915, the psychologist G. Stanley Hall made Clark University a child study factory. He and students sent questionnaires asking teachers to ask children about their thoughts, dreams, and play activities. The resulting returns—tens of thousands—resisted systematic analysis but encouraged imaginative reconstruction of childhood. Hall's major lesson was that children were qualitatively different from adults; they lived lives of primitive vitality and imagination, governed by distinctive beliefs and customs. Drawing upon evolutionary models of human culture as a sequence of ascending stages, Hall maintained that children recapitulated as instinctual drives those modes of action that proved useful for survival during each successive culture epoch. The stage of free play began at 2 or 3. Ages 6 and 7 were years of crisis, leading to a period from 8 to 12 when children resembled early savages. Then after a virtual new birth the adolescent emerged, similar to people of medieval times—imaginative, emotional, and idealistic but still not fully modern.[66] While in these premodern stages, therefore, children must be protected from the demands of modern adult life.

In Hall's extravagant phrase, childhood was "the paradise of the race." Accordingly, children must live each stage to the fullest. Failure to assimilate new instincts, warned Hall, led to "retrogression, degeneracy, or fall." Hall urged that every child "be at each stage of his life all that that stage called for . . . ; adult views and standards should not be prematurely enforced." Child study strongly reinforced beliefs that education should be child centered. The progressive educator John Dewey, who was influenced by child study in his early educational writings, warned that children should not be "hampered and stunted" by ignoring their current needs: "if we identify ourselves with the real instincts and needs of childhood, and ask only after its fullest assertion and growth, the discipline and information and culture of adult life shall all come in their due season."[67]

Living out each stage meant staying on schedule. In race history Hall hoped "to find true norms against the tendencies to precocity in home, school, church, and civilization generally." Though recapitulation theory came under attack by other psychologists, Hall's students continued to pursue questions of developmental timing. By 1916 Lewis Terman had standardized age-normed intelligence tests for American use (the Stanford-Binet tests), and Arnold Gesell was about to begin observational studies of child development from infancy to age six.[68]

Child study's prescriptive developmentalism furnished a rationale for the increasingly precise age grading of middle-class children's lives. By 1900 children's birthdays were almost universally celebrated with cake and presents by urban middle-class families, less frequently by farm families and the working class. Middle-class children's lives followed a schedule. Physicians checked their development against age norms. They advanced at regular intervals through graded elementary schools and entered high school at age 14.[69] Although Hall's popularity among public educators waned after 1900, his ideas reached the middle class through other channels and gained popular influence. For the National Congress of Mothers and Parent-Teacher Associations, Hall's sequence of stages remained gospel past 1920. Religious educators took Hall's developmentalism as a guide for reform, and his ideas furnished an ideology for Boy Scouting and YMCA boys' work.[70]

Staying on Hall's schedule was distinctly a class privilege, especially as he urged prolonging both infancy and adolescence for richer development. Child study bolstered the hegemony of middle-class childhood as the normative model for all urban children. Poorer children, however, often fell behind in school and began paid work young. Such precocity threatened the ideal of the sheltered childhood. Accordingly, progressive reformers tried to legislate age rules, especially concerning school leaving and child labor but also regarding evening curfews and the age of consent. These laws and ordinances aimed to prevent children from seizing independence too soon.[71]

Even as Hall's ideas shaped middle-class thinking about older children, the best-selling child-rearing advice of the era conveyed a very different image of children as infants. Extrapolating from William James's account of habit formation in terms that foreshadowed behaviorism, L. Emmett Holt's *Care and Feeding of Children* (1894–) and the Children's Bureau's *Infant Care* (1914–) portrayed babies as impressionable creatures forming lifelong habits and at grave risk of forming bad ones. Since babies were born with unformed impulses, the direction these took depended entirely on each baby's environment and training by mother or nurse. "The first nervous impulse which passes through the baby's eyes, ears, fingers or mouth to the tender brain makes a pathway for itself," explained Mary West, writing for the Children's Bureau, and "the next time another impulse travels over the same path it deepens the impression of the first. . . . If, therefore, these early stimuli are sent in orderly fashion, the habits thus established . . . will persist throughout life."[72]

The theoretical conflict between habit formation in response to external stimuli and instinct-driven developmentalism was not obvious because Hall's questionnaire method led him to say little about infancy. Seemingly, contemporaries thought separately about infants and older children. Whereas Hall urged taking each stage as it came and not forcing the pace of development, warnings that habits formed early and for life meant that mothers must impose control and sacrifice the present for the future. The little habit former shaped by environmental influences was in peril. As with slum children menaced by their surroundings, progressive-era experts on infant care urged control.

Child Saving and Progressive Reform

The United States has seldom lacked for reform movements. Rarely, however, have they proliferated and pursued their causes with such confidence as during the period from the 1890s to the late 1910s, commonly labeled the progressive era. The effort to capture all this activity within a single definition of "progressive reform" has proved so frustrating that one historian proposed "an obituary for 'the Progressive movement.' " Yet certain features were common to many reform campaigns, especially those for child welfare. Spurred by the depression of the 1890s, massive immigration, and corporate consolidations, progressive reform in the North centered on problems created by the growth of industry, big business, and cities. Rural nostalgia highlighted urban problems. The "ruddy poverty of the country," as Jane Addams characterized it, seemed more benign than the concentrated squalor "which even a small city presents in its shabbiest streets." Though reformers addressed some problems that could affect middle-class children—such as impure milk and rote teaching—concern centered on immigrant slum children. In the South, where progressive reform was weaker, it focused on problems of rural whites: child labor in small-town textile mills, hookworm, and bad schools in farm counties. Southern progressives proposed a racist bargain: if rural whites accepted reform, black children would get nothing.[73]

North or South, the basic pattern was that upper-middle-class, native-stock, urban whites would try to reform poorer whites. The reformers had some wealthy patrons and often allied with trade union leaders, but they were mostly professional and businesspeople. They drew inspiration from liberal Protestantism, which increasingly made service the crux of religion, and from the new social sciences. Progressive rhetoric blended moralism and scientific expertise; often progressives categorized children in some loosely social scientific way and then treated them moralistically. For themselves, reformers sought the sense of direction formerly afforded by religious conversion. Growing numbers of female college graduates built the prescription that women serve others into careers of dignity and authority. In an era when occupations were professionalizing in search of social authority and power in the job market, reformers often presented themselves as professional experts.[74]

For children, reformers prescribed mostly the sheltered, family-centered childhood of the nonfarm middle class, although they would modify it according to class circumstances, lengthening adolescence for the middle class and emphasizing vocational education for the working class. Only a few child savers still advocated a less sheltered childhood for city boys. John Gunckel, who won public acclaim by organizing the self-governing Toledo Newsboys' Association, clashed with child labor opponents over his staunch advocacy of newspaper selling.[75]

Progressive reform owed much of its success to a weakening of traditional partisanship that further opened the political system to organized pressure groups, including those formed by middle-class women who still lacked the vote. As described by historian Richard McCormick, progressive reformers "typically began by organizing a voluntary association, investigating a problem, gathering relevant facts, and analyzing them according to the precepts of one of the newer social sciences. From such an analysis a proposed solution would emerge, be popularized through campaigns of education and moral suasion, and . . . [frequently] be taken over by some level of government as a public function." This is a bit too neat. The rhetoric of Spargo and Kelley owed more to romanticism than to social science, but the pattern of organizational activity was typical. As they built reform networks, child welfare leaders followed the same trajectory as other progressive reformers—from mainly local and state activity in the 1890s and early 1900s to calls for federal initiatives by the 1910s.[76]

In part, progressive child saving descended from the practice of nineteenth-century agencies that combined relief with moral policing. Leaders of the

Charity Organization Societies, founded in the 1870s and 1880s to ration private charity and curb the irresponsibility of the poor, were chastened by the 1890s depression and began to consider environmental explanations of poverty. Leaders such as Edward T. Devine, editor of *Charities and the Commons*, backed child labor legislation and the institution of a federal Children's Bureau. By 1915 there were seven professional schools of social work whose new casework method put professional authority behind advice to the poor. Societies for the Prevention of Cruelty to Children, which had combated child abuse since the 1870s, came under the control of professional social workers after 1900. As with other progressive reforms, the changes were not revolutionary. Casework reaffirmed the concentration of welfare work on women and children, since they were more accessible than men. In some instances, casework amounted to little more than keeping all the records on one family in a single file instead of scattering them through huge ledger books. SPCC caseworkers continued to pronounce many of their clients immoral or feeble minded.[77]

For mass support, child welfare reforms drew on women's voluntary associations. Already by the 1880s women's missionary societies and the Woman's Christian Temperance Union were providing kindergartens and day-care centers in poor neighborhoods. Women's literary clubs, which enrolled middle-class wives and growing numbers of women with professional employment, joined in 1890 to form the General Federation of Women's Clubs. Many took up social and political topics in the 1890s, started demonstration projects such as kindergartens and playgrounds, and lobbied local governments on issues of health and child welfare. Increasingly, women justified activism as "municipal housekeeping." Club leaders argued that their mission was defensive: poor garbage pickup, bad schools, and tainted milk imperiled all households. But club women also found that reforms affecting children represented a field in which they could safely claim initiative. By the 1910s suffragists were arguing that women needed the vote to protect children. During the first two decades of the twentieth century, women's clubs launched countless projects: milk inspection, well-baby clinics, better school buildings, domestic science and manual training classes, playgrounds, vacation schools. The work of the National Association of Colored Women's Clubs (their motto was "Lifting as we climb") was vital to black schools because white officials provided so little. By supplying thousands of local volunteers, women's groups enabled the federal Children's Bureau, though a small agency, to secure state legislation and carry out extensive birth registration and child health projects.[78]

Much of the leadership and social awareness essential to progressive reforms came from new social settlements. By the 1880s and 1890s, colleges were graduating large classes of women, many of whom felt called to serve others but could not pursue the careers open to male graduates. Taking up residence in immigrant neighborhoods, such women hoped to Americanize and improve the surrounding community. Perhaps the two most famous settlements were Chicago's Hull House, founded by Jane Addams and Ellen Gates Starr in 1889, and New York's Henry Street Settlement, begun by Lillian Wald in 1893. Settlement women did not intend to specialize in serving children but found them particularly receptive. Hull House started a kindergarten early and Chicago's first public playground in 1893. Clubs and services for the young proved to be what the neighbors liked best. As settlement residents sought government support for their projects and made the settlements centers of social research, they began to build reform careers. Florence Kelley was an early example. Arriving at Hull House in 1891, Kelley persuaded the Illinois Bureau of Labor Statistics and the federal commissioner of labor to finance her studies of sweatshops. Using her findings, Hull House residents and the Illinois Woman's Alliance got the state legislature to pass a child labor law in 1893. Governor Altgeld then appointed Kelley to enforce it as the state's first chief factory inspector. After a change in governors, Kelley moved to New York in 1899, where she headed the National Consumers' League and remained a leading opponent of child labor.[79]

Other sources fed public awareness of child-related social problems. Photography brought slum life to the middle class. For a quarter century until his death in 1914, Jacob Riis toured his slide show "The Battle with the Slum," featuring the ragged children of the streets. Elaborate social surveys, many carried out by female social scientists who could not obtain academic posts, were a hallmark of progressive reform. European influences were powerful, as economic and political rivalries led European leaders to consider child welfare an investment in national efficiency. As in the U.S., male politicians tended to resist women's demands for political rights but to accept their welfare initiatives. Throughout western Europe and North America, women shared techniques of "maternalist" social action.[80]

In their quest for professional status, female reformers found that male colleagues ceded them most autonomy when they served only women and children. Accordingly, argues historian Robyn Muncy, female professionals shortened "the leash that tied most women to home and children. Insistence on the primacy of the mother-child relationship in child development, the obligation of mothers to stay home, and fathers to earn a family's living were critical tenets in shaping welfare policies." Thus the only federal agency run by women, the Children's Bureau, concentrated on improving maternal nurture. Originated by Florence Kelley and Lillian Wald, the idea finally passed Congress in 1912. Jane Addams secured the appointment of Julia Lathrop, a Hull House resident, to head the bureau; Lathrop staffed it almost exclusively with women. The bureau received only an advisory mandate "to investigate and report upon" child welfare and child life. Though the bureau briefly administered the Keating-Owen child labor act, Lathrop stuck mainly to safer issues. The bureau published child-care pamphlets, studied child health, and campaigned for better birth registration.[81]

Further discussion of specific reforms must await later chapters, but it is important to realize that progressive reformers achieved mixed results. Perhaps because public health programs promised to benefit all classes, they were moderately successful. Support for poor children was less satisfactory, as mothers' pensions were helpful but inadequate. Though family placement became dogma, institutions remained full. Kindergartens and playgrounds multiplied, but not enough to enroll every child or end street play. Educational reformers who favored vocational education achieved modest results. Those who hoped to transform classrooms and foster active learning had little impact on teaching. Of all progressive child-saving crusades, the campaign against nonfarm child labor aroused the most passionate commitment yet suffered the most painful defeats, though child labor did decline in urban settings. Almost every state adopted the juvenile court, yet most such courts remained more punitive than originally intended.[82]

Uniting these varied initiatives was a desire to insure each child an appropriately supervised and sheltered childhood, which reformers often conceived more clearly than the children or parents. Thus reformers would supply mothers' pensions and return many juvenile offenders to their homes—but under supervision of a caseworker in each instance. Alexander McKelway, the National Child Labor Committee's leading agent in the South, wrote a "Declaration of Independence" for children that described childhood as "endowed with certain rights that included 'the right to play and dream,' the right to sleep rather than work at night, and the right to schooling." Even in their right to play and dream, though, poor children needed guidance by kindergarten teachers and playground supervisors, plus protection from commercial entertainment. In the context of child protection, children's rights "did not mean the child's autonomy, self-determination, or self-government, but instead ideas of enforceable limits on adult conduct." Discretionary control by child welfare workers was most blatant in the juvenile court, which was "expressly devoted to children's best interests rather than to [their] legal rights."[83]

In practice, however, reformers had limited power to change children's lives. Some limitations were intrinsic to progressive reform. Because the evils they opposed seemed so self-evidently wrong and their Protestant backgrounds had taught them that change came through repentance and conversion, reformers tended to believe that if they simply exposed abuses such as child labor, all right-thinking people would agree and change would follow almost automatically. In the South, campaigns for public health and better schools copied evangelical revivals, producing enthusiastic group conversions but risking backsliding once the revivalists moved on. The social casework approach also had a built-in weakness: punitive sanctions undermined voluntary cooperation. Other progressive reforms were more "prohibitory" than "socially reconstructivist."[84] Thus child labor laws banned paid work by young children without providing resources for families to construct different family economies.

A further weakness was that reform typically came from outside the group being reformed. While white philanthropists pushed industrial education, black educators quietly read W. E. B. Du Bois on preparing African Americans for leadership. To Americanize immigrants, settlement workers sought to discourage them from developing too complete an institutional life of their own. Thus Hull House residents unavailingly opposed bilingual parochial schools and tried to enlist immigrants in multiethnic clubs. The local priest resisted and began a Catholic community center. Jewish immigrants set up their own cultural center, which outdrew Hull House in weekly attendance. Italian women were aghast that child labor opponents would topple their painstakingly constructed family economies: "Hull House ladies are dreaming to send so old a girl to school."[85] Reform was hard to impose where the value of a sheltered childhood was contested.

Progressives often had to settle for strong principles and weak enforcement. To prevail more fully against opposition, they needed more resources than they had. Although American women won considerable influence in the formation of policies for children, the American tradition of limited state activism meant that they secured only limited expenditure. Reformers often had to accept permissive legislation that left local authorities to decide how well to fund a program. Trends in school spending, by far the largest area of public expenditure for children, show that the progressive era was not a time of lavish outlays for the young. The share of Gross National Product spent on public elementary and high schools had risen 146 percent from 1860 to 1890 but increased only 9 percent from then until 1920.[86] Ironically, the "century of the child" began with slowed growth in educational spending. Progressive reformers were often attempting major changes with modest budgets.

It must be stressed that a sheltered childhood was not simply normal and natural, despite this presumption by progressive reformers and recent critics of the disappearance of childhood. Such an upbringing demanded resources and commitment. By the early 1900s commitment to this ideal of childhood was well established among the urban middle class and increasingly among the upper tier of the working class. Urbanization, declining ratios of children to adults, better living conditions, belief that children needed to develop at a measured pace through different stages—all were helping the sheltered childhood spread. But even in towns and cities it was still contested. And reformers had only limited resources to force the pace of change.

2

Infancy and Early Childhood

A child's early years were dangerous; in the late 1890s, more than one American child in six died without reaching his or her fifth birthday.[1] As growing faith in medical science and social reform spurred an impatient sense that something must and could be done, mothers, physicians, and child welfare workers made baby saving a progressive crusade. Mortality declined substantially by 1920, but infancy remained hazardous.

The early years were also those when children lived most closely confined within their families. Although the progressive era spawned efforts to regularize child rearing, reformers had less influence on small children than on older ones, whom they could reach through schools and other agencies. The idiosyncrasies of parents, contrasting rhythms of urban and rural life, and differences in social class and ethnic culture all worked against uniformity in early childhood.

Childbirth

Childbirth was changing from a home-centered experience, controlled by women, to a hospital-based experience dominated by mostly male physicians. In 1900, 90 to 95 percent of American mothers gave birth at home, but half employed a physician. The process was still fraught with hazard, however. Between 1900 and 1920, mothers died from childbirth at more than 30 times today's rate. In 1900 one child in 29 was stillborn and others suffered harm during delivery. Prenatal medical care was limited and so ineffective, according to data from the 1910s, that it produced no reduction in the mortality of newborns.[2]

Of necessity, pregnant farm wives and other working women carried on their regular routines—so completely that some farm children remember being startled when, after a day banished to a neighbor's, they returned to find a new sibling. A majority of black mothers in lowland North Carolina and a minority of white mothers continued field labor up to the day of birth. Although limited information suggests that white newborns of the late nineteenth and early twentieth century weighed no less than newborns of the mid-twentieth century, maternal malnutrition from overwork and underfeeding meant that black infants averaged 6 to 9 percent smaller than white babies—enough to lessen their chances for survival.[3]

In choosing who should deliver the baby, cost was influential; midwives charged less than half what physicians did. But cultural traditions mattered at least equally, for immigrants and African Americans were far less likely to summon a physician than were native-born women. Dr. Josephine Baker, director of New York City's Bureau of Child Hygiene, observed that first-generation immigrant women would have sought "amateur assistance from the janitor's wife or the woman across the hall [rather] than submit to this outlandish American custom of having a male doctor for a confinement."[4]

Midwives and doctors offered different advantages. Often members of the mother's ethnic community, midwives brought familiarity and understanding and a patient, noninterventionist approach: "When the fruit is ripe, it falls from the tree." Physicians, on the other hand, wore the badge of modern science; they often provided partial anesthesia and generally adopted a more active, take-charge approach. Even when mothers chose a midwife, medical doctors were commonly summoned if an emergency developed, but employing physicians for routine births brought no added safety. The greatest danger to mothers was puerperal sepsis, a virulent infection that killed about half the women who died from childbirth. Since midwives did not use forceps or probe by hand the way doctors did, their caution markedly reduced opportunities for infection. Untrained midwives usually neglected to put silver nitrate drops in the baby's eyes, a precaution against blindness, but general practitioners were equally lax. At least in northern cities, mortality was higher in deliveries by physicians than in midwife births.[5]

Even so, the tide was running heavily against midwifery by the 1910s. Claiming to represent scientific enlightenment, physicians successfully marketed their aspirations rather than their average performance. Most right-thinking progressives assumed the superiority of native-stock, middle-class folkways. Second-generation immigrants, Baker noted approvingly, "learned to insist upon employing doctors as stubbornly as any American girl."[6]

Beyond summoning the midwife or doctor, the father's role was shadowy. A Children's Bureau pamphlet prescribed all the preparations for delivery without once mentioning him. Yet when birth was at home, native-stock husbands were frequently in the room supporting their wives. As they had fewer children, couples perhaps treated each birth as an event to share. Only when birth moved to the hospital were fathers uniformly banished to the waiting room.[7]

The shift to hospitals gained momentum after 1910. In cities with large native-stock white populations, 30 to 50 percent of births occurred in hospitals by 1920, though the proportion was much lower nationwide. Originally for the poor, hospitals sought revenue by building maternity wings for prosperous patients, offering mothers rest and quiet. A combination of surgical intervention and anesthesia difficult to manage at home began to be standard.[8]

Two to three weeks in a hospital suited the contemporary prescription of a long lying-in period. A week or two's rest was standard, though many African-American women were obliged to get up sooner and to resume field work within a month. Mothers hired a girl for housework or neighbors came round. In about 10 percent of rural Kansas families the father nursed his wife or did all the housework; such helpfulness struck a Children's Bureau investigator as noteworthy.[9] For many husbands this was an interval of waiting for domestic routine to resume. For mothers and babies, it was a time to recover and establish patterns of feeding and nurture.

Nutrition in Infancy and Early Childhood

Although leading pediatricians prescribed bland uniformity in children's diet, different traditions persisted. As with childbirth, medical opinion was not always best for the child. The farm tradition was distinctive: mothers breast-fed babies longer than doctors advised and let babies share food from the family's regular meals at a far younger age. In the Midwest, the majority of farm babies nursed at 12 months and some past 18 months; in the South, almost all breast-fed past their first birthday, half or more beyond 18 months. Northern table feeding typically began between six and nine months; some southern babies, especially African-American infants, began sampling vegetables and fruit as early as three or four months. In contrast to the schedules recommended by child-rearing manuals, southern rural babies probably breast-fed on demand and older children snacked freely. Children's Bureau investigators complained that "in many homes the child is allowed to go to the 'safe' for leftovers whenever he can think of nothing else to do." Mothers applauded the speed with which babies began to share the family diet. Magnolia Le Guin, a Georgia farm wife, took pride in her little omnivore when five-month-old Ralph first consumed gravy with mashed sweet potato in it.[10] Such feeding patterns reflected the relatively undifferentiated togetherness of all ages in farm families.

The value of farm diets was easily compromised. The quality of a mother's milk depended on her own nutrition, which, if the mother was poor, was often deficient and further drained by heavy labor. Similarly, feeding from a poor sharecropper's table offered little benefit. Nor is it clear how well the food was mashed, though some parents prechewed it. But the potential benefits of farm-style feeding practices were considerable. Prolonged breast-feeding conferred substantial protection against disease, while supplementary feeding avoided both the undernutrition possible among infants exclusively breast-fed beyond nine months and the dietary deficiencies risked by adherence to contemporary pediatricians' restricted baby diets. Reflecting the medical opinion of their day, Children's Bureau agents were shocked by early table feeding and prolonged nursing.[11] Yet the farm tradition was closer to today's practices than were the dietary prescriptions of progressive-era pediatricians.

Urban traditions were less coherent. On average they involved less breast-feeding, earlier use of cows' milk, and slower progress toward adult foods. But ethnic practices differed markedly. Although Polish, Italian, and Jewish immigrants favored prolonged breast-feeding, a few smaller immigrant groups, including French Canadians and Portuguese, nursed babies briefly or not at all. Native white mothers' practices also varied. According to one study, 21 percent of their city-born babies received no breast-feeding as early as the third month, yet 58 percent were still breast-fed in the twelfth month. Working-class parents, who could not separate babies from family meals, probably supplemented breast-feeding with table scraps.[12]

What told against breast-feeding? Only modest numbers of mothers with small children worked away from home, but for women at all active outside their own households, nursing was difficult. Meanwhile business firms aggressively promoted substitutes for breast milk. Some preparations, like Mellin's Food, were concoctions of cereal flours and a little bicarbonate to add to cows' milk and water; others, such as Horlick's Malted Milk and Nestle's Food, included dry milk and needed only water. Borden's sweetened condensed milk also sold well in poor neighborhoods, where mothers often overdiluted it.[13]

Leading pediatricians made bottle-feeding respectable. Drawing on discoveries that human milk contained more water, sugar, and fat than cows' milk and less protein, Dr. Thomas Rotch of Harvard University devised an elaborate "percentage method" of diluting cows' milk with water and adding minutely calibrated volumes of sugar and cream. L. Emmett Holt, from 1899 medical director of the Babies' Hospital of the City of New York, an early president of the American Pediatric Society (founded in 1887), and in private practice the Rockefellers' pediatrician, championed Rotch's system, asserting that "the man who has mastered it will never lack for patients." Percentage feeding enabled well-to-do women to lead untrammeled social lives, and its complexity satisfied their concern to adopt the latest in scientific motherhood. Originating as instruction for nursemaids, Holt's *The Care and Feeding of Children* became the best-selling child-rearing guide of its day. The Children's Bureau spread pediatric ideas still further through its *Infant Care* manual, compiled by Mary West, a widowed mother of five; 1,500,000 copies were distributed between 1914 and 1920.[14]

Despite the germ theory's presumed ascendancy, pediatricians found it easier to explain health problems in terms of nutrition and environmental influences rather than infection. Both Holt's *Care and Feeding* and *Infant Care* blamed most maladies on improper feeding, sometimes exacerbated by hot weather. Neither text classified diarrhea, which was a major cause of infant mortality, with infectious diseases. As late as 1918 Holt even prescribed a "cathartic, usually castor oil," for severe diarrhea on the grounds that the disorder was caused by "fermenting food which has not been digested." Holt duly warned about sterilizing milk and bottles (though he was casual about nipples and stoppers), but his main interest lay in the mixing and scheduling of feedings.[15]

Untroubled digestion and steady gains in a baby's weight became the tests of a mother's success, to the point that *Infant Care* advised buying scales accurate to within one-half ounce. With the slightest pause in growth worrisome, bottle-feeding was tempting. On average, bottle-fed babies gained weight faster than breast-fed ones, especially if given a cereal supplement such as that in commercial baby foods. Although published advice recommended breast-feeding, magazine writers suggested that some modern women would be too nervous to nurse; indeed, nervousness was almost proof of refinement. Mrs. West warned that worry would check the flow of milk and advised weighing the baby after every feeding for 24 hours to determine how many supplementary bottles were needed. For their part, physicians were quick to tell mothers that their milk was insufficient. Thus advice to breast-feed came mixed with promptings to expect failure, and the advice literature devoted far more space to artificial feeding. Much published advice also advocated mixed feeding from the start; a bottle or more a day would free the mother, let her sleep at night, and make weaning easier. Unsurprisingly, by the 1910s "more and more women were reporting" that their milk gave out after a few months and they were "obliged to wean."[16]

Before and after weaning, Holt and his colleagues advocated a much more limited diet than that of rural or immigrant children; pediatricians feared digestive upsets far more than dietary deficiencies and believed in any case that modified cows' milk was a complete food for small children. Reliance on milk also curbed precocity, prolonging babyhood. This enthusiasm was widespread; milk sales multiplied ninefold between 1870 and 1900 and surged again between 1910 and 1920. Beyond milk, medical advice prescribed a severely restricted diet, although it broadened slightly by the 1910s. In 1894, Holt allowed only a little arrowroot, beef juice, or egg at 10 months and fruit only after the 15th month. By around 1913 a report of the American Medical Association coauthored by Holt recommended strained fruit juice at seven to eight months, though in tiny doses of one to three tablespoons a day. At 10 months babies might also have a crust of bread, but green vegetables must wait until age two. The second year's menu added only a spoonful or two of rare meat (scraped), cereals cooked several hours, and (by the 1910s) "mealy baked potato." Thereafter Holt still prohibited a long list of foods for children under age 10: pork products, corn, cabbage, fresh bread, pancakes, jam, raw tomatoes, cucumbers, pineapple, apples, and bananas.[17]

On one level, Holt merely reinforced the Anglo-American tradition of bland, overcooked food, made worse by contemporary home economists. But pediatric prescriptions also formed part of a broader project to set children apart and shelter them from overstimulation. Holt had taken the unbending rules of nineteenth-century child-saving institutions that he learned at the Babies' Hospital and translated them for home use. His advice reacted against companionable working-class and farm practices that integrated small children into family life, encouraged table feeding, and permitted between-meal snacks. Babies were to be fed separately, on a schedule, then left to sleep long hours apart. The pediatrician Dr. Benjamin Spock, whose mother devotedly followed Holt's advice (young Benny was forbidden bananas until age 12), reports an extreme version of this separation: the Spock children all had supper—typically cereal and applesauce—at 5:30 P.M. and were in bed by 6:45. Not until age 12 was Ben permitted to join his parents' dinner at 7 and eat adult food.[18]

Dietary deficiencies were fairly common. Average rural diets were reasonably healthy, but not in areas of poverty and pellagra. Most breast-fed infants were not at great risk; the problem lay with older children and the artificially fed. Although research into vitamins was underway during the 1910s, confusion prevailed past 1920. Babies whose formulas included cream probably got enough of the fat-soluble vitamins A and D, but some poor mothers economized with skim milk. Rickets, which results from lack of vitamin D, afflicted large numbers of tenement children. While cod liver oil had long been a known remedy, it fell into disuse in the late nineteenth century and did not again become common until the early 1920s. Instead, some babies found themselves stretched on a frame in a makeshift effort to straighten crooked bones. Pediatricians encountered numerous cases of scurvy in the 1890s, mainly at 7 to 14 months of age among bottle-fed children of prosperous parents. It was less common among children of the working class, because table feeding usually included foods with vitamin C. Curiously, a pediatrician noted the connection in 1894, observing, "The poorer classes . . . , too frequently allowing their offspring to have the run of the table, as it is called, seldom offer us cases of the disease." But physicians were above learning from their social inferiors. For infants fed only milk and cereals, the problem was that raw cows' milk, which furnished modest quantities of vitamin C, frequently contained dangerous bacteria. Consequently, prudent mothers boiled milk fed to infants. But heat destroyed the vitamin C, which explains the otherwise risky preference of some early pediatricians for raw milk. Although vitamin C was not chemically isolated until 1928, orange juice was increasingly accepted for babies after 1910. By 1918 Holt also recommended vegetables in late infancy, though his prescription of minute servings and advice that it was "almost impossible to cook [vegetables] too much" limited nutritional benefits.[19]

Fragmentary evidence suggests only trivial gains in body weight among one-year-old boys between the 1890s and the late 1910s. African-American boys remained substantially smaller than others. More comprehensive evidence for six-year-olds indicates that once past infancy, white boys grew faster in both height and weight by the early 1920s than they had in the 1890s. African-American boys gained only slightly, however, and advances among whites were confined to reasonably prosperous families. In 1920 sons of the poor were two to three pounds lighter and two inches shorter than other boys at age six.[20] Evidently the benefits of rising living standards were distributed unequally.

Infant and Child Mortality

Rates of infant and child mortality formed a direct, emotionally compelling measure of well-being. The improvement between 1890 and 1920 in children's chances of survival was substantial. So too were the advantages of being breast-fed, living in the country, and being born into a small, high-income family. Yet early death threatened even the most favored. Every urban undertaker maintained a white hearse for burials of little children. Remedial measures centered initially on cleaning up the urban environment, then on improving infant feeding, and during the 1910s on educating mothers.[21]

Although child mortality had probably been declining since at least the 1880s, rates were still high around 1900. That year the Census Bureau began collecting data from 10 northern states and selected cities. Within these states in 1901, infant mortality (under age one) was 124.5 per 1,000 babies born. At 1901 rates, a further 57.5 would die between ages one and five and 28 more between their 5th and 15th birthdays. Risk declined markedly with age. Nationwide, child mortality was only slightly lower than in the 1900 Death Registration Area. Though high by modern standards, such mortality was below that of most other countries in 1900. Knowledge of infant mortality increased as the Death Registration Area grew to 34 states by 1920, and the Census Bureau began a Birth Registration Area in 1915.[22]

Infant and child mortality declined substantially, mainly in the 1910s. Within the original Death Registration states, infant mortality decreased from

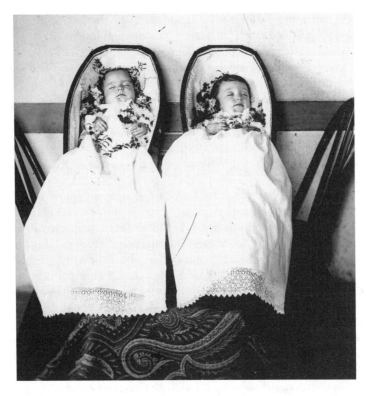

Studio portrait of Robert and Janet Fitzpatrick, twins who died of pneumonia at age nine months in 1886. Photographs of dead children would become less common as infant and child mortality declined. (Courtesy of the State Historical Society of Wisconsin: WHi [V2] 724)

133.5 per 1,000 white male babies in 1901 to 123 in 1910 and to 92 for 1919 to 1920. For white female babies, it dropped from 111 per 1,000 in 1901 to 102 in 1910 and to 74 in 1919 to 1920. Rates for African Americans were unrepresentative in those states, but they too declined. Mortality among older children also decreased. Within the original Death Registration states, the annual death rate for children ages 1 through 4 fell 48 percent between 1900 and 1920, while the rate for those 5 through 14 decreased 28 percent.[23]

In 1900 and 1910, the countryside was much safer than the city. Although public health programs improved urban conditions, in 1920 infant mortality was still 13 percent higher in cities of more than 10,000 than elsewhere. Country children gained from longer breast-feeding and a more varied diet, and distance protected farmers from each other's germs. Even highland North Carolina, where residents with misplaced ingenuity located their few privies directly over streams, had 28 percent lower infant mortality in the 1910s than the average of eight cities studied by the Children's Bureau.[24]

Although more children of immigrants died than those born to native parents, this reflected mainly clustering in cities and low incomes. Infant mortality varied markedly by ethnicity. Jewish immigrants had rates well below native whites, whereas French Canadians, who breast-fed only briefly, had mortality rates nearly double those of native whites.[25]

Marked differences in survival separated European-American and African-American children. Among those born in 1896, the probability of dying before age five was 16 percent for whites and 25.5 percent for blacks. Because poor nutrition and crowding made urban poverty especially lethal, the added risk for black children was more than twice as great in urban as in rural settings.[26]

Around 1900, physicians' children died at rates only 6 percent below the national average. Demographers Samuel Preston and Michael Haines conclude that the problem was ignorance, not income: even prosperous parents and doctors did not know how to prevent or cure threats to life. But income increasingly mattered, and differences in family size magnified the effect. In cities studied by the Children's Bureau between 1911 and 1915, infant mortality was 22 percent in families whose father earned less than $50 per family member but only 6 percent in families with incomes above $400 per capita. Crowding spread disease; even controlling for the father's income, these studies found infant mortality in families with two or more persons per room almost double the rate in families with fewer than one per room.[27] Together, several clusters of factors influenced child mortality. Where a child lived and the level of crowding markedly affected the diseases he or she encountered. Diet, including length of breast-feeding and degree of bacterial contamination, further determined a child's exposure to infection and his or her strength to resist it. And family income influenced diet, sanitation, and crowding.

One pattern was clear: more than half of child mortality came before the first birthday and most of the rest before age five. The result was a measure of security once children had passed the first few hazardous years. But for mothers of small babies who had already lost a child, fear of another death could be overwhelming.[28]

Three types of threat stood out. Of babies who died during their first year, between 27 and 36 percent never got a solid start in life and expired, mostly within the first month, of problems variously described as prematurity, debility, inanition, malformation, and injuries at birth. About 29 or 30 percent died of gastrointestinal problems, mainly diarrhea, often described as enteritis or cholera infantum. The third major cause of death was respiratory disease, which accounted for 18 or 19 percent of infant mortality. Among children ages one through four, respiratory afflictions, especially pneumonia, were the leading menace, responsible for almost one-third of all deaths. Except for whooping cough, which killed significant numbers of infants, the childhood diseases—measles, scarlet fever, and diphtheria—slew primarily children ages one through four. Diphtheria was also the largest single cause of death for children ages 5 through 14.

Adults took quite different attitudes toward the three main causes of infant mortality. Neonatal mortality (deaths within the first 30 days) impressed even health reformers as inevitable. Although respiratory disease did not inspire such explicit fatalism, it drew curiously little attention, possibly because airborne infections—still vaguely described in 1913 as " 'bad-air' diseases"—seemed hard to control without extensive housing reform. Instead, diarrheal diseases monopolized attention. The manner of death was appalling. After days of diarrhea, a baby would start vomiting and be unable to absorb liquids. "Almost overnight, the infant's body would become emaciated, its belly distended, and its eyes deeply sunk within their sockets. . . . Continuing to vomit and purge, the infant would cry without cessation until it sank into a coma . . . [and] died." The pediatric obsession with infant feeding and the concentration of cases in a few summer months made cholera infantum seem tantalizingly controllable.[29]

Once children fell sick, parents felt frighteningly helpless. "Ten days he lay there . . . wasting, wasting away," wrote W. E. B. Du Bois, describing his son's diphtheria, "and joy and sleep slipped away. . . . Then we two alone looked upon the child as he turned toward us with great eyes, and stretched his stringlike hands. . . . He died at eventide."[30]

Summoning a doctor did little good. Pediatrics had emerged as a specialty when physicians applied experience gained in hospitals and orphanages to the problems of feeding infants and preventing disease. Thus pediatricians offered dietary and preventive advice rather than cures. The main exception was diphtheria antitoxin, whose introduction around 1894 cut deaths from diphtheria by half or more. Yet in 1900 diphtheria still caused 14 percent of deaths between ages 5 and 14. In confronting the more common cholera infantum, physicians were powerless; not until the 1920s and 1930s did they begin to develop effective fluid and electrolyte therapies. Despite the absence of effective treatments, parents expected the doctor to prescribe something. So when William Owens's young sister took sick with croup in rural Texas in 1907, "Dr. Reeves came and tried his medicines." When they failed, all he could do was ride back into town, leaving the child to die in her mother's arms. Surgery was the family doctor's other weapon. Children of the 1910s remember tonsillectomy on the kitchen table. Occasionally, grisly errors occurred as the doctor labored in full view of the family.[31] Under these conditions, most reduction in child mortality stemmed from preventive measures, not treatment. There were so many possible sources of improvement, indeed, that it was uncertain which mattered most. Incomes were rising, families shrinking, and with them residential crowding. Both public health and domestic hygiene were improving.

In public health, the big money went into sewers and water. By 1896, 42 percent of the nation's population already had public water and 27 percent

had sewers, though cities were slow to filter water and even slower to chlori-
nate. Easily available water facilitated daily baths for babies and washing of
diapers after each use. (By 1918, Holt stipulated boiling diapers as well.) As
this example shows, there was no firm line between improved public health
and better home hygiene. Water closets gradually replaced unsanitary privies
where adults caring for children could not wash their hands after use and also
eliminated breeding places for flies. Surprisingly, however, rudimentary statistical studies have found no large reduction in infant or overall mortality
resulting from turn-of-the-century water and sewage projects. A similar suspicion apparently led child health reformers to advocate measures that directly
singled out children.[32]

Among the less effective were arrangements to separate sick children. In
the 1890s cities instituted home quarantine for childhood diseases, particularly diphtheria and scarlet fever, but the most elaborate precautions often
came after the child's most infectious period. School medical inspections to
detect children with infectious diseases were superficial and better at determining who needed eyeglasses. Perhaps more resulted from southern campaigns to install sanitary privies in schools and state laws banning the infamous common drinking cup.[33] In any case, school-age children faced far less
risk of death than babies.

For infants, the best measure required no public expenditure. Children's
Bureau studies of urban infants found that through the ninth month babies
who were exclusively breast-fed died less than one-third as frequently as
those who were entirely artificially fed. The benefits of breast-feeding were
smaller but still evident through the 12th month, although from the 9th
month onward babies who also received other foods died a little less often
than the exclusively breast-fed. Whereas artificially fed babies died from respiratory diseases at 1.85 times the rate of breast-fed infants, they died from
gastrointestinal diseases 7.7 times more often. This difference suggests that
breast milk's freedom from contamination counted for more than better
nutrition or shared immunities. The advantage of breast-feeding held constant across all income groups, casting doubt on pediatricians' claims to make
artificial feeding safe.[34]

Despite the superiority of breast-feeding, experts presumed that numbers
of mothers would not breast-feed and that all should stop by the baby's first
birthday. Thus the search for safe cows' milk assumed great urgency. Quality
problems abounded on the long route from cow to baby bottle. At worst,
milk from sickly cows went into unclean cans, then sat uncooled, breeding
bacteria. Middlemen added sugar, chalk, and bicarbonate of soda to whiten
the fluid and mask souring. Then storekeepers and street peddlers ladled it
from unrefrigerated cans into purchasers' unsterilized containers. Even
monied consumers had to wonder what had occurred upstream in a city's vast
milkshed. Early regulation focused on adulteration and skimming, yet bac-

terial contamination threatened infant survival much more. By 1900 pediatricians advised mothers to boil or pasteurize milk; though boiling was straightforward, home pasteurizing cannot have been easy. Bottle hygiene changed
slowly. As late as 1906, Sears Roebuck sold only bottles with long rubber
tubes leading to the nipple. These were convenient because the bottle did not
have to be held; it could lie beside the baby. But the tubes were virtually
impossible to keep clean. By 1909 Sears described bottles with the nipple set
directly on top as most sanitary but still sold the tube kind at half the price.
Commercial pasteurization was long unreliable, as many plants used a "flash

A tube bottle in use (1890s). (Courtesy of the State Historical Society of Wisconsin: WHi [X3]
51265)

process" (heating milk briefly to 175 degrees) that failed to kill dangerous bacteria. Henry Coit, a physician who had lost a son to bad milk, pioneered a quixotic scheme in the 1890s to organize private medical milk commissions that would certify raw milk produced under sanitary conditions. But pasteurization was inescapable for mass protection. In 1909, Chicago effectively required it and prohibited the flash method. Other cities followed, until by 1921 more than "90 percent of American cities with populations over 100,000 had the bulk of their milk supplies pasteurized," though many smaller cities lagged.[35]

In the 1910s, with pasteurization still coming into place, child welfare reformers emphasized maternal education. Privately funded milk stations urged breast-feeding, taught sanitary bottle feeding, and sometimes sent visiting nurses to teach home care. Charitable organizations bore much of the cost, since governmental expenditure for public health totaled just 20 cents per capita in 1917. Unlike the situation in France, where the original milk stations provided material (albeit insufficient) aid for nursing mothers, American projects offered the poor mostly good advice. Progressives' focus on ethnicity shifted attention from economic inequality to supposed cultural deficiencies. Although there was presumption in sending nurses to teach breast-feeding to ethnic groups that practiced it more consistently than native-stock mothers, instruction on subjects such as how to sterilize diapers and nipples as well as bottles had real health value.[36]

To cope with limited resources for public health, the Children's Bureau turned to pamphlets and educational programs, using club women for help. In 1916, the General Federation of Women's Clubs and the bureau jointly sponsored a National Baby Week that centered on maternal education and baby parades, ignoring socioeconomic issues. African-American mothers, who had the greatest need for help, got the least. The bureau's Children's Year (1918–1919) arranged more baby inspections; 11 states weighed and measured at least one-third of their children under age five. Rejection of 29 percent of World War I draftees for physical defects spurred new concern; by the end of 1920, 35 states employed public health nurses.[37] Although these projects raised awareness of infant health, many were transitory and easily sidetracked onto minor problems such as adenoids and mouth breathing. Maternal education often presented as vital medical knowledge what was merely the conventional wisdom of home economists and pediatricians who favored a bland diet and orderly child rearing.

Yet infant health *was* changing. While other causes of infant mortality lost little of their power, deaths from infant diarrhea abated dramatically in the 1910s. Rates of death from pneumonia and influenza declined only slightly and by 1922 surpassed death from diarrheal disease among infants. Meanwhile, infant deaths from diarrhea and enteritis within Death Registration States fell from 4,430 per 100,000 in 1900 to 3,779 in 1910 and then plummeted to 1,626 by 1920. Similarly, death rates from diarrhea among children ages one through four declined from 303 per 100,000 in 1900 to 272 in 1910 and to 141 by 1920. Although the reduction reflected in part the increasingly rural composition of the expanded Death Registration Area, it also represented real gains in child health. Clearly prevention was working, but which form? In Philadelphia, infant mortality declined fastest where infant hygiene clinics had opened; yet in Newark, infant mortality declined more rapidly *before* the city launched ambitious infant health programs than afterward. With purer water not a major factor, one might credit steadily rising living standards, but long-term trends cannot explain the acceleration of improvement around 1910. Since major progress was confined to deaths from diarrhea, the most plausible explanation is better home sanitation and safer feeding, achieved first by boiling milk and sterilizing bottles and nipples as advocated by the 1910s, and second through the spread of commercial pasteurization.[38] There was no progressive-era revolution in infant and child mortality, no full transition to a sheltered childhood medically speaking. But one major source of death for infants declined markedly.

Child Nurture: Mainly Parental

Child nurture was mainly female too, since mothers provided most routine care, and supplementary caregivers—daughters, nursemaids, baby tenders—were mostly female as well. In tune with nineteenth-century gender stereotyping, mothers were to rule by love. And as families shrank, mothers were expected to focus that love intensely on each remaining child, especially during the impressionable early years. For respectable mothers, full-time personal involvement was imperative: "I felt then, and still feel," wrote the antilynching crusader Ida B. Wells in explaining her retreat from public life while her children were young, "that if the mother does not have the training and control of her child's early and most plastic years, she will never gain that control."[39]

Conventional wisdom has held that progressive-era fathers were relatively uninvolved in child rearing. Believing that husbands should be breadwinners and wives exclusively homemakers and rearers of children, progressive-era reformers sought to insure that working-class fathers would do their duty as providers and support their wives in full-time domesticity. Historians have portrayed immigrant, working-class fathers as often insecure in their breadwinner role, emotionally withdrawn or locked in combat with their older children. These accounts may, however, overstate intergenerational tension by relying on the memoirs of children who Americanized unusually rapidly and on reports by social workers and journalists drawn to conflict in the immigrant community. In theory, farm fathers were closer to their children, yet a 1900 census taker suspected that many Nebraska farmers were unsure of their own children's ages.[40]

Advisers on the care of small children assumed that fathers played no role. Writing for the Children's Bureau, Mary West mentioned them only as nuisances: "It is a regrettable fact that the few minutes of play that the father has when he gets home at night, which is often almost the only time he has with the child, may result in nervous disturbance of the baby and upset his regular habits." That was about it for fathers in *Infant Care*, and they went unmentioned in West's *Child Care*. Yet when it came to older children, other authors exhorted middle-class husbands to spend time: "Open your heart and your arms wide for your daughters and . . . make a chum of your boy." Even so, as historian Robert Griswold has noted, the time men spent with wives and children was a "gift," not a shared assumption of child rearing.[41]

Through its influence on social policy, the division of labor favored by progressive child welfare experts—father as provider, mother as child rearer—tended to become a self-fulfilling prophecy. Institutional day care was scarce. Although female philanthropists and settlement houses sponsored day nurseries, in 1910 those affiliated with the Association of Day Nurseries served fewer than 50,000 children nationwide. Underfunded, many could not afford proper food. Fearful of disease, short of staff, and oblivious to children's need for stimulation, nursery managers emphasized hygiene and order. At first some matrons cared single-handedly for 30 or more children; in 1917 the Day Nursery Association of New York's standards still permitted 8 infants or 16 "runabouts" per staff member. Without space to play, children were herded into group singing and marching or learned to sit silently. According to an observer in 1917, many lapsed into the "sheep-like" apathy of "the institutional child." With charity day care inadequate, mothers turned to alternatives run for profit by working-class women. During the decade after 1910, social workers increasingly stigmatized nurseries of either sort as harmful makeshifts that encouraged fathers and mothers to neglect their respective duties.[42]

Although relatively few mothers worked for wages, ethnic groups differed. In 1900 only 3 percent of married white women earned wages, compared with 26 percent of black wives. European immigrants' children commonly contributed wages to the family economy, whereas African-American mothers more often worked for pay. These differences reflected economic need and child-rearing traditions. Whereas African-American mothers of necessity socialized their children for self-reliance at an early age, Italian immigrant mothers emphasized family ties and told their children to play with kin rather than with neighbors.[43]

Who cared for preschool children whose mothers worked for pay? Studies in the 1910s found only one child in 5 or 10 receiving nursery care. In

Philadelphia, almost one child in 5 was cared for by a father, though the investigator dismissed fatherly surveillance as perfunctory—sleeping off a night shift or glancing aside from work. On the other hand, Mary White Ovington's study of black life in New York City gave generous credit to African-American fathers as daytime caregivers. In general, children were tended by female relatives or neighbors. Some baby tenders were incompetent; Ovington found two puny infants lying beside a sick old woman who "talked to me enthusiastically of salvation and gave filthy bottles to her charges." But many children probably received adequate care, with more free play than at most day nurseries; middle-class investigators were predisposed to criticize working-class child care. Estimates of the number of preschoolers left on their own or with older siblings ranged from very few to almost half, as investigators varied in their willingness to credit relatively casual adult surveillance as care.[44]

Some children of wage-earning mothers undoubtedly felt emotionally neglected, but less from child-care arrangements than from the long working hours, with housework before and after, that drained their mothers' energy. As Jane Addams recalled, a factory worker's saddest memory of her dead five-year-old was that he begged her to hold him, and she never had time. Laws limiting women's working hours made little difference.[45]

Farm mothers who did field work could take a child with them. William Owens, a white Texan, was first left propped in a rocking chair with a "sugar tit" in his mouth while his widowed mother plowed, then laid on a quilt beside the field, and then staked out with a rope once old enough to crawl. As he grew too big to stake, his mother sent him to an aunt's to run errands. Black preschoolers were often left with neighbors, relatives, or older siblings.[46]

The common practice of leaving children in the care of other children or on their own alarmed social investigators, not because of developmental damage but because of the physical risk. The first three crippled children Jane Addams met at Hull House had all suffered their injuries while home alone. Control was weak even when an older sister or brother was present: "You're not the boss of me," insisted a Detroit girl's brothers when she was left in charge. The problem was acute when caregivers were as young as six or seven. In the rural South, burns and falls were common among African-American babies, whose mothers were likely to be in the fields. In one North Carolina county, fires and accidents caused more than one-quarter of the deaths of black children between ages one and six.[47]

While some observers gazed fondly upon "little mothers" (the term for young baby tenders), child welfare advocates decried their employment as a double crime against the ideal of sheltered childhood. Jacob Riis photographed big babies spilling out of laps of little mothers scarcely a foot taller. A Chicago settlement worker found an 11-year-old boy responsible all day for a 15-month-old with diarrhea. Some children sacrificed schooling as well as playtime to care for babies. Yet the average situation was less grim. Many little mothers were simply helping after school or in summer. A New York girl recalled "long, chattering, comfortable afternoons" with her friends beside the baby carriages. Doubtless it seemed easier in memory; an 11-year-old's comment was more guarded: "I think my brother is nice but I get tired minding him sometimes." However onerous, child care sometimes freed boys from constraints of gender; by age nine Benny Spock "had changed a lot of diapers and given a lot of bottles." For children born late into large families, this nurture was vital, and such children frequently express great affection for older sisters or brothers who shepherded them through childhood.[48]

A small fraction of mothers could hire a nursemaid or housekeeper; in 1890 there averaged one domestic servant for every eight households nationwide. In the North, women in the upper middle class or above could afford a full-time servant, whereas the marginally middle class might have part-time help. Most northern servants were immigrant or rural girls and young women. In the South, even white families of modest means could hire black servants at oppressively low wages. Ideally, children remembered longtime nursemaids with deep affection. Ethel Spencer praised Mollie Reagan, who lived with her family from 1893 to 1905: "We all adored her. Mark [Ethel's brother], as a baby, would not eat unless she held the spoon." Short of such perfection, however, the family stood ready to judge. Although she stayed four years, "young, plump, and foolish Augusta" was dismissed in memory as "by no means a jewel." Strains were endemic in mothers' relations with servants and can hardly have left children unaffected. Turnover was rapid. Southern nursemaids were often very young for the responsibility, and older women found themselves in the galling position of leaving their own children to tend someone else's.[49]

As fewer immigrant girls entered domestic service, servants became markedly less available during the 1910s, until by 1920 there was only one for every 16 households. A growing proportion were African-American day workers. Meanwhile the middle class of mothers who might have employed assistance was expanding. More and more, they were on their own. Since an average urban housewife of the 1910s spent roughly 40 hours a week on housework in addition to 20 directly on child care, mothers were *not* free to devote themselves full-time to child rearing.[50] When advice writers tried to make child care efficient, they were responding to this predicament.

Historians have long recognized a trend toward milder measures in nineteenth-century child-rearing advice. More liberal Protestant theology and reliance on love for moral nurture led authors to advocate affectionate guidance suited to a small child's capacities. This trend culminated in advice that emphasized redirecting rather than challenging children's energies. In *The Science of Motherhood* (1894), Hannah Whitall Smith told mothers whose girls cut holes in curtains to give them colored paper instead: "The will is one of the most sacred parts of our nature and should no more be broken than the main shaft of a steam engine."[51]

It is conventional to see a sharp reaction against permissive advice after 1900. L. Emmett Holt's *Care and Feeding of Children*, from which most other writers drew, originated as a manual for nursemaids and reflected a hospital physician's obsession with measured nutrition, hygiene, and order, plus impatience with babies' attention-seeking behavior such as crying. Translated into the middle-class household, Holt's regimen became a prescription for controlling babies, differentiating infancy from later life, and keeping babies at a distance from their parents, both physically and emotionally.

Control required that bad habits, in Holt's words, "be broken up just as early as possible." Of these masturbation was the "most injurious." Although Holt's warning was relatively unemotional, Mary West was fiercer. "Children are sometimes wrecked for life by habits learned from vicious nurses," she claimed, adding that more girls than boys masturbated in infancy. Restless little girls (perhaps bored by the lack of attention West and Holt recommended) easily fell under suspicion: any baby "rubbing its thighs together or rocking backward and forward with its legs crossed" must be diverted at once. To keep control, West recommended placing pads between the baby's thighs or tying its feet to opposite sides of the crib. For thumb sucking, which Holt thought unsanitary, unsightly, and bad for digestion, he prescribed restraint by imposing mittens or forcing the elbow straight with pasteboard splints. The baby's own inclinations were no guide: "Thumb and finger sucking babies will rebel fiercely at being deprived of this comfort when they are going to sleep," West noted, "but this must be done if the habit is to be broken up."[52] Any babies raised on this widely circulated advice experienced sustained frustration of their attempts to secure pleasure and comfort.

The same disdain for babies' desires marked advice on feeding. "The baby should be nursed regularly, by the clock, from the very first," wrote West, "and should have nothing between meals save water to drink." Sessions should be businesslike and brief: "Babies like to nurse a little, then sleep a little, then take the bottle again; but this should not be allowed," warned West, "as it unduly prolongs the feeding." The penalty for falling asleep was no more bottle until the next scheduled time.[53]

Mothers were likewise to take early and forceful charge of bowel movements. Unscheduled urination was tolerable, but diapers soiled by bowel movements presented a health hazard and a mess for mothers. During its third month, Holt and West agreed, the baby should be placed upon the "chamber," supported by the mother, "at exactly the same time each day." If the infant failed to perform promptly, Holt and West suggested inserting a piece of soap "to indicate to the baby what is wanted." Then the mother could escalate to suppositories or enemas, as West explained how to inject up to a pint of water.[54]

Besides imposing control, Holt's and West's advice aimed to isolate the child the way the nursemaid in a monied household had done—only now in most cases without the nursemaid. Babies were to sleep apart in their own crib, in a room kept cooler than the rest of the house—55 degrees at night—or outdoors during the day. Holt believed a baby should sleep 16 hours a day at six months; West estimated 18 to 20 hours for young babies and 14 at one year. These figures were high by recent standards.[55] If followed in practice, this isolation barred fathers from any sustained interaction with infant children and reinforced a pattern of denying babies stimulation.

Though West told mothers to pick their babies up frequently and hold them quietly, both she and Holt discouraged kissing for fear of germs. Active play with the baby was to be minimized, lest it encourage wakefulness. Holt was brusquely dismissive: "Babies under six months should never be played with; and the less of it at any time the better for the infant." West more regretfully conceded that "it is a great pleasure to hear the baby laugh and crow in apparent [sic] delight" but affirmed that the rule against play, especially by father in the evening, was "a safe one." Older babies should learn to sit alone, West advised, since minding a baby consumed "nervous energy" that a mother should not "waste" in "useless" activity.[56]

Should the baby seek attention by crying, mothers were to judge whether it was crying from physical pain; if not, they should ignore it. "It is the baby's exercise," Holt observed complacently. The alternative, warned West, was to "make a slave of the mother." To be sure, Holt admitted, babies thus neglected might cry hard enough for mothers to fear rupture. But that was unlikely, he assured them, "if the abdominal band is properly applied, and not after a year under any circumstances."[57] According to this advice, parents were to suppress their impulse to respond to the baby, while the infant was to learn that it could not control its human environment.

The campaign for an isolated, self-reliant baby had a pronounced middle-class animus. Child welfare reformers attacked the means whereby tenement mothers kept babies reasonably quiet and content amid noise and crowding. Social investigators disparaged demand feeding. Immigrants from varied backgrounds used swaddling, which tends to quiet infants, as routine covering; social workers bluntly told them to stop. The abusive practice of sedating babies with opiate-laden soothing syrups declined as labeling laws led manufacturers to purge their products. Still, social workers accused immigrant mothers of giving their children alcohol. With equal indignation, apostles of scientific motherhood inveighed against the "deadly pacifier" and the thumb.[58] Then, having denied restless babies swaddling, sedation, nursing on demand, or sucking, the experts told mothers not to pick them up if they cried. Such advice virtually required middle-class spaciousness in housing, since the baby needed "a room to himself" to sleep undisturbed and cry relatively inaudibly. For older, mobile babies, a high-sided crib became standard equipment. Whereas in 1897 the majority of cribs offered by Sears Roebuck were low sided and half folded up, by 1917 most were high sided and did not fold, suggesting that they would occupy a fixed space within the home. An illustration showed a baby standing (not sleeping) securely confined within the crib, hands on the rail.[59]

Holt's ideas won over women's magazines. Whereas in 1890 almost all articles accepted loose scheduling for infants, by 1920 virtually all advocated tight scheduling and letting recalcitrant babies cry it out. Like Holt, magazine writers had no sense of babies as curious learners with social and emotional needs. Science, declared one apt student of scientific motherhood, teaches that "babies are vegetative organisms, not social ones."[60] Compared with the regimen of farm or tenement, Holt-style rules prescribed sensory deprivation.

What lay behind this narrow view of infant care in part was unthinking continuity, as Holt adapted impersonal hospital routines to instruct nurse-maids and then mothers. Yet this advice mimicked the regimented institutional care that progressive reformers deplored. Mary West's explanation was that "systematic care" benefited the child and reduced "the work of the mother to the minimum." Despite West's professed belief that her regimen would inculcate habits of lifelong value, building such habits mattered less to her and Holt than it would to later behaviorists. Inattention to the baby's intellectual, social, and emotional needs stemmed less from considered psychology than from preoccupation with the child's physical health and the mother's convenience. A primary goal of *Infant Care* was to help harried mothers manage routine child care. West's directions on how to make a sleeping bag occupied as much space as her strictures against bad habits. (With her baby securely encased [as if swaddled!], a mother need never interrupt housework to check whether the infant had thrown off its blankets.) Scientific motherhood was the domestic analogue of the contemporary enthusiasm for scientific management. West preached early bedtimes: "If you have not tried putting away your children at six o'clock, you have no idea what a relief it will be to you." And when she urged that children sleep long hours, her rationale referred to the mother, not the child: "Plenty of sleep is of special importance in this day when so many parents are nervous and high strung." As increasing numbers of mothers felt entitled to a life beyond the household and yet faced housework unaided by servants or husbands, systematizing child care addressed an urgently felt need. Although the prescriptions were unrealistically rigid, they spoke to the dream of controlling the well-nigh uncontrollable details of domesticity.[61]

The other great concern was pediatric. More than half of *Infant Care* dealt with health and nutrition, as did the majority of magazine articles on care of small children. Pediatric concerns—fear of germs and misshapen mouths—outweighed maternal convenience in the prohibition of thumb sucking and pacifiers.[62] Unbending rules promised to transform mere child care into scientific motherhood, much as precise measurements were turning cookery into domestic science. Exactness was what made formula feeding seem scientific—certainly not the spirit of experimental inquiry—and this approach carried over into all aspects of infant care. To be tentative was to be unscientific. To be uncertain was also to be anxious. For this was an era when it seemed that all infant mortality *ought* to be preventable—and yet was not. In this predicament, rigid rules offered the assurance that one had done one's best.

Important features of the new infant care advice carried over into prescriptions for toddlers and preschoolers—bland diet, careful scheduling, fresh air, cool bedrooms, and early bedtimes. In Mary West's *Child Care*, a sequel to *Infant Care* also published by the Children's Bureau, quirky details of hygiene still assumed outsize significance: adenoid removal cured all manner of ills, and baths as cold as 40 degrees would bring "a glow and a tingle" to the child's skin.[63] Yet the overall tenor of advice differed from that in guides to infant care. For slightly older children, the nineteenth-century trend toward milder measures continued—not quite unabated, but only mildly checked by the new concerns for hygiene and the mother's convenience. Except concerning diet, Holt's repressive *Care and Feeding of Children* focused almost exclusively on infancy, whereas West drew a sharp distinction between rote habit formation in infancy and the freer activity needed by toddlers: "As the child grows older . . . his hereditary traits appear, and the simple routine of babyhood is complicated by the necessity of providing for his developing energies and interests." Whereas baby training proceeded by sheer imposition, West now told parents to grant their child "freedom of expression." Since mortality declined rapidly with age, even by the second year parents could relax somewhat and enjoy their child's developing personality. Beyond the first birthday, awareness of the child's growing individuality and the influence of child study (which in Hall's hands never reached down into infancy) compelled recognition of a child's need to play and grow freely. Ellen Key, whose book *The Century of the Child* gave its title as a slogan to child welfare workers, wrote with characteristic hyperbole of "the religion of development."[64]

Continuity with the nineteenth-century trend towards milder measures was most evident in unqualified denunciations of physical punishment. From its first issue, the *Ladies' Home Journal* denounced spanking. West condemned whipping and spanking as outbursts of "animal rage" that engendered "fear, anger, and hatred" in the child. Key claimed to "experience physical disgust in touching the hand of a human being that I know has struck a child."[65]

Under the influence of child study, progressive-era writers took an increasingly nuanced view of children's emotions and de-emphasized gender distinctions among small children. Advice literature discussed temper tantrums as a problem for both sexes. Hall and his student Alice Birney described young children of either sex as subject to troubling fears, and subsequent writers urged parents to reassure fearful children—boys as much as girls.[66]

The same light touch can be seen in Gelett Burgess's popular book of moral instruction for preschoolers, *Goop Tales* (1904). In rhyme and story Burgess described 52 alphabetically named cartoon characters, all about age four or five, each of whom "while mainly virtuous, yet has some one human and redeeming fault." For example, DESTROYA was generous and helpful, "But Books and Papers, Every Day, / She'd Tear, in quite an Awful Way!"[67] Stories portrayed the Goops as pampered children who misbehaved. A few toys were broken and one party canceled, but punishments amounted to little more than mild reproof. Then after each story appeared the cautionary question "Are you a Goop?" Boys and girls had similar faults: making messes, balking at instructions, being mean to playmates. Gender differences were mostly shades of emphasis: more boys were dirty and aggressively bad, whereas girls' shortcomings were more often faults of manners. Still, a few faults were blatantly gendered: only boys, Bawlfred and Krysoe, were condemned for crying, and only a girl was Verivaine.

Determining how parents actually raised their children is harder, however, than merely ascertaining what experts advised, since admonitions may have gone unheeded. Historian Jay Mechling has cautioned that child-rearing advice may be a poor guide to practice because the writers were attempting, often in vain, to *correct* their contemporaries' behavior. Yet one's first newborn can be daunting. Faced with this little unknown, mothers who were isolated or deferential to experts may well have turned to child-rearing manuals. Furthermore, retrospective descriptions of actual practice may also be problematic. Autobiographies and oral histories may include false or distorted memories and can convey only hearsay about the years before conscious memory, although older brothers and sisters may remember how parents raised their younger siblings.[68]

Clearly, printed advice went largely unheeded outside the urban middle class. For a mother in the highland South to follow manuals was to court ridicule. "People here in the mountains raise them very rough and call mine a book baby," reported a Virginia mother in 1917. Another case shows the limited influence of published advice. Magnolia Le Guin, a fairly prosperous Georgia farm woman, was an avid reader of the *Ladies' Home Journal* and a close observer of her children's development. Yet her child rearing was highly individualized; she weaned her children at ages varying from 11 months to 18 months. Her fourth child, Ralph, demanded and got a lot of attention: at five months he was "a real pretty, fat, playful, sweet, baby; but my! my! my! the trouble!!! He never lets me catch up night or day light and keeps me up rocking him long and late at night and sometimes (yes often times) I am up thro' the night with him. He sleeps cat naps and I rarely ever finish anything I undertake to do while he sleeps—he wakes too soon." Her two-year-old customarily slept with Magnolia and the four-year-old with her husband.[69] This was a far more intimate style of child rearing than the new advice prescribed: no schedule, no separate nursery for sleeping, and no leaving babies to cry it out.

Some infants were more amenable to scheduling than Ralph, but mothers took cues from babies far more than Holt or West advocated. Despite the Children's Bureau's role in promulgating the let-them-cry dogma, men probably advocated this course more easily than women. When a self-described "very foolish mother" wrote the bureau for advice in 1920, she reported, "My husband tells me to feed [the baby] good & let him cry himself to sleep but this seems very cruel." Even within the core constituency for the new advice, compliance was very spotty. "Some of my friends laugh at what they call my 'schedule babies,'" reported one enthusiast in 1912. Holt's simpler dietary prohibitions won more compliance than his fussy directions for formula feeding. A critical observer complained in 1911: "While the intelligent portion of the community may not feed their babies cabbage or bananas, the welfare of bottle-fed babies, even among the educated classes, is largely a matter of chance." As for Holt's strictures against emotionally responsive parenting, these could be ignored as meriting exception for one's own children. The anthropologist Margaret Mead recalls that her mother served her children the approved bland diet. "She accepted [Holt's] admonition about never picking up a crying child unless it was in pain. But she said her babies were good babies who would cry only if something was wrong, and so she picked them up."[70]

The most conscientious systematizer might diverge in practice. In *How I Kept My Baby Well* (1913), Anna Noyes told how she reared her infant son Leonard under pediatric guidance, with Holt's manual "at my right hand." The book might have been subtitled *Feces Observed*, so extensively did Noyes report Leonard's bowel movements. Yet he set his own pace. Though Noyes began toilet training in his third month and sometimes used soap suppositories, she "caught" only one bowel movement in six. Only in the 25th month were all "caught in the chamber." Leonard won out even more obviously regarding thumb sucking, which he used to fall asleep. Despite being slapped and pinched and having his thumbs coated with quinine, bound in adhesive plaster, and encased in pasteboard, Leonard persisted "and became most efficient in freeing his thumb from bondage." After two years, the habit remained unbroken. More importantly, Leonard's delight in active play won him lots of it. Photos show infant Leonard being dangled by his heels, carried on his father's back, and helped to walk on his hands.[71] Although Holt's advice served for diet and hygiene, even earnest followers might ignore his admonitions against play.

As children in their second year began to assert themselves, many parents traditionally turned to punishment. On the evidence of chastisements recalled

Walking wheelbarrow fashion: Anna Noyes and her son Leonard, age 20 months. (Anna G. Noyes, *How I Kept My Baby Well* [Baltimore: Warwick & York, 1913], 89)

from later childhood, parental discipline in the early twentieth century diverged as much from published advice as infant care did, although in this instance toward greater strictness. In both cases, parents did not distance themselves from their children the way advice manuals urged. Although Philip Greven believes that harsh punishment of children has been fairly constant through American history, fueled by Protestant fears of hell, other historians think that the severity of ordinary punishments has declined since the 1700s. Rising incomes and smaller families probably reduced stresses on parents; mainstream Protestantism adopted a developmental model of religious nurture; and recognition that mothers were primary disciplinarians legitimized lighter punishments. Outside liberal Protestantism, however, harsher traditions retained their power in the early 1900s. Mainstream Protestant missionaries were appalled at how severely southern mountaineers beat their children. Many Catholic children also remember beatings at home and at school.[72]

At the outer limits, the humane movement probably narrowed the range of permissible punishment, although its agents sometimes believed that lower-class children needed harsher punishment than those from respectable families. Beginning in the 1870s, Societies for the Prevention of Cruelty to Children proliferated. Their emphasis shifted to neglect after 1900, as social workers excused beatings by hardworking parents, while juvenile courts concentrated on acting out by older children and ignored its possible roots in earlier abuse. Even so, the societies served an educative function, as did state laws against cruelty to children. Ned Cobb, a black farmer who grew up in Alabama in the 1890s, recalls how his father's white employer stopped him beating Ned: "He's your boy. He's your boy. But there's a law for the way you beat him up."[73] Deference to paternal authority remained strong, but the balance shifted slightly toward the needs—more than the rights—of children.

In European- and African-American cultures, physical chastisement was a ritual of submission, enforced by pain. By contrast, since they idealized physical courage and endurance, most Native American tribes used corporal punishment sparingly against children if at all. As measures grew milder, some European- and African-American children had to learn to submit to a spanking or even less. A rare spanking recalled by Ethel Spencer illustrates the lesson. Elizabeth, Ethel's little sister, was stretched across their mother's knee. "Intent upon interrupted play," Elizabeth called heedlessly to her brother: " 'Wait for me. I'll be there in a minute.' Mother, outraged by such indifference to punishment, said sternly, 'Elizabeth Spencer, don't you know that I'm spanking you?' whereupon tears obligingly flowed."[74]

In many families, though, the problem was still controlling violence. The use of objects as tools for chastisement, rather than simply one's hand, represented an attempt to ritualize punishment and, possibly, give the adult a moment to reflect. When seven-year-old Askew carelessly let his baby brother fall from the bed, Magnolia Le Guin "slapped him with my fist several licks on [his] back" but then felt "ashamed." "If I had composedly used a switch I would have felt alright.... I am sorry I did not controll self and use a switch." For children, use of implements heightened the psychological impact and physical pain. Although belts, shingles, and sticks were all in common use, switches—flexible tree branches applied to the child's buttocks or bare legs—were most popular. Their relatively light weight reduced the risk of internal injuries while maximizing surface impact, and they lent themselves to ritual, since the child often had to choose his or her own switch and then wait while the adult trimmed off leaves and twigs. A Minnesota farm girl, raised by her widowed father and aunt, recalls the anticipation: "After we brought her the branch we would be in tears because we knew what was going to happen. Then my Aunt would strip the leaves off slowly in front of us and ask the unforgettable question: Now who deserves the punishment?" A Michigan farm boy remembers straightforward pain: "We really never got in too much trouble. . . . But if you did, you were in a world of hurting. Dad did the punishing. He would go grab a limb from a maple sapling, strip it down and whip you with it. Plus you wouldn't get to eat supper that night."[75]

In practice, children had to take what came their way. A flawed but suggestive 1894 study found children surprisingly accepting of punishment. For example, a girl who cried so hard at having her hair washed that her aunt whipped her and locked her in a room wrote, "I think I deserved it." Only when punishment was imposed for something a child really had not done or approached battery did children dare to call it unfair or too severe.[76]

Popular culture commonly treated punishment of children as a joke. From Mark Twain's Tom Sawyer to Booth Tarkington's Penrod, authors made the whipping of older boys an occasion for facetious humor resting on empathetic nostalgia for boyhood, but elsewhere the joking extended to small children in forms void of empathy. At age three, Buster Keaton appeared on-stage as "the human mop," knocked about by his father. A card from about 1890 advertising the Red Cross Base Burner (a heating stove) featured a mother beating her crying toddler's backside with a stick labeled "a base burner."[77] Such easy amusement suggests a sensibility far removed from the tenderheartedness of writers such as Ellen Key.

Starved for systematic evidence, historians have occasionally read back into earlier eras the results of recent studies, which find that working-class parents use more corporal punishment than middle-class parents. Such studies have not achieved fully consistent results and tend to overemphasize the modest class distinctions they find; nor is there any guarantee that class differences have remained stable over time. Still, impressionistic evidence does suggest that poor children of the early twentieth century often experienced harsh controls. Conceivably some lower-class parents consciously sought early mastery as a foundation for later dominance. When a speaker on kindergarten urged a club of working women to renounce despotic discipline, one responded that "if you did not keep control over them from the time they were little, you would never get their wages when they are grown up." Yet if poor parents punished more harshly than the middle class, the difference probably stemmed more from immediate stresses. At the extreme, German immigrants from Russia, their families near starving in winter on the North Dakota plains, beat oxen, women, and children alike in their desperation to appear manly and master their own fears. The novelist Ralph Ellison

The Red Cross Base Burner: trade card, c. 1890. (Courtesy, The Winterthur Library: Joseph Downs Collection of Manuscripts and Printed Ephemera)

described the beating of children by southern black mothers as protective—"a homeopathic dose of the violence generated by black and white relationships." Parents hard pressed to supervise children punished in an effort to make them behave safely. Street culture menaced their children; so too did hazards at home. In prosperous homes with basement furnaces, elevated gas jets, and eventually electric lights, open flames were retreating beyond the reach of small children, whereas fireplaces and kerosene lamps remained common in homes of the poor. Without excusing abuse, one may recognize that poor parents were sometimes frantic. Even people who report little physical punishment as children often recall a memorable spanking or whipping inflicted after they had alarmed their parents. Hurting a sibling, killing or injuring animals, stealing, uttering blasphemy, and playing with fire or matches all could drive parents to anxious extremes.[78]

Attempts to generate more systematic information suggest a modest nineteenth-century trend toward milder discipline and *possibly* a slight return to sterner punishment in the early twentieth century. A small sample of published recollections, mostly middle- and upper-class, indicates a limited trend toward mere spanking or complete avoidance of corporal punishment: of 18 children born between 1750 and 1799, all were hit at some time with an object; of 46 born between 1850 and 1899, about three-quarters were. A survey of childhood recollections found slightly higher rates of physical punishment in the first two decades of the 1900s than before or after, although small samples render the results merely suggestive. Twelve percent of white respondents born before 1904 claimed *never* to have been spanked, but only 6 percent born between 1904 and 1917 made this claim. In addition, 43 percent of the white working-class respondents born between 1904 and 1917 reported having been spanked *frequently*, compared with 36 percent of those born before 1904. But the overriding impression is one of relative stability over time and little difference between white and black respondents. The only consistent disparity—9 to 12 percent more working-class than middle-class respondents reported having been spanked frequently—is still relatively small.[79] These results suggest that most American children of the late nineteenth and early twentieth centuries suffered at least occasional spanking (or worse) but that less than a majority did so frequently.

A similar though slightly bleaker picture emerges from a small sample of interviews with people who were children during the 1910s, about three-fifths in Michigan, one-fifth elsewhere in the Midwest, and most of the rest in the South.[80] Half were farm children, a majority of the rest working class. Approximately 14 percent reported never receiving physical punishment, about 43 percent recalled only infrequent corporal punishment, and an equal number remembered frequent physical punishment. Farm and nonfarm children differed little. Unsurprisingly, a larger proportion of boys than girls reported frequent corporal punishment. Indeed, these results may understate the severity of discipline, since almost three-quarters of the narrators were women. The picture also darkens a shade when one considers the mode of punishment. Although a large minority of those reporting corporal punishment recalled only spanking, slightly more than half remembered being hit with objects, most often switches and leather straps or belts. Just over one-fourth of all those interviewed reported being hit *frequently* with a switch or other object. Harsh punishment was less common when both parents shared disciplinary responsibility than when either acted alone. This pattern may help explain why mild measures were slow to spread: if parents disagreed, the one who felt impelled to whip would take the initiative and become the main disciplinarian. Mothers served as primary disciplinarians almost twice as often as fathers. Relative to their smaller numbers in this role, fathers were more likely than mothers to inflict frequent, severe punishment; but in absolute numbers, mothers and other female relatives comprised half the adults meting out frequent switchings and whippings. Many decades later, a few of those interviewed endorsed their beatings as beneficial, more reported them matter-of-factly, and a few spoke bitterly.

Only about one-third mentioned nonphysical discipline, either alone or combined with blows. It is unclear, however, whether physical discipline predominated or simply lodged more firmly in memory. People who recalled noncorporal discipline remembered mainly being talked to or scolded and being confined to a chair, corner, or bedroom; a few also lost supper or some privilege. Most respondents who received little corporal punishment gratefully remembered their parents' discipline as mild. "We were almost never scolded," recalled one. "My parents were wonderful people."[81] Such recollections suggest that children associated mild discipline with love. Yet occasionally parents who avoided spanking also seemed cold and distant. Conversely, people whose mother or father had beaten them insisted nonetheless that their parents were loving. Intensity of parental affection cannot be inferred directly from punishment practices.

Unfortunately, affection seems often to have left few tracks in conscious memory as vivid as those of punishment. Maternal love was buried in routine care. There was enough expectation of physical affection for an immigrant girl whose parents never hugged her the way the neighbors did to ask whether she was adopted. Yet many of those interviewed recalled undemonstrative parents. Although most families ate at least the evening meal together, the children often had to remain silent. Their togetherness was stolid, buttressed by patriarchy. Poverty and large families wore many mothers down. "I cannot ever remember Ma taking time to hold me," recalled the daughter of Russian-German immigrants to North Dakota. "It seemed so many pioneer mothers had no time to talk or teach, only punish when something went wrong."[82] Although families vary in every generation, the average emotional tone as remembered seems less effusive than today's.

A glum view of parental care pervaded the judgments of child welfare workers, yet their gaze often fastened on faults of hygiene and housekeeping while ignoring family affection. A case in point is a 1912 photograph by Lewis Hine showing a teenage millhand and his family. Hine's caption offers the sole dismissive comment "Crowded, dirty home."[83] Yet the photo depicts an affectionate family grouping. In her lap the mother holds a baby, carefully arrayed in a long, ruffled white dress and baby boots. The older boy has playfully inserted the baby's fingers in his mouth, while the mother, her head leaning forward almost against her son's, smiles fondly at the baby.

Some families built affection into daily routines; meals were lively and evenings companionable. Growing up poor in rural Texas, William Owens's early memories included evenings when his widowed mother sang funny songs, told stories, and then led Bible reading and prayer. A world away in a big house in Pittsburgh, Ethel Spencer's mother began reading to her children while they were young and worked through most of Dickens as they grew older. An Indiana farmer's daughter remembered evenings by the fireplace while her father played dominoes or cards with his children. She watched Halley's Comet beside her mother on a blanket in the yard.[84] Typically,

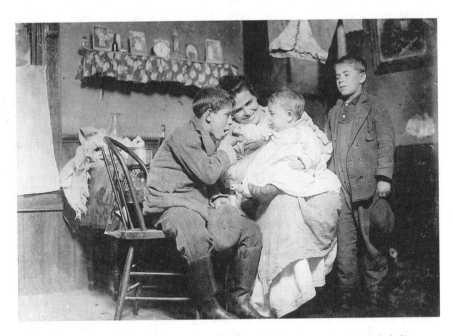

"Flash light photo of John Sousa, his mother and some brothers and sisters. Crowded, dirty home." Photograph by Lewis Hine, 1912, New Bedford, Massachusetts. (Library of Congress, LC-USZ62-86267)

mothers read to children, whereas fathers played games with them. Such social evenings were common, however, among only a minority of families.

Although both parents were important, mothers provided the basic care that structured a small child's daily life. Yet that disproportion is less clear in recollections, partly because they reflect events later in childhood but also because maternal nurture often seems to have been taken for granted. Some fathers were indeed distant. Ethel Spencer's regularly came home "tired, nerves on edge, [and] found his seven children hard to take." By contrast, they "adored" their mother. Certainly more children recalled distant fathers than distant mothers. Yet many remembered being close to their fathers: a janitor's daughter sitting in his lap until age seven or eight; an auto worker's son tussling on the floor with his father; a farm boy feeling close to his father while doing chores with him. Fathers' intermittent involvement often gained disproportionate attention, as they budgeted their time for influence. A widely approved practice was to schedule a children's hour each evening. Fathers might also put themselves in charge of treats and expeditions. Magnolia Le Guin commented regretfully when Ghu, her husband, took their young boys to town: "What a treat it would be to go and carry them to different places just for their pleasure—that would please me to see them pleased. I am denied that sweet pleasure and Ghu carries them to town." This guarded "masculine domesticity," which was not confined to the suburban middle class, suggests that the stereotype of the turn-of-the-century father as mere breadwinner was overstated.[85]

The conclusion that maternal influence was paramount but that fathers also seemed important to their children gains support from a survey of 100 California couples (61 middle-class and only 4 African-American) who had been children between 1910 and 1920. The men rated 73 percent of their mothers but only 43 percent of their fathers as having been highly involved and influential in their growth and development. Women, on the other hand, rated their two parents nearly equal. Both sexes rated mothers high in authority more often than fathers, reflecting the mothers' frequent disciplinary role. Yet whereas men ranked their mothers high in affection much more often than their fathers, women by a tiny margin favored their fathers as the affectionate parent.[86] Both sons and daughters rated parents of the 1910s higher in authority than affection. Perhaps discipline did outweigh affection, but our memories of parents are often unfair.

Child-rearing practices between 1890 and 1920 varied widely, as parents only intermittently followed printed advice. Infant care was less distant and controlling than Holt desired, yet older children faced more punitive discipline than West or Key wanted. Mothers, daughters, and female servants provided most basic care, but many fathers furnished additional discipline and affection. Although typical nurture was not grimly repressive, neither was this a golden age of childhood.

Clothing

Some mixture of practicality and empathy for small children changed fashions between 1890 and 1920 in ways that facilitated active play. Growing practicality was also evident in baby carriage design. Well-to-do infants of the 1890s were paraded in carriages that bulged with upholstery and crawled with ornamentation. All but the cheapest sported a fringed parasol awkwardly mounted on a pole. By 1917, simpler wicker carriages, with a hood that afforded more reliable shade, were common. And Sears Roebuck now sold go-carts that enabled children to sit up and look around. Clothing for infants changed more slowly. Those of the 1890s were arrayed in gowns up to a yard and a half long, little heads above a cascade of white cloth. By 1917 the Sears catalog decried "cumbersome long dresses" but considered 24 inches "practical." At around six months old, babies got shorter dresses ending just above the ankle. Though formal dress for slightly older children remained quite fancy, lighter, freer play clothing began to appear. As late as 1900, in hot weather the Spencer children of Pittsburgh played in their underwear for lack of lighter garb. From about 1906 onward "rompers" and other clothing intended for mobility and play became widely available. For one- and two-year-olds, rompers were loose, one-piece outfits with baggy bloomers that left room for diapers. Those for older children to age six had more sharply defined short pant legs. By 1917, the baggy kind were called creepers; those for older children were rompers. Overalls also appeared in small child sizes, and in 1909 Sears advertised "play in the mud suits" sized 2 through 7.[87]

The new fashions slightly complicated the process whereby small children learned age and gender roles through clothing. Surprisingly, turn-of-the-century children's clothing was completely androgynous for the first years of life. Children of both sexes wore first long and then shorter dresses, white for infants and sometimes pastel for toddlers but with no color coding by gender; pink and blue were interchangeable. At least through 1900, for formal occasions both boys and girls wore dresses or suits with skirts, distinguished at most by minor details of headgear and trim, until age five or six. Using white for infants and dressing both sexes in skirts emphasized childish innocence, identified small children with their mothers' domestic world, and differentiated early childhood from the sharply gendered world of older children. Since parents knew their children's sex, androgynous clothing cannot markedly have altered their child rearing, but it may have encouraged muting gender differentiation. From age 2 or 2 1/2 onward, by which time most children would have been capable of elaborate gender distinctions, unisex dress may have slowed intensification of these distinctions.[88]

By the 1890s, though, some male opinion leaders were anxiously decrying gender blurring and feminization in home, school, and church. Perhaps coincidentally, dresses began to seem wrong for boys age five; some were reportedly humiliated to be mistaken for girls. Boys began putting on knee pants as young as 3; from then until 12 or 14, boys' suits featured knicker-bocker pants. Not all parents complied, however, for Sears still offered some "children's" dresses for ages up to six in 1909, though few past age four by 1917. Hair styles also varied through the 1910s, with some boys having short hair while others still had bangs and side curls. Fathers often hurried the process, whereas mothers resisted change as the first step in los-ing their baby to the world outside the home. When Fred Le Guin put on pants in 1902, his mother had hoped for delay, but Fred and his father "both wanted him to don pants today and leave dresses forever behind." Magnolia reflected ruefully: "Fred is 4 years and 2 months and several days old. . . . Sad to see babies growing from innocent babyhood to 'boys grown tall' so fast. . . . Gentle baby Fred—in pants." Lyndon Johnson's father made his first haircut at age four or five a brutal imposition of gender. Claiming that Lyndon's long curls, which his mother treasured, made the boy a "sissy," his father cut them all off one morning when she had gone to church. "When my mother came home," the president recalled, "she refused to speak to him for a week."[89] To mothers, pants and short hair marked loss of innocence. To boys, they demonstrated the exclusivity of male gender roles. Nineteenth-century girls experienced no equivalent change. They simply continued to wear skirts and dresses, eventually cut and trimmed more like women's but well off the floor until adolescence. Dress linked childhood, domesticity, and womanhood, reinforcing continu-ous socialization, whereas boys' pants signified readiness to venture outside the home.

The advent of rompers and other playwear added a new element. Boys received tacit encouragement to start early on energetic activities associated with boyhood. For girls the sequence was more confusing. When little, they too wore creepers. But after early childhood, girls had to return to skirts and dresses. Straight-cut or long pants seemed overbold. When Sears Roebuck offered "play in the mud" suits, only those with bloomer pants were for either sex, and overalls were for boys only. Although some sportswear with pants became available for wealthy and athletic older girls, otherwise even bloomers saw little use as outerwear except in the gymnasium.[90] When inter-viewed about childhood, women who grew up in the 1910s insist—with the force of a taboo still strong in memory—that they never wore pants. Whether little girls felt inhibited at play by wearing dresses after the romper phase is uncertain. But girls now faced an early transition from gender-neutral rompers to dress for one sex only. This transition made dresses even more definite gender markers. Thus the new children's clothing, while encouraging active play for little boys and girls, also distinguished gender at younger ages.

Play and Work

Recognizing children's need for play, progressive-era adults began to give small children specialized space as well as clothing. Although some parents strapped active babies into safety swings and jumpers, the bounded freedom of the playpen grew more common.[91] Yet as they grew, children's activities depended on family circumstances. Even by age five, the ideal of a sheltered childhood devoted to play was seriously compromised for many children. Movement toward the ideal owed less to reform crusades than to expansion of the urban middle class.

Although rural nostalgia suffused writing on children's play, young children on farms were at the mercy of family size and location. Those blessed with siblings close in age or near neighbors with small children led a sociable life. Children especially treasured occasions when relatives or neighbors gathered and the young split off to play as a group. Then older children often let the little ones join games beyond their capacities. Otherwise, as even farm families shrank, by the 1910s numbers of farm children passed solitary childhoods. "On the farm, you played alone," recalled a former Michigan farm boy. Nature could be playground or prison, depending on grown-ups' anxiety levels and the availability of children to create safety in numbers. Little Dorothy Howard and her friends roamed freely in the woods of east Texas, armed with knotted sticks in case of snakes. By contrast, in South Dakota Mildred Renaud could not leave her yard for fear of rattlesnakes.[92]

Young children of the nonfarm middle class commonly played in small groups or alone. The well-to-do often had roomy houses and yards, but apartment life could be confining; a Chicago dentist's son remembers his parents' rooms in minute detail because he spent his preschool years there as an only child. As families shrank, more children fell back on solitary indoor play. Even in small towns, health workers in the 1910s found many children who lacked outdoor exercise because "they would not stay out of doors alone" and their mothers "did not have time" to stay with them.[93]

Crowded housing drove working-class city children out to play at early ages. Toddlers occupied the stoops alongside their "little mothers," while preschoolers moved down onto the sidewalk and street. Though busy streets were unsafe even in the horse-drawn era, the advent of asphalt pavement and better street lighting in the 1880s and 1890s ushered in a brief golden age of street play. Older children gained most, as balls bounced higher and truer and play continued after dark. Soon, however, automobiles made streets even more hazardous. Though big cities criminalized street play, traffic deaths of children nationwide nearly doubled between 1915 and 1920. Still, from 1890 into the 1910s school-age children owned the streets.[94]

Reformers were not pleased. Their distaste for street play, in which they saw seeds of criminality, combined with concern that children needed safer play areas to foster a playground movement that became one of the progressive era's foremost child-saving crusades. The public playground began as a German idea to benefit small children. In imitation of Berlin's "sand gardens," Boston philanthropists in 1885 dumped sand piles outside a nursery and a chapel; the next year saw 10 sand heaps. Very early, the organizers determined to keep limited hours, emphasizing supervised rather than free play. By 1899, philanthropists in 14 cities had established supervised playgrounds, most with sandboxes and swings. Soon, however, swarms of older children and the dream of combating juvenile delinquency brought a shift in emphasis. In New York City, where benefactors converted three lots to playgrounds by 1892, Jacob Riis reported that they brought in sand, plus "little wheelbarrows, toy-spades and pails to go round." But Riis's photos show a large bare lot, with the wheelbarrows in the hands of older boys and few preschoolers evident. Riis praised the playground at Poverty Gap not for amusing preschoolers but for transforming the Gap from a zone of juvenile mayhem into one of peaceful play.[95]

This emphasis gained impetus in 1906 when Henry Curtis, then director of Washington, D.C.'s playgrounds, and Luther Gulick, director of physical education for New York City public schools, formed the Playground Association of America. They were soon joined by Joseph Lee, a patrician Boston nativist. Heavily influenced by G. Stanley Hall, all three men espoused group play for gang-age and adolescent boys to counter delinquent individualism and to Americanize immigrants. In Lee's words, "playgrounds for big boys" assumed central importance. The model playground introduced careful age grading, and as in teaching, prestige accrued to youth workers who dealt with older children.[96] Promoted as remedies for street play, commercial recreation, and juvenile delinquency, public playgrounds spread rapidly between 1906 and 1917. Proponents followed the classic progressive reform strategy: start with privately supported demonstration projects, then secure government funding to expand services. With municipal backing, playgrounds spread into middle-class neighborhoods after 1910. Even so, funds were insufficient to serve all districts. Built-up land was costly, and of 432 cities reporting supervised play in 1915, only 182 had full public funding.[97]

Consequently, the playground movement's direct influence on children's lives was limited. Even where playgrounds were fairly common, most children preferred the unsupervised streets. In Milwaukee and Cleveland no more than 4 percent of school-age children frequented playgrounds, in Chicago perhaps 10 or 20 percent. Smaller children often stayed away. In Chicago, Curtis found that preschoolers would not regularly venture to a playground more than two blocks from home.[98]

Instead, the example of sand gardens convinced some parents to turn their yards into playgrounds. Sandboxes permitted children the freedom of mud play without the mess. By 1918 Mary West was urging mothers to furnish sandboxes, swings, teeter boards, and low ladders.[99] This equipment encouraged vigorous play, loosely shaped by physical settings rather than tightly focused on specific toys.

Mass-produced toys that children could own individually encouraged children to play privately indoors. Inexpensive and durable—the poor boy's Christmas present—American-made cast-iron pull toys began to displace German-made tin toys in the 1890s. Spring-powered trains acquired sectional track in the 1880s and 1890s, then electric trains appeared around 1905. Construction toys proliferated: Meccano (1901), Erector sets (1913), Tinkertoys (1914), and Lincoln Logs (1916). At an age when children normally need free play for development, the profusion of elaborate toys risked narrowing their imagination. Mechanically intricate toys quickly bored them. But the much-reproduced stereograph of a small boy seated in dulled satiation two days after Christmas 1909, with his toys massed on the porch steps, was a joke, playing upon adult suspicion that children were overindulged. Many children enjoyed no such profusion. Poor children improvised: clothespins for dolls, dried corn cobs for building blocks, a wooden spool carved into a top. Even Benjamin Spock, raised in affluence, treasured in memory the toy boats he built from scavenged shingles and scraps of wood. Like the sandbox, moreover, some of the new toys spurred activity by small children. Admittedly the squeak toys that proliferated after about 1895—when manufacturers gained the right to patent funny noises—promoted repetitive play, but they did reward action by infants. For preschoolers, Mary West recommended wooden blocks and modeling clay, and the advent of Tinkertoys opened elaborate construction play to much smaller children. Wagons, sleds, and tricycles all grew increasingly available.[100] On balance the new objects probably promoted free play at least as much as it narrowed it.

Although more boys than girls owned sleds and bicycles, gender distinctions were far from absolute among preschoolers. Girls owned tricycles. Magnolia Le Guin's boys (ages seven, four, and two) were pleased with "chop axes" for Christmas 1902, and she worried about their fondness for toy pistols. Yet the four-year-old cried because Santa had not brought him a doll. Three-quarters of city boys played with dolls, stopping on average at about age six or seven. Though virtually all little girls played with dolls, many came to prefer outdoor play as they grew older.[101]

Whereas antebellum doll play had taught sewing skills, by the 1890s the endless stitching that formerly filled a genteel girl's every spare moment had subsided. Dolls now served more for role-playing but only gradually assumed forms that encouraged identification and mothering. Despite surveys showing that children under age five preferred baby dolls and that their older sisters wanted child dolls, European imports fashioned like little women dominated the American market until World War I. Accordingly, adult dolls whose wigs came off might be pressed into service as babies. By the 1910s American manu-

"Boy on porch with toys," 27 December 1909, stereograph by Underwood and Underwood. (Library of Congress, LC-USZ62-42228)

facturers were producing more childlike dolls that encouraged identification with quite varied gender roles: romper-clad New Kid dolls that exuded energy, "Goo-Goo"–eyed flirtatious dolls, and demure Fairy dolls with the latest lingerie.[102] Since many dolls had fragile heads, breakage plagued young owners and disrupted identification. Older girls often remembered a particular lost or broken doll the rest of their lives. Yet new doll heads were a standard Christmas gift, and many girls enjoyed these changing identities. One who was forever breaking dolls' heads on the sidewalk remembers her father teasing: "Did you really break that, or did you just want another pretty head?"[103]

Because dolls represent humans—small children of the 1890s occasionally blurred the line by calling infants "meat dolls"—they lend themselves more readily than other toys to dramatic interpretation. Some girls mutilated and smashed dolls; others fought to defend them against vandalizing boys. Historian Miriam Formanek-Brunell interprets both forms of behavior as challenges to established gender prescriptions. Girls commonly used dolls to try out roles and work through troubling issues. School-age children explored self-other relationships and socialized themselves for motherhood, commonly rocking dolls to sleep and shushing others while the dolls slept. Younger girls used dolls as externalized representations of themselves. As they struggled to gain self-control and cope with parental discipline, children below age eight punished their dolls more frequently and harshly than older children did. In 1890s surveys, 108 children whipped their dolls; 108 never punished; 80 sent them to bed; 75 spanked; 39 slapped; 35 stood them in the corner; 34 scolded; 21 shook dolls; 20 put them in a dark closet; and 5 threw them on the floor. Some children reported great restraint, others abusive harshness, like the six-year-old who "beats and almost breaks her doll because 'she wets herself most every day.' "[104] Doubtless such extremes reflected parental abuse, but surveys cannot disentangle how much the overall pattern represented imitation of parents, how much reactive anger or anxiety, and how much longed-for gentleness.

Perhaps it was fitting that not all dolls embodied the spirit of carefree play, since some were made by home-working women and children as young as four. Reluctance to condemn expedients whereby poor and single mothers scraped together a living has inspired some effort to rehabilitate homework, highlighting children's pride in contributing to their family's income and mothers' closeness to their children as they gathered round the worktable. But small children performed monotonous tasks for trivial pay. Fortunately, by a 1911 estimate, only 6 percent of households did piecework.[105]

By age five or so, many boys and girls faced only domestic chores, being expected to help set the table or mount a chair and dry dishes. In towns and villages where many nonfarmers still kept animals and grew large gardens, small children commonly fed the chickens and picked bugs off potato plants.[106] But such light chores impinged only marginally on playtime.

Farm children worked harder. Around ages four to six, most began doing light housework, feeding chickens and livestock, herding cattle, watering stock, and carrying water to the house or to field workers. Texas folklorist Dorothy Howard reported that children soon demanded "jobs to prove they were no longer babies." At age five she carried water daily to the men in the fields and stayed on to play; one memorable day they let her drive the wagon home. Not all observers, however, shared her faith in the rightness of folkways. Water was heavy in a small child's bucket. A former Michigan farm girl remembers pumping water for cattle as such hard work that it took her and her two young sisters in turn to pump enough. Similarly, buttermaking on an Indiana farm required the younger children to "churn, churn, churn," and they "hated" it. Chores often depended more upon the luck of birth order than upon any parental notion of what children needed. Small children with competent older siblings could sometimes parlay initial clumsiness into nearly total exemption from chores such as milking or gathering eggs.[107]

Since cotton, tobacco, and corn demanded vast amounts of labor at peak seasons, southern children were pushed especially hard and early. When asked why he did not buy a corn planter, one hill country farmer replied, "I already have eight." In lowland North Carolina in the 1910s, two-thirds of white and three-quarters of black farm children ages 5 to 15 did field work in addition to chores, typically starting as a "toddler of 5 or 6." No child was exempt; a mother explained that "when she puts 'one at it,' [she] puts 'them all at it.' " Parents so wanted children to learn hard work that children of prosperous

Worming and suckering tobacco: "5-year old Jack and 13-year old Bitsey are regular workers on their father's farm." Photograph by Lewis Hine, August 1916, Gracey, Kentucky. (Courtesy of Photography Collections, University of Maryland Baltimore County)

farmers were almost as likely to labor as those of poor tenants. When Magnolia Le Guin's father hired Askew, age seven, and Fred, age four, to pick cotton, she commented approvingly: "Fred is real industrious in the cotton patch. Works more regular than Askew. Ghu [her husband] says he is a very industrious cotton-picker for his age." Prosperity diminished the pressure, however, for his mother gave no hint that Askew would suffer for slowness.[108]

In 1918 an international conference on childhood promulgated a "New Bill of Rights of Childhood," including "*a right to play*. Free, 'unbossed' play is the most serious business of the child. It is the way in which his faculties are best brought to their highest capabilities."[109] Yet as young as age five, many American children's playtime was still narrowed by demands for monotonous labor of no developmental value. At the same time, growing adult recognition that children learn through play strengthened the impulse to channel even small children's play and make it constructive. Although the playground movement exerted only marginal influence on small children, trends in private play space and toy design opened new possibilities for free play.

Kindergarten

The kindergarten movement embodied the controlling impulse. Its pioneers idealized play but carefully structured it to teach moral and cultural lessons. By the 1910s, many schools also used kindergartens to steer children from unbossed play toward the discipline of schoolwork. Except for infant health, kindergartens constituted the progressive era's foremost program for small children's welfare; yet only a minority enrolled by 1920.

Friedrich Froebel (1782–1852), the German originator of the kindergarten, designed a complex regimen. Children were to arrange "gifts" (balls, blocks, geometrical shapes, sticks, rings, and pellets) according to precise directions, then progress to handiwork (called "occupations") with materials such as clay, paper, and beads. Nature study, stories, songs, and rhythmic movement completed the program. A romantic idealist, Froebel expected the gifts and occupations to draw out metaphysical ideas innate in the child's psyche. Although his program allowed little freedom, the idea that children could learn through play made it revolutionary.[110]

By the 1870s kindergartens had spread thinly in the U.S. as fee-paying institutions for well-to-do children. Then in the 1880s reformers transformed kindergartning into an outreach movement to bring maternal nurture to poor children. Philanthropists such as Pauline Agassiz Shaw in Boston financed dozens of free kindergartens, and genteel young women took up kindergarten teaching as social service. In the 1890s women's clubs, both black and white, also began sponsoring free kindergartens. Supporters made extravagant promises that structured play, plus songs and stories filled with blacksmiths, birds, and flowers, would remedy the unnatural conditions of city life and prevent crime. Outreach went beyond teaching children, as most kindergartens ran mornings only; in the afternoon teachers visited homes and held mothers' meetings to preach better hygiene and milder discipline.[111]

Private philanthropy soon reached its limits, however. As early as 1888, Boston and Philadelphia took over charitably financed kindergartens. By 1912, public kindergartens had 312,000 pupils and private ones just 52,000. Contending that school administrators destroyed kindergarten's reform potential and that progressive kindergartners substituted conformist peer control for education that fostered moral autonomy, some historians have sharply criticized progressive-era kindergartens.[112] But the story was more complex. Campaigns for public kindergartens became a regular feature of progressive child saving, with publicity exposing the regular schools' failure to meet poor children's needs and contrasting kindergarten methods to ordinary rote teaching. Yet success brought control by school superintendents who were divided concerning the kindergartens' purpose and cautious about expanding them. A few, such as Herbert Weet of Rochester, New York, where every school had a kindergarten, discounted "efficiency" and praised kindergartens as giving "a joy and happiness to childhood." Others were blunt Americanizers, describing kindergartens for immigrant children as "self-preservation" for the state. Many confined kindergartens to neighborhoods where "home conditions" were "artificial," primarily "poor" and "immigrant" districts.[113]

Would kindergartens retain an independent ethos or merely socialize immigrant children to primary classroom routine? Home visits often ceased by the 1910s, as most kindergartners now had to teach both morning and afternoon. Yet insofar as such visits had been culturally patronizing, their cancellation democratized the kindergarten. Debate over classroom activities moved within a narrow spectrum. Grace Parsons, who supervised kindergartens in Denver, argued for a distinctive program: "A child who is unable to arrange blocks and sticks, to use sand and clay, to play simple games with his fellows, is not ready for the detailed work of the school." On the other side, advocates of efficiency seldom proposed completely transforming the kindergarten or introducing early reading. At most, school officials sometimes divided the day or year between " 'pure' kindergarten . . . and 'beginning' first-grade work." Commonly, kindergartens and primary schools effected a partial accommodation; some primary teachers even sought to meet the expectations of kindergarten graduates by trying games and songs and granting pupils slightly greater physical freedom. Although public kindergartens were routinized and often underfunded, the ideal of enrichment through play did not wholly disappear.[114]

Whereas critics of progressive-era kindergartens have emphasized administrative constraints, apologists have praised liberating curricular changes. Nineteenth-century Froebelian orthodoxy had severely limited classroom freedom. Kindergartners whose training had obliged them to copy "700 paper folding forms" would not lightly abandon established techniques. Indeed, all but two kindergartners walked out in 1895 when G. Stanley Hall criticized Froebel's gifts as too small and precise for young children. Subsequently, however, kindergarten reformers accepted Hall's belief that children needed larger, more varied playthings. John Dewey's experimental school and kindergarten at the University of Chicago made instructional practices more flexible by organizing the classroom as a learning community. Even Edward L. Thorndike's view that children learn by establishing highly specific stimulus-response patterns justified proliferation of kindergarten activities. At Teachers College, Columbia University, Patty Smith Hill (who wrote "Happy Birthday" as a kindergarten song) wove these influences into a rationale for freer, more varied classroom practices.[115] Her ideas prevailed by 1920.

Kindergarten reformers still sought to teach orderly behavior, but like many other progressive-era managers of childhood, they turned from drills toward group pressure. In *Children's Rights*, Kate Douglas Wiggin, a veteran of kindergartens in San Francisco, wrote approvingly, "If the child is unruly in play, he leaves the circle and sits or stands by himself, a miserable, lonely unit until he feels again in sympathy with the community." In practice, adults ran the groups. A Detroit boy who attended kindergarten in 1920 remembers mainly being read to in a circle and then being placed apart on a table for talking.[116]

Whatever their methods, kindergarten teachers directed activity fairly closely. It was a concession when kindergartens of the early 1900s began permitting children to draw and model clay according to their own imaginations. Since many primary teachers thought kindergarten children loud and restless, those of the first two decades of the 1900s probably enjoyed some freedom to make noise and move around. Yet some first-grade teachers complained that kindergarten children, trained to expect adult direction, had trouble working on their own.[117]

In any case, only a minority had the experience. Public and private kindergarten enrollment increased from about 5 percent of children ages four and five in 1902 to 9 percent in 1912. Public kindergartens alone registered more than 10 percent of children those ages in 1920. As more kindergartens took five-year-olds only, the proportion enrolled at that age approached 20 percent. Yet this was less than half the nonfarm population, and children attended irregularly—only 61 percent of those enrolled on any given day in 1911. This record implies that many parents did not think kindergartens vital for their children. If school superintendents' views were representative, middle-class parents believed their own five-year-olds needed only mother's care and play in the yard.[118]

If parents were to bother with preschool education, many wanted direct preparation for schooling; they favored early reading, which educators often resisted. Rural children started school informally at varying ages, some tagging along early with an older sibling, others going alone at age five if the school was close; yet a few parents held children back until age seven. When asked about kindergarten, some former country children recalled "chart" classes, but these were distinctly reading oriented, focused on practicing the alphabet from a big chart. Country children commonly came ready to read. In large families, small fry imitated older siblings' lessons. Many onetime farm children remember mothers and fathers who themselves had limited education teaching them basic reading before they went to school. Some city children have similar memories. A former working-class girl observed that "in those days when kids came to school, they didn't need a kindergarten. There would be [a] very few that came from illiterate families, maybe. But as a rule, we all knew our ABC's, we knew our numbers, we knew our colors, we could draw. This was part of the things we did at home after the house quieted down."[119] Many parents with limited schooling recognized literacy as a valuable skill and may have questioned the value of marking time in kindergarten. Yet public kindergartens were placed first in working-class neighborhoods.

In the progressive era formal education grew to occupy a larger share of children's lives. Age-graded schooling lengthened conspicuously at both ends of childhood. With its distinctive program for children of four and five, the kindergarten's expansion paralleled the high school's. But the high school's utility was more evident to parents and children; kindergartens grew more slowly, and early childhood was less institutionally distinctive than adolescence.

Overall, early childhood by 1920 remained less securely set apart than reformers wished. Despite their efforts to make middle-class standards hegemonic, widely varying practices prevailed in infant diet, parental nurture, preschool education, play, and work. Even by age five, many children began to face responsibilities that ran counter to the ideal of the sheltered childhood. Without much more equally distributed prosperity, many parents would or could not free even small children from the demands of the family economy. For the sheltered, play-centered childhood was not, as many reformers seemingly believed, simply normal because it was developmentally beneficial. It demanded cultural commitment and economic resources.

3

Later Childhood: Schooling

$\mathbf{F}$rom around age 6 to 12 or 14, turn-of-the-century children's social contacts expanded rapidly beyond the family. Despite the ideology of the sheltered childhood, their socialization now began more directly to foreshadow adult roles. As theorists have since noted, children within this age range display new developmental possibilities much more akin to adult capacities than are those of early childhood. In Jean Piaget's terms, between ages 7 and 11 children develop concrete operational thinking; they can classify and rank things and understand arithmetical and spatial relationships. Erik Erikson describes later childhood as an age of apprenticeship through formal or informal education, when children develop a confident sense of industry or, sadly, come to believe in their own inferiority.[1] Recognizing the possibilities of childhood for growth and socialization, progressive-era educators undertook to develop individual possibilities to their fullest, while increasingly defining that maximum as low for some children. On balance, educators shifted between 1890 and 1920 from imperfectly realized universalism toward frankly proclaimed (though also imperfectly realized) prescriptive diversification.

School Expansion and Progressive Reform

Even in the progressive era, expansion characterized American schools more than fundamental reform. Commitment to universal elementary schooling was already widespread in the North and West. Symbolizing extension of this commitment were compulsory attendance laws, enacted in all states by 1918; by then 7 states required attendance until age 15, and 31 until age 16. Southern legislation remained little more than symbolic, however. North Carolina's

1917 law, for instance, mandated only four months of annual attendance from ages 8 through 13—a lifetime total of 24 months—and exempted anyone whose parents wanted the child's work at home. Legal coercion was almost certainly not the primary cause of rising school attendance. Not until school enrollment spread widely did states pass more than token legislation; statistical analysis suggests that even strong laws boosted enrollments by no more than 2 percent. Increased availability of schools, parents' recognition that literacy was valuable, and declining employment of children probably mattered more.[2]

Schools achieved nearly universal enrollment only within a narrow age range. In 1890, almost 80 percent of American children ages 10 through 14 already attended school sometime during the year; by 1910, 88 percent did so. Yet only 49 percent of children ages six through nine attended school in 1890 and 62 percent in 1910. As late as 1920, it was only from ages 9 through 13 that more than 90 percent of American children attended school, although more than 80 percent of children ages 7, 8, and 14 did so. Although secondary schools grew dramatically, they enrolled only 2.4 million students in 1920, compared with 20.4 million attending elementary schools. Children still got most of their education in the elementary grades.[3]

Racial and regional disparities narrowed, but only slightly. In the South, only 51 percent of African-American children ages 10 through 14 attended school at any time during 1890, compared with 78 percent of white children the same age. By 1920, 78 percent of black children ages 10 through 14 and 90 percent of whites managed at least brief attendance. But how brief? Nationwide, the average school term lengthened from 135 days in 1890 to 162 in 1920. Though still irregular, average attendance per enrolled pupil rose from 86 days in 1890 (less than two-thirds of the term) to 121 in 1920 (nearly three-quarters). Assuming 20 school days to the month, average attendance had increased from just over four months a year in 1890 to six by 1920. Children were spending more of their childhood in school—although the 121-day average still represented fewer than one-third of the days in a year, and increases were unevenly distributed. Public schools in towns above 4,000 early approximated the modern standard with terms averaging 186 days in 1910. Other schools averaged just 140 days. And nonurban pupils attended less of their shorter terms (68 percent versus 79 percent for urban pupils in 1910). Northern rural school terms ran fairly long, but the rural South, with its huge child population, lagged badly. In 1919 to 1920, South Carolina had the nation's briefest average term (110 days) and lowest attendance per pupil (76 days). Skewed school funding produced terms for African Americans 9 to 51 percent shorter than whites' by 1910.[4] For many children, schooling was still a sometime thing—and for black farm children it was scarcely that.

Despite the contemporary rhetoric of concern for children, progressive-era schools operated with limited resources. In 1890, average spending per day per pupil in attendance stood at 12.8 cents. This rose slightly to 15.1 cents (in 1890 prices) by 1900, and more substantially to 20.2 cents in 1910. During the late 1910s, inflation ravaged school budgets, producing a decline to 18 cents in 1920 at 1890 prices. By contrast, the figure surged to 34.2 cents by 1930—larger than the entire gain for the preceding three decades. While not a time of extreme stringency, neither was the progressive era an unusually flush time for schools. Progressive invocations of efficiency, which grew in fervor during the inflationary 1910s, reflected real pressures on educators.[5]

With per capita income half the national average and far higher ratios of children to adults, the South spent less than half the national average per capita on education in 1900. In 1901, formation of the Rockefeller-financed Southern Education Board allied southern reformers and northern philanthropists in a crusade for better schools. To appease southern whites, the northerners supported plans that offered African Americans preparation for menial labor or nothing. Though miserably low, southern school funding had been more equal racially in 1890 than ever again before 1954. But court decisions during the 1890s sanctioned blatantly unequal facilities. As disfranchisement cost African Americans virtually all political power, crusaders seeking higher taxes assured white voters that the revenues would not go to black schools. By siphoning off funds, white schools in heavily black areas thrived, whereas those in predominantly white counties still fared poorly. In 1917, many mountain schools still lacked desks; pupils hunched all day on benches with papers in their laps.[6]

By 1910, African Americans were left with school expenditures per pupil that ranged from two-thirds of those for whites in Tennessee to one-sixth in Louisiana. In a typical North Carolina township, only two of four black schools reached past the fourth grade; enrollments ranged from 44 to 96 in one room; and painted planks served for blackboards. Although hundreds of private schools, many church controlled, mitigated these deficiencies, private resources could not furnish mass education. Most northern philanthropists favored Booker T. Washington's Tuskegee Institute, where future teachers studied at a common school level, labored in the fields, and prepared to teach rudimentary skills underlying menial labor, but Washington did not convince most black educators. Whereas industrial education fell flat, African Americans had long given labor and cash for schools that offered hope of advancement—to the point that private support for black public schools outweighed tax money in some states. So when Julius Rosenwald, the president of Sears Roebuck, offered seed money for buildings, black donors and taxpayers in effect shouldered double taxation to construct almost 5,000 schools between 1914 and 1932.[7]

As African Americans moved north in increasing numbers after about 1916, they found a mixed though intensifying pattern of school segregation.

Only the more segregated systems had any number of black teachers. Some white teachers were blatantly racist, and even the well intentioned assumed that recent arrivals needed uplift. Burdened by low expectations and weak southern education, many migrants found themselves placed far below their age level. Even so, an enhanced supply of schooling released pent-up demand. Black migrants typically stayed in school farther into their teens than first- or second-generation European immigrants did.[8]

Many immigrant parents found the public schools' Protestantism religiously threatening. Although some educators had grown cautious by the early 1900s, opening exercises often featured hymns, Bible readings, and the Lord's Prayer. Yet wholly secular education also drew Catholic criticism. Either way, churchmen promoted parochial schools to defend the faith.[9]

Parish schools could also defend parents' language and cultural identity. German immigration, which had swelled both Catholic and Lutheran schools, waned toward 1900, but new Catholic immigrants flooded in. Whereas Italians were relatively indifferent, Poles, Lithuanians, Czechs, and Slovaks made schools centers of ethnic identity, staffed by teaching sisters from the homeland who recruited American-born girls into their orders to carry on national traditions. Increasingly, however, prominent bishops tried to position Catholic schools alongside public schools as part of a larger Americanizing system. By the late 1910s, state legislation and Americanizers such as Chicago's Archbishop Mundelein began moving church schools toward exclusively English-language instruction. Yet Polish still predominated in many Chicago-area schools where teaching sisters spoke little English. Although little more than half of all Catholic children attended parochial schools, between 1890 and 1920 their elementary enrollments roughly trebled to 1.8 million. Lutheran parochial schools fared less well. Lacking inexpensive nuns, they averaged huge classes and often drafted the pastor to teach. As use of English in church eroded commitment to separate schools, enrollment fell from 212,000 children in 1895 to below 100,000 by 1925.[10]

The harshest struggle between acculturation and diversity pitted the federal government's insistence on formal schooling against Native Americans' kin- and community-based education. Appearing on every reservation by the late 1880s, government schools adopted an unbending English-only policy. On paper, children progressed from day school to a reservation boarding school to a more advanced and distant boarding school. In practice, off-reservation boarding schools scrambled for pupils, took some as young as five, and seldom offered older youths instruction beyond the eighth grade. In the decade after 1910 federal support shifted to favor contracts with local public systems. By 1919, these reportedly enrolled half of all Native American pupils, but local officials left many American Indian children unschooled. Ironically, neglectful federal policy mitigated damage to Native American cultures.[11]

Progressive reforms left parochial and American Indian schools untouched. Except for a few experimental private schools, reformers had to find niches in the public school system. There it proved easier to add new subjects and services than to change the basic elementary curriculum and classroom procedures.

By the late nineteenth century, teachers had settled into a routine of marching students through textbooks. Some teachers, described by historian Barbara Finkelstein as "overseers," merely prescribed assignments and checked their completion, commonly by catechizing students. Others, the "drillmasters," organized exercises, unison recitations, and competitions. A third group, "interpreters of culture," actually "clarified and elaborated" materials for students. Yet all three teaching styles settled for rote reproduction of skills or knowledge.[12] On their own, teachers were unlikely to change much. Contemporary gender stereotypes suggest that increasing numbers of female teachers—from 66 percent in public schools in 1890 to 86 percent by 1920—should have fostered empathetic, less peremptory teaching. But fear of superintendents made city teachers cautious. Rural teachers' limited training emphasized subject content over teaching methods. Young and inexperienced (on average teachers taught only five years), most would teach as they had been taught.[13]

Routines in most one-room schools followed the overseer pattern. One subject at a time, for 10 minutes or so each, a cluster of pupils came forward to the recitation bench, recited memorized passages, answered questions, presented scraps of writing, or worked arithmetic problems, then received a new assignment and returned to their desks. Pupils got ample scrutiny but limited explanation. Although former pupils boasted of learning advanced subjects early from overheard recitations, concentration was difficult. A critical journalist described the scene as two squads recited: "another group wrote in their copy-books pages of such inspiring themes as 'O barn burn barn O.' . . . One group read geography questions and hunted upon the map for answers; one studied history; one did sums; and several groups did nothing with great proficiency." The week's highlights for eager students were Friday afternoon ciphering and spelling contests, where victory rewarded mastery of detail.[14]

In graded city schools, teachers could drill classes en masse. Writing in 1892 and 1893, reformer Joseph Rice left caustic portraits of these drillmasters at work. In Baltimore, pupils chanted arithmetic and even state boundaries in concert. A New York City principal's motto was "Save the minutes." In her school, children screamed "ready-made" answers at top speed, the next pupil rising to perform while the previous one recited. Forbidden to move their heads, pupils passed papers blindly across the rows.[15]

In contrast, Rice praised schools elsewhere that encouraged children to be active learners. With this sharply drawn distinction between "old . . . unscientific or mechanical" methods and the "new," "progressive" education, Lawrence Cremin believes that Rice first gave progressive education self-awareness as a national movement. Women's clubs and child study enthusiasts took up the call for a "new education" that "emphasized individuality, mild forms of discipline, and an end to excessive memorization, recitation, and testing."[16]

Somewhat incongruously, Rice's main remedy was structural. He wanted to end ward-based control of schools, substituting a centralized board of education appointed by the mayor from the city's professional and business leaders. The board would hire a professional superintendent of schools to teach teachers proper methods and fire the recalcitrant. Similar attacks on local control became staples of reform discourse, and centralization proceeded apace during the progressive era. These administrative changes did not necessarily foster Rice's vision of joyful, liberating education, however. Efficiency could reduce graft but also justified further regimenting teachers and cutting budgets. Toledo's board, newly centralized in 1898, opposed "fads and frills" such as kindergartens and playgrounds.[17] Above all, loss of local autonomy made it easier for administrators to categorize children, consigning many to schooling that reinforced social inequality.

Rice believed that progressive pedagogical principles were already widely known. As John Dewey observed, the necessity of active learning had long prevailed in educational preaching—just not in practice. In 1892, the psychologist William James warned teachers: "An impression which simply flows in at the pupil's eyes or ears, and in no way modifies his active life, is an impression gone to waste." G. Stanley Hall preached that children must learn through activities suited to their stage of cultural development. Yet much psychology also bolstered traditional pedagogy and differentiation among children. Hall believed the years from 8 to 12 "should be mainly devoted to drill, habituation, and mechanism." Similarly, James told teachers that *we must make automatic and habitual, as early as possible, as many useful actions as we can.*" Wrenched from James's subtler context, such statements supported old-fashioned drills. James's student Edward L. Thorndike sharpened James's conclusion that habits are highly specific. Doubting that teachers could develop pupils' general abilities, Thorndike urged that schools concentrate on sorting the worthy from the unworthy.[18]

The most celebrated attempt to change classroom practice—much more generously conceived than this protobehaviorist testing and sorting—was John and Alice Chipman Dewey's Laboratory School, which opened in 1896 at the University of Chicago. The Deweys wholeheartedly endorsed active learning but went beyond individual psychology to try, in John Dewey's words, to remake the school into "an embryonic community, active with types of occupations that reflect the life of the larger society, and permeated with the spirit of art, history, and science." In practice, the Deweys sought to integrate learning through shared undertakings of interest to children; arithmetic, for instance, would emerge from the needs of cooking and chemistry.[19]

The Deweys' ideas had limited effect on classroom practice. With a clientele of faculty children and 23 instructors for just 140 pupils in 1902, the Laboratory School remained strictly experimental, not a model that public educators could replicate. When John Dewey left Chicago for Columbia University in 1904, the couple had not fully tested their ideas' validity and had no plan for overcoming resistance. Yet many parents respected only formal, highly controlled classrooms; nor were administrators about to grant teachers or pupils the autonomy that the Deweys' approach required. Meanwhile the two largest graduate schools of education fell under the dominance of "measurers"—Thorndike at Columbia and Charles Judd at Chicago—who lacked the Deweys' concern for individual development and social renewal. Instead, both men viewed education as "matching individuals to existing social and economic roles." In defining the "mainstream" of educational expertise, writes Ellen Condliffe Lagemann, by the late 1910s "Thorndike had won and Dewey had lost." Proponents of manual training and sundry causes invoked Dewey's name, but even disciples diluted his challenge to existing practice. The best-known attempt to encapsulate Dewey's ideas for classroom teachers, William H. Kilpatrick's 1918 essay "The Project Method," endorsed group undertakings to counter the "selfish individualism" of "our customary set-task sit-alone-at-your-desk procedure." Yet Kilpatrick asserted that traditional drill qualified if undertaken in a "hearty purposeful" spirit. While Deweyan methods survived in scattered private schools, public schools held mostly to formal, teacher-centered instruction.[20]

Enthusiasm for testing and hierarchical categorization of children—an approach incompatible with the Deweys' ideal of a cooperative community—drew strength from studies of "retardation" in city schools. (The term did not imply mental deficiency, merely failure to advance one grade per year.) In a landmark compilation, *Laggards in Our Schools* (1909), Leonard Ayres estimated that one-third of urban schoolchildren were two years or more below the proper grade for their age. *"These conditions,"* Ayres charged, *"mean that our courses of study as at present constituted are fitted not to the slow child or to the average child but to the unusually bright one."* Since discouraged pupils quit school, he estimated that only half of city children reached the eighth grade. Ayres wrote with feeling of the hurt to children taught "the habit of failure" but also invoked the progressive cult of efficiency by likening schools to wasteful factories. Although promotion statistics spurred educators to tighten grading by age, they also encouraged invidious distinctions. High retardation rates reinforced belief that an academic curriculum was too demanding for most immigrants. Ignoring the shortcomings of black schools, many educators concluded that African Americans' large percentage of children too old for the grades in which they were placed proved them unfit for academic studies. And girls' superior progress led Ayres to pronounce schools *"far better fitted to the needs of the girls than . . . to those of the boys."* Immigrants, nonwhites, and boys in general began to be labeled "hand-minded." Much of what passed for progressive education was an effort to adapt schools to the purported needs of pupils considered academically untalented on ethnic, class, and gender grounds.[21]

Drawing on business models of measured efficiency, the quest to regularize student advancement triggered an "orgy of tabulation" as educational researchers sought to quantify current achievement levels and embody them in standardized tests. Such tests, Stanford's Elwood Cubberley assured teachers, "set 'limited objectives' . . . which the teacher is expected to reach, but beyond which she is not expected to go."[22] Proponents of standardization charged that teachers using traditional examinations bestowed wildly varying grades and, by allowing pupils all the time they needed, failed to reward efficient, high-speed workers. Despite assurances that the new tests were "scientifically devised," however, their creators had trouble choosing which nuggets of information to include and found complex skills intractable. Thorndike himself failed to reduce grades for handwriting to more than average scores by "competent judges." This was far from his dream of "tests which can be scored by persons utterly devoid of judgment concerning the products in question." Formats varied, as pupils wrote short answers and crossed out, circled, or underlined items. Mechanical scoring with stencils awaited invention of the multiple choice format, first widely used to screen draftees during World War I.[23]

Although Lewis Terman published his "Stanford-Binet" revision of French psychologist Alfred Binet's intelligence tests in 1916, such tests saw limited use until psychologists pressed them on the army in World War I. Terman and Robert Yerkes revised the army tests for school use, and World Book printed 400,000 in 1920. Intelligence tests won deserved notoriety for cultural bias, since Terman normed the Stanford-Binet set using native-born, middle-class children and excluded both rural and African-American children when standardizing the 1920 tests.[24]

In claiming to evaluate narrowly defined competencies rather than general intelligence, achievement tests seemed more objective. Yet they too embodied cultural hegemony in their choices of knowledge to test and children to use for age norming. Slipping into use a bit sooner, achievement tests proved more important than IQ tests for sorting pupils and bolstering administrative control of teachers. By 1918, a testing proponent could describe 84 standardized tests of elementary school subjects. As surveys of city school systems gained popularity in the 1910s, they used standardized tests to assess instructional efficiency. Since test makers surveyed educators' opinions and textbook contents to determine essential knowledge, then tested current pupils to set achievement norms, their tests mostly reinforced existing curricula.[25]

Standardized testing did accelerate one major shift—from oral to silent reading. Critics had long mocked mindless recitations; now Thorndike showed that many pupils could not answer questions about passages they had read. Educators of the 1910s urged that children learn to read silently "to acquire ideas rapidly and effectively" and not for "oral exhibition." Functionalists could explain this as a shift from an oral culture of preachers, politicians, and lawyers to one dominated by large organizations that required orderly processing of written information. This change also marked a gendered reorientation from public oratory toward a private realm of sensibility more familiar to girls than to boys. Despite progressive educators' professed fondness for physical activity, suppression of vocalization in reading marked another step toward stillness in the classroom. The new emphasis culminated a trend away from the programs of showpiece declamations by which country teachers displayed their pupils' achievements to parents and community.[26] Instead, the ability to read silently and answer short questions became the pupil's core skill.

Parallel changes—away from superlative, competitive performance and toward steady, age-graded improvement—were under way after 1910 in arithmetic and spelling. Superintendents sought to replace prodigious feats of computation and obscure topics such as "apothecaries' weight, alligation, [and] aliquot parts" with "carefully graded, simple problems." Spelling lists shrank to focus on commonly used and frequently misspelled words. Unthinkable in city schools was the open competition of all ages that had excited country pupils at Friday spelldowns and interschool ciphering contests. In rural Kansas in the 1890s, when "eleven-year-old Roscoe Conaway went down on a problem of cancellation, bested by a sixteen-year-old girl," nobody charged unfairness due to age.[27] Progressive educators would have been horrified.

The new experts did not go unchallenged, however, for the wars over how to teach reading had already begun. Teachers of the early 1900s commonly started with words and added phonics fairly soon, though immigrant children recall only memorizing words. Reading specialists, who believed that vocalizing slowed silent reading, wanted phonics delayed. Then as now, however, lay critics favored early phonics. Many parents also wanted quick literacy. As advocates of a slower pace, Arnold and Beatrice Gesell blamed "the impatient anxiety of A-B-C-minded parents" for creating "an artificially precocious atmosphere in the primary school."[28]

Beyond the primary grades, conservatives such as William T. Harris, U.S. Commissioner of Education from 1889 to 1906, favored grammar, literature, mathematics, geography, and history. Rhetorically, however, liberal education could not compete with the language of utility and social efficiency that increasingly dominated public discourse on education and represented conventional wisdom by the 1910s. Preaching his New Nationalism, Theodore Roosevelt urged that schools furnish "practical training for daily life and work." Yet little changed. Manual training had entered elementary schools in the 1880s as a device for holding boys in school and teaching accuracy and diligence—not as directly vocational preparation. The most popular system, sloyd, promoted formalized wood carving. Manual training classes grew fairly common by the early 1900s, but only as "carpentry kindergartens." Recalling his fifth-grade work with scroll saws, B. F. Skinner observed that he had better tools and supplies at home. Proposals to differentiate elementary instruction had little effect. In 1914, city school systems allotted 77 percent of instructional time to reading, arithmetic, language, spelling, penmanship, and geography—the traditional core studies. Drawing, music, and history each claimed slightly more time than manual training, science a trifle less. Although the advent of junior high schools in the 1910s facilitated tinkering with curriculum, junior highs spread widely only after 1920.[29]

Nonwhites faced graver threats to dilute their curriculum. In an era when racism was respectable, many educators favored consigning whole groups to preparation for lowly work. Federal officials wrote explicitly after 1900 of training Native American children for wage labor and domestic service, but underfunded boarding schools had long imposed daunting workloads. Many girls did not even develop all-round domestic skills, since they labored exclusively in one workroom, doing laundry, sewing, or cooking for the whole school. Racism and white enthusiasm for Tuskegee's program to train laborers forced African-American parents to fight on two fronts, seeking to upgrade underfunded public schools while fending off schemes to consign their children to rudimentary industrial and domestic training. In Atlanta the Women's Civic and Social Improvement Committee petitioned the board of education in 1913 to end double shifts in black schools. When the board responded by proposing to provide only industrial education past the sixth grade, the committee had to oppose the plan. In rural North Carolina, black schoolchildren's "industrial" training consisted of darning, embroidery, and basketmaking. Northern school officials likewise hurried to "industrialize" elementary schools for African Americans. When challenged by parents, the Philadelphia school board defended industrial education as suiting black pupils' "educational aptitudes."[30]

Unable to transform the core of common schooling for white pupils, reformers sought to help the poor and to Americanize immigrants by adding services outside the regular curriculum: school playgrounds and vacation schools offered supervised recreation; visiting teachers advised poor parents; "steamer" classes served recent immigrants. Social settlements and women's organizations pioneered the majority of these innovations. Yet most voluntary associations could fund only demonstration projects; city-wide application required adoption by the school authorities, who often resisted or complied only pro forma. When the Woman's School Alliance of Milwaukee served hot meals, for instance, they could average fewer than 300 per school day across a large city. Coverage broadened only when the school board provided funding in 1917. Nationwide, school meals—like other new social services—"never reached the majority of children."[31]

School health programs exemplified the problems of services that were underfunded and superficial. Following studies that linked physical defects to retardation, examinations for faults such as bad teeth became a panacea for school improvement. As often happened, reformers confused symptoms of poverty with causes of social problems. Although there was value in urging parents to provide spectacles and dental care, huge variations in defect rates from city to city (7 percent in Bayonne, New Jersey, 80 percent in Sioux City, Iowa) and age to age (except for vision, reported defects fell by almost two-thirds between ages 6 and 15 in New York City) suggest that inspections detected mostly passing trivialities. Adenoids and mouth breathing became obsessions. "*Adenoids* dull the mind" by impeding respiration, explained Arnold and Beatrice Gesell, resulting in "distractible attention (*aprosexia nasalis*), disturbed emotion, and weak memory." Surgery promised swift cures. "In one instance a primary-school child had spent a whole year in school without learning the alphabet," reported the Gesells. "An operation removed the adenoids, and the alphabet was learned in a week." Such certitude favored cultural imposition. In an extreme instance, a principal on New York's Lower East Side responded to parents' failure to have children's adenoids removed by bringing in a surgeon. When the rumor spread that the goyim were cutting throats, parents besieged the school. More commonly, as in other areas of child welfare, reformers lacked funds to pay for changes or power to force them and fell back on blaming parents. Rather than provide treatment, school health officials sent notes home urging parents to take their children to physicians and dentists. Parents "were far from cooperative," complained New York's Josephine Baker, "and this money might have been spent with better results in almost any other field of public health."[32]

Surprisingly, the most celebrated attempt to combine progressive zeal for efficiency with enhanced school services sprouted in United States Steel's new city of Gary, Indiana. The school superintendent, William Wirt, got a fresh start, with business backing and a recently arrived immigrant population unorganized to resist innovation. Wirt also segregated black children and excluded them from many activities. By housing all grades from kindergarten through high school in the same large buildings, he provided gymnasiums, manual training shops, libraries, and playgrounds for all ages. And by platooning students so that some occupied classrooms while others used shops or playgrounds, Wirt claimed to furnish an enriched program as cheaply as conventional schooling. Yet Wirt eschewed narrow vocationalism and won effusive praise from Dewey's disciple Randolph Bourne for educating the "whole child" without class bias.[33]

Trouble ensued when reformers bent on lower taxes made Gary their model. Hoping to avoid new construction, Mayor John P. Mitchel hired Wirt in 1914 to advise on reorganizing New York City's schools. An upper-class xenophobe, Mitchel advocated coercive Americanization. Under such sponsorship, the Gary plan alarmed immigrant parents, who feared it would impose vocationalism on and deny advancement to their children. When voters ousted Mitchel in 1917, his successor eliminated the Gary plan. Meanwhile Wirt had responded to criticism by requesting that the Rockefeller-financed General Education Board evaluate Gary's schools. Foreshadowing later critics of progressive education, Abraham Flexner and Frank Bachman's report complained of low scores on standardized achievement tests, alleging that children were being "habituated to inferior performance." This criticism cooled enthusiasm for the Gary plan among reformers, although platooning survived as an economy measure.[34] Gary's failure as a transforming model left administrative efficiency and traditional pedagogy, supplemented by a few new subjects and services, dominant in urban education.

Most proposals to reform rural schooling sought to impose these urban patterns: centralization, close supervision, and age-graded, large-group instruction. The National Education Association's Committee of Twelve on Rural Schools framed the reform agenda in 1897. Decrying the current system of virtually autonomous district schools staffed by "untrained, immature" teachers, the committee prescribed consolidation. Although larger, centralized schools had to transport distant pupils in horse-drawn wagons, reformers promised compensating gains. With separate classes grouped by age, closely supervised teachers could substitute "more rational methods of instruction" for the flexible makeshifts of one-room schools, inculcating the "regularity, punctuality, obedience, industry, [and] self-control" prized in city schools. Since school boards and parents commonly resisted, however, consolidation proceeded fitfully. As of 1920, 195,000 one-room schools survived nationwide; just 10,000 had consolidated and many only to two rooms.[35]

Reformers sought to uplift the rural community through its children. In the South, the Woman's Association for the Betterment of Public School Houses made practical improvements: ceiling vents, sanitary privies, water coolers to replace the common dipper. But a leader voiced the grander ambition that fresh paint and landscaped grounds would inspire pupils to scorn their "low, groveling, canine conditions of life." By the 1910s, schoolhouse modernization merged into a campaign to cure hookworm and with it southern lethargy. As elsewhere, reformers dreamed of shortcuts to social efficiency. Thus sanitation officers in North Carolina organized school adenoid and tonsil clubs for removal at group rates.[36]

Agitation to change rural education gained impetus after 1900 from belief among opinion leaders that farm communities were dreary and dispirited, that agricultural inefficiency inflated food prices, and that outmigration by young people was weakening the nation's demographic backbone. These concerns received official sanction in 1908 when Theodore Roosevelt appointed a Country Life Commission to report on rural deficiencies. Charging that rural schools trained children for white-collar work and encouraged them to leave the farm, Country Lifers advocated nature study to inspire farm children and home economics and agricultural education to inculcate receptiveness to technological change.[37]

Two exemplary teachers, Missouri's Marie Harvey Turner and Iowa's Sarah Gillespie Huftalen, won renown for transforming one-room schools. Harvey assigned agricultural bulletins and centered arithmetic around the young farmers' account books. Not one pupil, she claimed, subsequently left the community. Huftalen likewise integrated instruction with local materials; the children studied trees and landscaped the school yard. Few rural teachers, however, equaled Harvey's and Huftalen's initiative. In 1919, just 21 percent of rural Nebraska teachers attempted vocational or domestic instruction, and 71 percent of those few considered the subjects "burdensome."[38]

Despite pressures toward consolidation, one-room schools had articulate defenders. Turner and Huftalen showed that such schools could offer rich programs. Dorothy Canfield Fisher's popular 1917 children's story, *Understood Betsy*, idealized country childhood. Displaced from a midwestern city to rural Vermont, Betsy transfers to a one-room school with only 12 pupils. Initially disconcerted by her teacher's flexible grading (she is placed with the seventh grade for reading, the second for arithmetic), Betsy soon thrives. At home, the technology of dairy farming—weighing, measuring, making butter—lies open to Betsy's observation and participation. Fisher's Vermont needed no Country Life reformers.[39]

Many farmers and their children viewed reform with indifference or hostility. Former pupils reminisced favorably about one-room schools. Even critics, such as a onetime North Dakota farm boy who recalled his school's barnyard odors and neglected bookshelf, were more likely to decry the one-room schools' low academic standards than their insufficient ruralism. Complaints that rural teachers—themselves country bred—counseled ambitious pupils towards urban, white-collar vocations suggest that rural young people assessed occupational rewards more realistically than reformers. Indeed, one skeptical farmer asked the Country Life commissioners "why they wanted rural boys and girls to stay on the farm when they themselves had left it." When allowed to vote, farmers defeated a majority of consolidation proposals. Farm parents complained that their children faced long waits, immorality on the wagons, and snobbery from classmates who lived in town. Some rode nearly two hours each way and got home late for chores. And consolidation almost always meant higher taxes. On curricular issues, fragmentary evidence suggests a rural perspective different from the reformers'. To farm parents, schools had a specific function—teaching children to "read, write, spell, and figure," not dabbling in "fads." A teacher who experimented with nature study, agriculture, or domestic science could face an angry parent who "sent his children to school to learn something useful." Parents resented implications that they were incompetent to teach their children farming and that a callow schoolteacher knew better.[40]

Like the urban working class, farmers valued the literacy and numeracy that elementary schooling conferred but had no desire to see schools engulf their children's socialization. The reformers' dream of socializing whole communities of culturally deficient immigrants and farmers through their children brought only peripheral changes to elementary schooling.

Experiences of Schooling

For children entering school, the relative failure of progressive educators to reshape the system in some ways buffered and in others sharpened the transition. Weak administrative rationalization permitted children to start at varying ages from five through seven and then attend somewhat irregularly, as parents often kept them home to do farmwork or household chores, nurse sick relatives, or mind babies. Investigators in Chicago in the 1910s found that 93 percent of truant boys and 98 percent of truant girls skipped school with their parents' knowledge.[41]

The persistent focus of primary education on a limited range of skills reduced the risk of being subjected to the wholesale resocialization advocated by reformers. But physical constraints were immediate and pressing, especially in city schools, as children sat at desks bolted to the floor, obliged to keep still and silent. Demands for testable mastery of school skills put even successful pupils under strain. Entering the first grade in 1914 in small-town Kentucky, Harriette Simpson received monthly report cards. Six decades later, what stood out in her memory was not the string of Es (for Excellent) but the lone G (Good—not even VG, Very Good) each month in penmanship. Many pupils faced harsher challenges, especially if they started partway through the year. So many repeated the first grade that the 1920 census recorded 65 percent more first than second graders.[42] For children needing to develop a sense of industry and competence, repeating the first grade cannot have seemed auspicious.

Language differences heightened the strain. Although some children of immigrants began parochial schooling in languages other than English, many public and parochial school pupils recall offhandedly learning English "soon enough" by what amounted to total immersion. Among the older children who came as immigrants themselves and entered school beyond age seven, surprising numbers also learned English quickly, although autobiographical testimony skews the record toward success stories. Entering a New York school at age nine in 1908, Marie Jastrow sat "alone and miserable. . . . I had no choice but to learn the new language, quickly and without fuss. Not much help was offered. Few teachers were linguists, and the feelings of the green-horns in the class were not spared. This method led to miracles of accomplishment."[43]

Beyond language, other rituals of difference invited or required compromises of identity. Faced with chapel-style opening exercises, Jewish students hesitated. When Mary Antin dutifully repeated the Lord's Prayer, a Jewish classmate reproved her and she argued back. Ironically, Mary was demoted from the honor row for whispering. Since they involved no equally clear principle, name changes were harder to resist, especially when presented as tokens of success. Rebecca Green would have been Bayla, her parents' choice, but the doctor wrote Beckie on her birth certificate. So when her eighth-grade teacher pronounced the name Beckie too undignified for graduation, she obediently became Rebecca. Similarly, Herschele Golden entered high school as Harry at his teacher's urging.[44]

Inspections for health and cleanliness left even less room for open resistance, though plenty for noncompliance with the directives that followed. Lice probes were rituals of humiliation. In a study of former New York City pupils, all the aged women recalled a teacher exploring their hair "with two pencils used in the manner of knitting needles." Although parents routinely ignored advice sent home, few voiced their resentment as boldly as one (possibly apocryphal) Italian mother in Cleveland. Told that her daughter needed more baths, she responded, "Maria is not a rose, do not smell her, teach her!"[45]

Yet immigrants' children often felt divided loyalties. Although many remembered censorious judgments, many also gained from teachers a taste of the emotionally sheltered childhood prescribed by reformers. On the bleak plains of North Dakota, even students who learned little found that school gave "relief from work, the company of other children, and some attention from well-meaning if often harried teachers." In the judgment of historian Elizabeth Hampsten, these children of work-obsessed immigrant parents remembered their schooling gratefully because it offered "a little leisure and the feeling of being looked after." Pardee Lowe, the son of a prospering Chinese businessman in California, recalled fondly how Miss McIntyre had nurtured his class of first graders: "Coming mainly from immigrant homes where parents were too preoccupied with earning a living to devote much time to their children, we transferred our youthful affections to this one person who had both the time and the disposition to mother us." Jewish girls remembered how they "loved" teachers, some Jewish themselves, who hugged and held first graders in their laps—this in contrast to recollections of mother as "not a nurturer" or "not demonstratively affectionate."[46] Time might temper children's enthusiasm for schooling, but early encounters could prove seductive as well as scary.

For Native American children, government schools were less seductive and the choices more daunting. Whereas most immigrants came from cultures with formal, text-based education for literacy, Native American education relied on imitative games, community practice, apprenticeship, and ritual. Yet European-American educators aimed to break this acculturation. Unlike immigrant parents who sent their children to elementary school fairly readily, therefore, Native American families delayed and agonized. The poor hoped their children would be fed and clothed; some family members thought English useful; others resisted or yielded only to compulsion. This ranged from withholding rations to sending Navajo police to seize children of Hopi traditionalists. Children were drawn by curiosity, boredom with farmwork, the lure of food, and the example of friends. As the daughter of conservative Hopi, Polingaysi Qoyawayma had dodged the Navajo police. But the prospect of a cotton dress, curiosity about *Bahana* food, and the sound of children playing drew her down off her mesa to be captured by friends and delivered to the teacher.[47]

The day schooling that followed relied on coercion without the power to make it fully effective. If European immigrant children accepted Americanized names, this often followed years of assimilation and the new name bore some relation to the old one. But Native American pupils entering day school faced abrupt shocks intended to strip them of identity: short haircuts, traditional garb confiscated, and a new moniker imposed at random. So arbitrary was this labeling that when a Hopi dubbed Nellie escaped and was recaptured, the teachers then called her Gladys. Teaching was equally impersonal—drills repeating uncomprehended words and making marks on paper. With pupils living at home, day schools could not prevail. In a year when teachers thought him a prize pupil, Don Talayesva learned only "bright boy," "smart boy," "yes," "no," "nail," and "candy."[48]

Forced change required the power of a total institution, the boarding school where pupils lost the "warm blanket" of attentive kinfolk, lived alongside members of different tribes, and learned to speak English all the time on pain of punishment. The majority did not go off until age 10 or older, but some children left home around age 6. New arrivals cried themselves to sleep and greeted the day with fresh tears. And yet while runaways were common, so were long-term residents who disliked going home and felt like strangers there.[49] Such children did not necessarily feel uprooted because new ideas had effectively displaced old ones but because school attendance had disrupted the practices required to learn traditional culture, such as work alongside elders and vision quests in which youths sought guardian spirits. Formal schooling interfered with the "never-ending" lectures by elders and the snow baths and long runs at dawn expected of Navajo boys and girls. And yet when Navajo adults who had attended Anglo schools told their life stories, they singled out parental advice as their most important education.[50]

Despite the expressed resolve of a prominent New York educator to "wrest" immigrant pupils from their parents, public schools did not challenge parents as directly as schools for Native Americans did. Most educators assumed that parents would support the schools' disciplinary authority. A punishment at school often meant a second one at home if parents found out. More positively, some parents also helped with homework. Academically, however, power shifted. Public presentations in rural schools invited collective judgment upon the pupils and thus upon the teacher. Since rural school routines left ample time for seat work, farm children seldom had homework to challenge parental control of their time after school. The urban practice of sending home monthly report cards reversed the burden of judgment, making clear the school's power to assess each pupil individually. Immigrant parents ambitious for their children were particularly vulnerable. Whereas a home visit by the teacher was an honor, a summons to school meant rebuke; yet a Jewish father in New York came anyway, losing half a day's pay. Report cards exposed some children to double jeopardy; a Chicago boy complained, "When you works a whole month at school, the teacher she gives you a card to take home that says how you ain't any good. And yer folks hollers on yer an' hits yer."[51]

Despite unison drills, city schools tried to isolate pupils. Grading and classroom discipline underlined the unimportance of each pupil's relationship to anyone but the teacher. "Sitting up, for half an hour, looking straight ahead. A very cruel life," complained a former New York schoolboy. When not receiving large-group instruction, pupils silently did textbook assignments and repetitive "busy-work." The main impediment to isolation was crowding so severe that a schoolgirl remembers gripping her seatmate to keep from falling.[52]

With the failure of consolidation, rural schools remained different. Teachers quizzing a succession of small groups necessarily tolerated more physical movement; restless children paraded to the water bucket. Older pupils sometimes helped teach the youngest. Academic achievement was rivalrous and thus social, certified by triumph in Friday afternoon contests, not just a teacher's grade. Despite low incomes, many country teachers gave prizes. A former Michigan farm girl remembers winning a gold Eversharp pencil and hankies. She loved school. Since recollections tend to come from winners, they neglect the chagrin of regular losers; but acceptance into a community where all participated may have cushioned defeat. Rural teachers fostered inclusiveness, sometimes as targets of group pranks such as stuffing the stovepipe with grass, more often as play leaders. If discipline was causing tensions, a teacher could seek reconciliation with the group at play.[53]

Of course not all schools ran smoothly, although they seemed calmer than in the mid-nineteenth century, when male teachers often battled older students. Amid poverty in southwestern Kansas in 1918, Maude Elliott's students stole from each other and fought at recess. Alternatively, pupils could unite against the teacher. In William Owens's school in rural Texas the boys and girls broke a teacher who never gave time off for basketball, drove his successor to quit, and forced the young woman who followed to make every day "a play day."[54]

In theory, close control could obviate conflict and harsh retribution. Yet agencies that most nearly approximated total institutions—juvenile reformatories, orphanages, and schools for Native Americans—punished especially severely. American Indian boarding schools scheduled every detail of daily life; meals, for example, required three bells—one to sit, one to say grace, and one to eat. Even the compliant Charles Eastman had trouble with the "wearisome regularity, like walking railway ties—the step was too short for me." Strict rules made infractions endemic. At the Phoenix School, young girls scrubbed the floor on hands and knees, racing against a strapping if not finished by 8 A.M. For talking with his seatmate, Don Talayesva had to chew laundry soap. Still harsher punishment awaited escapees: girl runaways cut grass with scissors; boys cried for days in prison.[55]

Although Joseph Rice depicted city schools as rule bound, he believed that physical punishment was declining. At the level of declared policy, 55 of 83 school superintendents surveyed in 1908 "adamantly" opposed corporal punishment or called it a "last resort." But congratulations were premature. Helen Todd, a factory inspector in Chicago, where corporal punishment had, officially, long been abolished, reported in 1913 that 269 of 800 wage-earning children "gave as their one reason for preferring a factory to school, that they were not hit there." An underage boy she returned to school protested: "They hits ye if ye don't learn, and they hits ye if ye whisper, and they hits ye if ye have string in yer pocket, and they hits ye if yer seat squeaks, and they hits ye if ye scrape yer feet, and they hits ye if ye don't stan' up in time, and they hits ye if yer late, and they hits ye if ye ferget the page."[56]

Classroom practice was still in volatile transition. In rural schools, to expel troublemakers offended their taxpaying parents. So parents and school boards expected teachers to whip pupils—but not too harshly. In the cities, Florence Kelley charged school officials with expelling difficult children and conniving at truancy. After 1900 city systems began consigning troublesome children, mostly boys, to special classes—but only the worst problems. Teachers and pupils had to negotiate a relationship. Lacking institutional backup, rural teachers' tempers could escalate easily. Even Sarah Huftalen, a teacher celebrated for program innovation, had trouble. When a boy "saucily responded 'All Right!' " to her repeated command he keep still, she slapped him twice and threatened a whipping. The boy's mother responded with threats. Since work offered a ready alternative, children in mill towns challenged teachers. Thus an unschooled 12-year-old reported, "Jim—he's my pal—he tried it an' he said twan't nothin' but jist to be bossed by 'er stuck-up woman and he cussed her out an' quit—so he did." Yet many teachers and pupils were learning mutual forbearance. Confronting a new class of rural Nebraskans in September of 1918, Bessie Tucker confessed concern at pranks such as "sticking pins through the rubbers of their pencils and then sticking each other with them or tapping them on their tablets in unison which sounds about like a flock of woodpeckers." Young Tucker did not panic. Though she "asserted authority with a will," she remained friendly, joining in play at recess; and her pupils responded in kind, cleaning the schoolhouse and convincing her by October 5 that they were "under control now."[57]

As these examples suggest, classrooms varied. In summary accounts, harshness often stands out. Boys who attended New York City schools between 1900 and 1925 recalled frequent blows with pointers and rulers for talking out of turn or reading for fun instead of studying. Accounts of schools in southern mill villages emphasized "whoopin' " with hickories. But schools were gradually modulating discipline. Multiroom schools increasingly reserved heavy hitting for the principal or priest, whereas classroom teachers merely smacked pupils' hands with rulers. This was common punishment for fairly serious indiscipline, recalled matter-of-factly by a majority of those who attended school in the 1910s. Against minor breaches of discipline or failure to learn assigned lessons, teachers increasingly employed milder measures. In one-room schools, children stood in the corner; in larger buildings, teachers banished them to the cloakroom or hall. Misdemeanants lost recess or stayed after school to write penalty sentences. Although a majority of teachers and principals still hit children in the 1910s and perhaps half did so frequently, a large minority are remembered by their pupils as having used only nonviolent sanctions, and others struck only rarely. Differences followed no clear pattern, although southern and rural teachers may have remained somewhat rougher. Teaching sisters and priests differed little from their public school counterparts. Only in crowded Lutheran parochial schools, often taught by overburdened clergymen, do the teachers seem to have relied routinely on physical punishments.[58]

Urban pupils survived by cultivating resigned acceptance. "I must not slam the door when I am mad, nor answer back the teacher," wrote a knowing Boston schoolgirl. "Teachers are sometimes aggravating, but we must put up with them because the city pays them to be like that." A parochial school graduate from Detroit put the matter more simply to an interviewer: " 'Were your teachers strict?' 'Yes, they were Catholic nuns.' "[59]

As at home, boys received more beatings than girls. Though not invincible to pain and humiliation, boys could respect a teacher who was forceful, even rough. Morris Schappes of New York City told without resentment how Miss Slaughterhouse banged his head against the blackboard for saying "Jesus Christ." It was "the last time I took the name of the Lord in vain. But, I got an education." A quarry worker's son from rural Michigan recalled a big teacher, Mother Smith, who had thrown him to the floor. She was "the only teacher that any of us remember." Girls were not immune to whipping, and they suffered vicariously as horrified observers of excesses. Yet girls also needed protection from boys who dipped their pigtails in inkwells and kept the classroom in turmoil. "We have hard times with the boys at school. They are so bad," complained a Mississippi schoolgirl in 1890. "Mortimer Mason is the terror of the school. Miss Hester has not whipped any yet. . . . [She] is not strict enough with the boys."[60]

Like forgotten teachers, much of elementary schooling—instruction more than discipline—lies hidden from individual and historical memory. As we have seen, critics dismissed turn-of-the-century pedagogy as dreary and ineffective. With an essayist's disdain, Henry Seidel Canby summed up his miseducation: "We went to school for facts and got them." Yet this description best suited the upper elementary and high school grades that many children never reached. The early grades emphasized basic literacy and computation. Since many teachers taught these skills as a succession of details, did children's knowledge cohere as poorly and dissipate as readily as the facts that thronged through more advanced pupils' memories? This seems improbable, since further schooling and daily life reinforced basic skills. But the history of education provides few answers. Despite a vast literature on educational policy, classroom teaching has scarcely been sketched, and the history of children's learning is a blank slate.[61]

Reported literacy rates rose markedly between 1890 and 1920, but the Census Bureau merely asked who could write. As illiteracy began to seem shameful, the inaccuracy of self-reporting became evident. Still, the census set a minimum: almost everyone counted as illiterate really was. In northern states, self-reported illiteracy virtually disappeared among native-born whites. Fifteen percent of native white southerners over age 10 admitted illiteracy in 1890 but fewer than 6 percent did so in 1920. Despite extreme underfunding, southern black schools reduced reported illiteracy for girls ages 10 through 14 from 40 percent in 1890 to 10 percent by 1920 and for boys the same age from 44 percent in 1890 to 14.5 percent by 1920.[62] Complete illiteracy was almost certainly declining.

Yet schooling did not guarantee functional literacy. An extreme illustration was the experience of a Michigan farm boy born in 1906 who attended school intermittently until age 16 and yet left illiterate. His father wanted his labor and a school official connived, saying to "go ahead and stay home; farming is more important than school; you'll probably be a farmer anyway." As a result, his wife had to teach him to read: "I didn't learn anything in school. I still can't write or spell. . . . I think it's because I stayed home and cut corn." Hearing damage from measles exacerbated his problems, but he thought he had at least partial company: whereas girls heeded the teacher, the "boys had a hard time reading. They thought they knew it all." Certainly boys fell behind in school more often and were more restive than girls, but this boy's illiteracy was exceptional enough in Michigan that he avoided Sunday school for fear of betraying his ignorance. In contrast, frank ignorance formed almost a point of pride among the touchy plain folk of southern mill towns. Jessie Lee Carter, who quit school at age 12, recalled, "I never did learn to read and write. But I loved to work. Yes, I did." Still in school in 1917, when he was 13, Curtis Enlow decided "I wasn't learning nothing." His father agreed, and he left for the mill.[63]

Assessing the skills with which children left school requires more than census tabulations. Although the census classified about one-tenth of whites in Georgia and the Carolinas as illiterate in 1910, historian I. A. Newby judges that "most plain folk were what we today call functionally illiterate." Reading specialists of the 1910s were working toward standards that anticipated functional literacy, emphasizing "ability to understand an unfamiliar text, rather than simply declaim a familiar one." E. L. Thorndike tested sixth graders by having them read a statement of school rules: "In Franklin, attendance upon school is required of every child between the ages of seven and fourteen on every day when school is in session unless the child is so ill as to be unable to go to school, or some person in his house is ill with a contagious disease, or the roads are impassable." Faced with this turgid sentence, many children could not state when pupils had to attend and when they could stay away.[64] As long as reading meant oral performance, a child who could stumble along with prompts and coaching seemed minimally literate. Tests of silent reading, with the teacher unavailable to help, raised the standard.

When World War I enabled psychologists to undertake large-scale "intelligence" testing, the sergeants who sorted army recruits judged that 25 percent lacked the "ability to read and understand newspapers and write letters home" and thus could not take the written ("alpha") test. Another 6 percent performed so badly on it that they too were referred for pictographic ("beta") testing. Although these results reflected poorly on the schools, the sample of draftees underrepresented the schools' educational successes by excluding women, skilled workers, others with essential jobs, and officers. And the sorters made hasty, often prejudiced judgments, summarily consigning many African Americans and foreign-born recruits to the beta group. In one large sample, 59 percent of foreign-born draftees took the beta test, 54 percent of African Americans from the deep South, 39 percent of African Americans from the North, and just 19 percent of native whites. At a South Carolina camp, 37 percent of southern white recruits but only 8 percent of northern whites took the beta test.[65] Thus the army tests suggest that northern schools cultivated the era's equivalent of functional literacy among a large majority of native-born whites. On the other hand, even discounting for racism, it appears that many white southerners and African Americans had not learned to read at the level required by twentieth-century bureaucracies and printed communication.

Even if a substantial minority remained deficient, average reading skills almost certainly improved over the course of the progressive era, since children on average spent considerably more years in school by 1920. Testing in the mid-1910s found that pupils' silent reading sped up markedly between the second and fourth grades and continued to accelerate, although more slowly, through the eighth grade. On the other hand, even advanced readers still learned to value overprecision in detail more than broad understanding. When S. A. Courtis studied reading for the NEA's Committee on Economy of Time, he reported good average speeds: 161 words per minute by the fourth grade and 262 by the eighth. Yet he advocated assigning shorter texts so that pupils could read each bit four times. Perhaps this was progress, since in the 1890s, according to Joseph Rice, assigning textbook passages too long to memorize verbatim—so that students had to answer in their own words—constituted innovation.[66] In other branches of language instruction— literature, composition, grammar, spelling, pronunciation, handwriting— school pupils faced similar demands that they conform exactly to detailed conventions. Although children who were eager to please teachers or prove themselves respectable learned in detail, overall the evidence suggests a drawn battle between rule givers on one side and children's persistent habits on the other.

With the breakdown of a common literary culture shared by all ages, literature retreated from reading and composition instruction, withdrawing toward the later elementary grades as a "content subject." By the 1910s, lists of "readings" rated selections by grade level; literary classics appeared mainly in versions retold for children. In addition, the average child memorized (more or less) several hundred lines of poetry a year—most often Robert Louis Stevenson and Eugene Field for young pupils, Longfellow and Tennyson for older ones. Literary diversity was of course unknown; children learned an Anglo-American canon.[67]

As literature became a separate realm, composition merged instead with grammar. Leading teachers of English encouraged a relatively plain style and put their main efforts into repressing grammatical errors. Many students did little creative writing, concentrating instead on learning rules of grammar and diagramming sentences. As a former pupil complained, "dissection" outweighed "construction."[68] Oral instruction settled into an inconclusive conflict between rule givers and popular speech habits, with many poorly educated teachers fighting erratically on both sides. (In reports on ill-taught schools, Joseph Rice pointedly italicized teachers' solecisms.) New Yorker Sadie Rehstock never forgot her embarrassment when a teacher refused her permission to leave the room until she asked "*may* I" instead of "can I." By attacking popular usage, educators kept immigrants and native speakers alike

off balance. W. W. Charters, a zealous enumerator of errors, believed ethnicity did not affect children's propensity to grammatical error; only the
accents differed. When he had teachers in Cincinnati and Boise count pupils'
oral mistakes, they recorded many double negatives and recurrent substitu-
tion of "seen" and "done" for "saw" and "did." But the teachers also tabu-
lated minor redundancies ("I haven't *got* any"), small infelicities ("I and my
brother" instead of "my brother and I"), and colloquialisms such as "mad" for
angry and "lots" for many. Apparently schooling had little aggregate effect on
children's speech, since the distribution of errors dropped from first to second grade but changed little thereafter.[69]

Similar suspicions of futility troubled efforts to teach spelling and handwriting. Although on average spelling improved with age, it seemed not to
matter whether school systems used short word lists or long ones, brief drill
sessions or lengthy ordeals. Instruction in penmanship was often coercive; the
widely used Palmer system tried to make children write with their whole arm,
drawing endless circles "around and around and around." Left-handers faced
harsh sanctions. Still angry after seven decades, a Detroit woman remembers
how the nuns hit her left hand and tied it behind her back. Yet many children
persisted in forming their own writing, and not every school system imposed
a single standard. Contemporary studies showed that practice exercises made
little difference, leading E. L. Thorndike to conclude that handwriting, "like
spelling," was "not very much influenced by the management of the
schools."[70]

More pressing for many immigrant children was their struggle with English pronunciation. New York City Jews, who left the fullest accounts,
expressed almost uniform gratitude to teachers. Mary Antin effusively praised
Miss Dillingham for enabling her to master the letter *w:* "When at last I could
say 'village' and 'water' in rapid alternation . . . that memorable word was
sweet on my lips. For we had conquered, and Teacher was pleased." More
grudgingly, Aaron Katz praised Miss Prescott: "She was an old biddy, but she
made us talk precisely."[71]

Arithmetic reportedly held students' interest better than most "drill subjects," but they still labored long for modest gains. Ideally children learned
simple addition and subtraction, memorized multiplication tables, and began
long division in the first four grades. Computation was the core skill; children
typically learned by memorizing rules and then applying them mechanically,
since teachers often could not explain them. Most commonly, at each lesson
the teacher gave out one rule and a long set of computations for pupils to
work at their seats or on the board. With their teachers' encouragement,
pupils recited mental litanies at each step. To gain speed, they had to suppress
physical manifestations such as finger counting and streamline the mono-
logue. As in teaching reading, advanced pedagogy sought to silence children.
Curiously, pupils were spared one source of extrinsic pressure: although oral

recitation required speedy responses, for written examinations students usually had almost unlimited time; slow pupils were graded only on those questions they completed.[72] Despite educators' talk of training efficient workers, children did not yet have to race.

Average skills had unquestionably advanced since the early nineteenth century, when basic arithmetic was an advanced subject and the study of fractions an impressive feat. But typical levels of numeracy among schoolchildren of the early twentieth century were still quite modest. A survey of urban schools found multiplication tables "predominantly present" even at the sixth grade. Rural pupils probably lagged a bit behind their nonfarm peers, and a woman who attended black schools in rural Virginia around 1910 claimed that her untrained teachers taught no arithmetic at all. Tests indicated problems with basic computation even among urban eighth graders—and many pupils did not get that far. Instructors distracted pupils from intuitive understanding by testing computation with numbers up to eight or nine digits, well beyond what was necessary for real-world use. Because encouraging pupils to estimate was still a novel idea, missteps routinely produced absurd answers. Certainly the army alpha tests anticipated modest numeracy. Whereas advanced questions elsewhere in the tests presumed extensive literary and historical education, the hardest numerical questions did not reach beyond basic arithmetic.[73]

Geography and history, two leading content subjects of the upper elementary grades, in theory set children's lives in broader contexts of place and time. In practice they showered pupils with disconnected facts. In both subjects, the glue binding the details together was a compound of Anglo-American ethnocentrism and more principled patriotism. Textbooks echoed geographer Matthew Fontaine Maury's assurance: "People who live as we do are called *enlightened*."[74] Geography won particular notoriety for cramming pupils with details. Typical of this approach was an oral examination for fifth graders observed by Joseph Rice. For each country, the pupil recited boundaries, mountains, rivers, productions, inhabitants, and other "facts." If the child paused, "the teacher remarked abruptly, *'Don't stop to think, but tell me what you know.'* " By the early 1900s more innovative teachers had pupils use sand tables to build landforms and tried to teach such principles as how physical resources shaped economies. An inspiring teacher could, as a former Wisconsin schoolgirl put it, make "you want to go places." But memorization still predominated and gained strength from the testing movement of the 1910s.[75]

By the 1910s, study questions in history texts were changing from who, what, and when to causal issues. Despite modestly increased attention to social and economic developments, however, military and political events and heroic leaders still dominated the textbooks. The roots of contemporary reform concerns received little consideration, and racial issues were slighted as impediments to sectional harmony or dismissed with casual bigotry. David Muzzey's standard text preached that enfranchisement "set the ignorant, superstitious, gullible slave in power over his former master." Perhaps it was fortunate that much instruction remained mired in distasteful memorization. When a centenarian recalled her elementary schooling in Jackson, Michigan, around 1900, the way her teacher taught history stood out: "For History, instead of having any connection at all, she'd say, recite paragraph ten on page two. You didn't have any connection in History. That's the way she taught History." Yet Jewish immigrants who attended school in New York City before World War I remembered differently; history, they testified, taught abiding love of country.[76]

Between 1900 and 1920, the proportion of children reaching the upper elementary grades rose dramatically. When the commissioner of education first ventured an estimate in 1903, public schools nationwide enrolled only about 11 eighth graders for every 100 second graders. By contrast, reasonably reliable 1920 reports showed almost 60 eighth grade students for every 100 in the second grade. Most children who reached the eighth grade were functionally literate. Their mathematical skills, though weaker than later generations', surpassed their ancestors'. By the 1890s, midwestern county superintendents prepared searching examinations for eighth-grade graduation. Avis Carlson, who passed hers in Kansas in the early 1900s, had to spell *obscene* and *assassination;* calculate 8 percent interest on $900 for two years, plus 67 days; convert pecks to bushels; define *zenith* and *panegyric;* write a temperance essay; describe colleges, printing, and religion in colonial America; name rivers and wheat-producing counties; diagram sentences and parse words. Such examinations were not mere formalities; in Nebraska in 1900, barely half the candidates passed. Graduates took pride in their success.[77]

Although enthusiasm does not prove learning, a good many girls and some boys "just loved" their elementary schooling. As remembered by Jewish immigrants, even the "rigid, rote method" of New York schools fostered learning. Still, students had to muster enthusiasm for arbitrary tasks; boys proudly brought home carpentry projects but considered them wholly unrelated to adult work. Spellers gloried in words such as *obliquity* and *aberration.* "It may not have been the best way to train the mind," observed Leonard Covello, an academically talented Italian immigrant, "but it did teach you to concentrate on mastering difficult jobs."[78] Despite cultural narrowness and mechanical teaching, early-twentieth-century schools were bringing extended education to many children. On the other hand, we cannot idealize those schools as models either of progressive innovation or of superior grounding in the three Rs.

Many children, moreover, could not stay the course—whether driven out by brutality or failure or drawn out by the lure of wages or the demands of family. While southern migrants to Chicago advanced at rates comparable with European immigrants, overage pupils piled up in the impoverished black schools of the South. And at boarding schools like Phoenix, almost no Native Americans graduated from the eighth grade.[79] Besides the schools' shortcomings—and despite their strengths as well—they did not operate in a vacuum. Racism and poverty blighted lives. Many families could not afford the sheltered childhood that gave education first priority. For many children, household chores, farm work, and earning money mattered more than any distant future tenuously tied to schooling.

4

Later Childhood: Work, Play, and Values

Progressive-era authorities made lengthened schooling normative for all children, and some children's playtime expanded, but many children still contributed largely to the family economy. And as children's social contacts widened, prescriptive identities came into sharper focus. Even as they extended real benefits, progressive reformers often reified and reinforced distinctions of gender, race, ethnicity, urban or rural residence, and social class. The concept of a sheltered childhood began to grow permanent teeth. For city children, the accepted standard became the middle-class childhood with extended schooling, supervised recreation, and careful cultivation of moral and religious ideals. Nonfarm families that fell short faced stigma. Yet quite different patterns of work and play continued, relatively unchallenged, to shape farm childhoods.

Work

Despite rapid expansion, schools commanded only a small fraction of children's waking hours; far more time remained for work or play. Progressive reformers conceived the child labor issue as a direct conflict between work and schooling—and with reason, for work compromised school enrollment and attendance. Yet in focusing outrage on the exploitation of modest numbers of full-time, mostly nonfarm workers, the reform crusade bypassed many more children who combined dauntingly long hours of work with a modicum of schooling. For large numbers of progressive-era children, work formed an integral part of childhood. This was especially true on farms, where half of American children lived in 1900 and 36 percent still did in 1920. As we have seen, many preschoolers already did significant tasks. Over children's next few years these coalesced into a stream that swelled and shrank with the seasons but never ran dry. Though not absolute, gender distinctions deepened, chores grew more demanding, and by the early teens most boys and girls were fully initiated into the work of farm men and women.

"My father believed in keeping his children busy as soon as they were able to perform simple tasks," reported Clifford Drury, the son of a progressive Iowa farmer. At age six or seven, children routinely dried dishes, set the table, hauled wood and water, weeded gardens, picked berries, fed the hens, gathered eggs, and herded cattle. Some girls and boys began milking this young. The next few years brought progressively heavier tasks: raking hay and doing other field work, feeding animals and cleaning barns, pumping water, sawing wood, and churning butter. Sometime between ages 8 and 10 or 11, these settled into a daily schedule of morning and evening chores. Fairly frequently children's duties outpaced their size, as in the case of a West Virginia farm boy who stood on a nail keg to harness horses. Ages 8 to 12 saw the beginnings of gender differentiation as girls—but rarely boys—began doing laundry and ironing, cleaning house, cooking, preserving food, and caring for children.[1]

Around 12 to 14, boys moved decisively toward heavier field work. Some had already been plowing for several years. Even at 12 or 13, Frank Webster of North Carolina was too small to reach the plow handles and had to use a crossbar; yet he "was doing almost a man's work by that time," he recalled. By age 14, practically all West Virginia farm boys described themselves as "regular farm hands." Some boys eased into the role as half hands; when Drury was 13 and his brother nearly 12, they "together took a man's place in the fields and on the threshing crew." For midwestern boys, acceptance in the threshing party signified initiation into manhood, completed by promotion at 14 or 15 to the manly tasks of binding and reaping.[2]

No equivalent marked a farm girl's maturity as a worker, but her tasks too grew heavier with age. Although in times of peak labor demand older girls drove teams, shocked wheat, and husked corn, this intermittent work counted only as "helping." By necessity or choice, however, a number of girls went further and substituted for sons. If a family lacked boys old enough, the eldest daughter typically did few indoor chores or none and assumed the full range of boys' tasks. A few simply disliked housework and insisted on a "tomboy" role. These gender reversals often inspired lifelong pride. One Michigan girl delighted to have become "my father's 'hired man,' as he called me," and another gloried in the memory of a neighbor mistaking her for a boy. Yet Country Life reformers, eager to reconstruct farm families on urban lines, were outraged that "many girls" were doing field work "whether required or not." Except to save a crop, declared William McKeever of Kansas State Agricultural College, the practice was "abominable" and should be outlawed.[3]

Meanwhile, many farm girls found ample labor within the household sphere. Without running water, laundry was a weekly ordeal. Daughters often did the ironing, sweltering in summer as they pushed heavy irons heated on the wood stove. Cooking, housecleaning, and food processing all required repetitive, often strenuous work. A former Michigan farm girl mostly left the fields and barns to her brothers and yet remembers summer as nearly unbroken work helping her mother can or string beans and dry pork. In wheat country, feeding the threshers was an annual crisis when sisters could labor in the cook car from 4 A.M. till 10 P.M. Other chores ran year round. "Washing the sticky separator with its innumerable tin parts was the bane of my existence," Era Bell Thompson of North Dakota complained. "Every night when I came home from school it stood waiting for me." For many girls, child care was the chore that never ended. A farm daughter recalls giving the cradle a push to start it rocking and then rushing outdoors before the baby could cry. African-American girls, whose mothers often worked out of the home, were especially burdened. All 97 women interviewed by historian Elizabeth Clark-Lewis, most born in the rural South around 1900, reported having "washed, watched, and whipped" younger siblings or the children of relatives or neighbors.[4]

Boys crossed gender lines much less than girls did. When a black boy in Arkansas dared ring the dinner bell, "he was in trouble," according to his cousin. "He got told straight that was not a job a boy or man ever did." A former southern farm girl, this one white, recalled with seeming pride, "I had the kind of brothers that really were men. They didn't do anything around the house." A son of Dutch parents in Michigan said that while he worked outdoors his younger brother's "job was to stay in the house and help mother." But such role reversals were rare for boys. As they approached their teens, most shed housekeeping chores and helped only rarely.[5]

Children could duck occasional chores they found upsetting. Thus a Michigan farm girl helped cut up slaughtered cattle because her brother next in age "could not handle the blood. He was in charge of eggs." Any further exemption required unusually indulgent parents or good fortune in the birth order lottery. The daughter of kindly Universalists recalled only that she helped her mother with fancy baking and that "when we got older we had to keep our rooms kind of ship-shape." A girl who was the "baby" of a large family often did only cursory chores.[6] Otherwise, few escaped. Up to a point, prosperity meant more land, more livestock, and more work. On the other hand, poverty imposed a grim regimen on African-American girls in the South whose mothers farmed and took in laundry. Chores began, one reported, "on the day you stood up!" By age nine, a girl could cook, clean house and " 'mash wrinkles out of most pieces sent by whites to be laundered. . . .' Outside, she could wash, boil, and hang clothes out to dry. In the field she could plant, weed, and harvest most crops." "By ten you'd be trained" and ready to work out, recalled a North Carolinian. "Your training was early and hard . . . no play ever for a girl. That's just how [women were] on girls. Work, work, work. No play, 'cause they told you, 'Life was to be hardest on you—always.' "[7]

Even under less dire conditions, many farm children resented and resisted work, often taking shortcuts and fooling around. Instead of planting beans three per hole, for instance, they might dump in whole handfuls to get the job over with. Children would "fuss and rassle" instead of working. Unable to withhold nonexistent pay, many parents resorted to force, and even reformers approved. McKeever considered a father exemplary who started his son gardening at age six: "Punishment was necessary more than once," the father reported, "but slowly he began to catch my point of view." Many mothers slapped, spanked, or switched girls to make them work. Some fathers whipped sons to work until their middle teens. "Man, in those days everybody beat their kids something awful," observed a farm woman from southern Illinois. Besides punishment, criticism and constant work demands sapped affection for taskmaster parents. "No, we never did enough," recalled one hardworking son. "My Dad was never satisfied." Whereas the women Clark-Lewis interviewed described their fathers as "often playful and attentive," they remembered their mothers as showing "little or no affection." To her mother, complained one woman, "we were there to work and mind grown people."[8]

Except for those with girls who took the son's role and sometimes with boys remembering harvest time, interviews with former farm children seldom yield memories of satisfaction at building skills. "Always the same work on the farm," recalled a son of Polish immigrants. "Everyday . . . young or old . . . doesn't make any difference." A onetime North Dakota farm girl voiced similar tedium: "As we got older, each time the shovel got a little bigger, and the pitchfork got a little bigger, because we lived on the farm." Reformers empathized with a 14-year-old West Virginia boy: "I have to work myself to death and don't get nothing out of it; never get to go *nowhurs*. I don't like it and ain't goin' to stay."[9] What redeemed farm drudgery was not personal gain but duty to family, the sober satisfaction of doing "our job" and "what was expected of you." In retrospect, a Michigan boy pronounced the lack of pay "fine because I was always supplied with meals, family, shelter, and love. Every Saturday us kids would get a nickel for an ice cream cone."[10]

Work allotments by age often followed a farm girl's simple formula: "As you grew up you would do a little more and a little more until you reached a limit." For boys, William McKeever proposed "five hours solid work per day" at age 10 and six hours at 11. Beyond that, he urged restraint: "Many 12-year-old boys are required to do a man's work every day." Warning that "girls are more readily enslaved to work than boys," McKeever declined to suggest hours. But these were reform proposals, routinely exceeded on many farms. McKeever endorsed a "thoughtful" farmer's summer schedule for sons ages 14 and 16: "I never permit them to work more than ten hours a day, while they are allowed a full half day off each week to use as they please, and about once each month they have an entire day to themselves." Despite McKeever's adjuration to "permit some crops to be lost rather than abuse the boy," children younger than these commonly worked more than 10 hours daily at peak seasons. As another reformer phrased it, rural parents had "not caught the newer vision of childhood, in which the parent owes all to the child till he reaches maturity."[11]

Pressures on children varied with the crops and the scale on which farms specialized. Butter and eggs for petty cash furnished year-round but relatively undemanding chores. Larger-scale dairying imposed heavy daily chores but caused no seasonal crises except at haying. Though gardening and canning gave children hot afternoons, only commercial market gardening subjected children to whole days of stoop labor. Wheat required little work from small children. But corn, the most widely grown field crop, employed all ages. Across the South, children from age five upward hoed corn; in autumn the older ones skipped school for heavy work pulling fodder (stripping leaves from the standing stalks). Still, the burden varied from intermittent work on

"Edna Smilley, R. D. 1, eighteen years old and sister seven years old who pick seventy-five pounds of cotton a day. 'We'd ruther do *anything* than pick cotton,' Edna said." Photograph by Lewis Hine, September 1913, Denison, Texas. (Courtesy of Photography Collections, University of Maryland Baltimore County)

patches in the mountains to sustained drudgery in the market-driven agriculture of the low country.[12]

Cotton was the classic child-labor crop. From late April through early July, it had to be thinned and then weeds repeatedly "chopped" with hoes. As soon as they could tell weeds from cotton, boys and girls began chopping. With aching arms and cramped hands, many children worked from "sun to sun," others only once the dew had dried. In September and October, every child within reach picked cotton. Although the burrs hurt, picking rewarded speed more than strength and made children almost as valuable as adults. Children rose before the sun and quit only at dusk; pickers competed, and children took pride in outdoing others.[13]

Between 1900 and 1920 sugar quotas spawned a new agribusiness employing child labor, as processing companies contracted with families to grow sugar beets. In Colorado, the industry employed German immigrants from Russia, who drove their children hard, and Mexican migrants. Elsewhere immigrants from cities combined with local owners and tenants. Beets required two great bursts of work: thinning in spring and pulling and topping in autumn. In Colorado in 1920, three-fifths of eight-year-olds in families under contract and almost all those over age 10 worked at least the seasonal peaks, averaging 9 to 13 hours daily.[14]

Despite their specialized tasks, beet workers shared one characteristic with other farm children: most worked unpaid for parents. Town children who picked cotton or fruit stood a better chance of keeping some earnings. To gain spending money, farm youths needed a sideline such as trapping for pelts or selling home products, but most lacked time or opportunity.[15]

By age 12 and often younger, the average farm child spent much more time at work than in school. Three hours of daily chores (a reasonable estimate), 4 more each Saturday, plus 30 added hours for each of 15 weeks in spring, summer, and fall would have totaled 1,753 hours in one year, approaching the equivalent of an adult work year in the 1990s and substantially exceeding the average school pupil's 516 classroom hours at 1890 attendance rates or 726 hours at 1920 rates.[16]

For nonfarm children, possibilities varied more widely—from taxing workloads to the classic sheltered childhood of schooling, limited chores, and abundant play. Among those faring worst were temporary migrants. In old age, retired black domestics recalled vividly the loneliness of leaving home each summer, as young as eight, to "do" for white families; every April found them in an employer's buggy, crying. Other migrants at least came with parents. Canneries nationwide, Gulf coast seafood processors, and Louisiana sugar refineries all hired mothers and children for seasonal work. Families camped in squalid makeshift housing, though canneries also hired local children. Hanging around the sheds, little children drifted into intermittent employment as "helpers," then steady work by age seven or eight. Investigators excoriated immigrant parents who hit children to make them work and hazards such as sharp oyster shells and alkaline liquids from shrimp that shredded and burned children's hands. Yet many children seemed disconcertingly persistent, drawn by the sociability of group work, proud of contributing to their family's welfare, and flattered by praise for speedy work.[17] This difference in attitude between reformers and young workers recurred in other industries.

More notorious than canning was coal mining, in which boys suffered accidents at three times their elders' rate. In the 1910s, as states banned underground work before age 16, jobs for boys disappeared in bituminous mining. In anthracite towns, though, thousands worked at 14 or younger aboveground, hunched over conveyor belts amid a fog of dust, risking lung and limb to pick unwanted slate from the rumbling stream of coal.[18]

What became the most controverted form of child labor mushroomed in the new whites-only cotton mills of the southern piedmont. Young girls spooled and spun, mainly checking rows of spinning frames for broken threads, while small boys doffed, replacing empty bobbins. Although still dwarfed by the numbers in agriculture, employment of southern cotton mill operatives age 14 or younger surged from 9,000 in 1890 to 25,000 in 1900; almost half were under 12. Tired of poor soil and hard labor, farmers delivered their whole family to the mill, expecting somewhat easier indoor work and higher total family income. Children contributed substantially; for girls under 14, no job in the South paid better.[19] Thus the rural family economy moved to town, though it was rendered vulnerable by the calculation of individual children's wages.

Two contrasting perspectives have shaped the history of child labor in the mills. Progressive reformers and later chroniclers of child labor reform decried children's frequent illiteracy and their long hours breathing humid, lint-filled air. Less reasonably, reformers blamed exploitive fathers and idealized the farm life that mill workers had fled. Nor did reformers such as Senator Albert Beveridge and the National Child Labor Committee's Alexander McKelway scruple to play the race card, making the preposterous claim that black children received ample schooling while the worthy race labored.[20] Drawing on oral history, recent historians have attempted to reconstruct the millhands' quite different perspective. While recognizing that early employment imposed hardships, these writers have portrayed children as relatively willing workers, motivated partly by antipathy for schooling but more positively by family and community ties. With the mill the center of activity, small fry drifted in to be with family or friends. Adults recall chatting with friends before and after school while turning freshly knit stockings right side out at 10 cents per 100. Others began helping family members; such aid enabled a sister, for instance, to take on more spinning sides. As children proved their value, family or the foreman often pressured them to return regularly.[21]

Helping at the mill resembled a farm child's initiation into chores, except that mill work was easier and more gregarious.

Many mill children came eagerly, encouraged by kinfolk to replicate their own life course. Such children won praise as "smart"—not for being intellectually acute but for working "willingly and well." "I took on right quick to learn," boasted a former prodigy who entered the mill at age seven, "and before long I could spin right up with some of the big ones." So small she pushed along a box to stand on, she became a prize exhibit: "The boss told Pa I was peart, and when folks come visitin' at the mill he'd bring them to see the youngun that could spin good." Spurred by piece rates, beginners gained reasonable proficiency in a few weeks: "They had to learn us, but it didn't take me long to learn," recalled one lady proudly. Industrial child labor could be seductive. Unlike school, where each bit memorized only led to more and where grades told children their shortcomings, simple factory tasks offered a sense of mastery. However meretricious that feeling of accomplishment appeared to child labor opponents, it satisfied many children's sense of industry. And yet, since neither spinning nor doffing required unremitting concentration, children had time each hour to chat, roughhouse, or even play outside. When not deprecating child labor as slavery, reformers complained that

Learning to spin: photograph by Lewis Hine, c. 1910. (Courtesy of the Archives of Labor and Urban Affairs, Wayne State University)

mill children had too much leisure to "just loaf and talk" instead of engaging in organized play.[22]

Partly because of this freedom, children's relations with supervisors were not all praise and pride. Although mill managers liked young workers' low pay, underbosses often found them "aggravating" and, like farmers and teachers in similar situations, reacted harshly. According to a contemporary, boys spent slack time " 'scuffling,' or making life miserable for the girls and women." Girls and boys alike absconded to go fishing. So when "hat-stomping" rages failed to overawe the children, some bosses progressed to spanking, whipping, or hanging recalcitrants by the heels out second-story windows.[23]

Because the family labor system permitted low adult wages, the children's pay furnished little margin of prosperity. Former mill workers recall vividly their sorrow at rare candy spoiled by ants or cheap dolls ruined by rain. Because many families kept animals and raised large gardens, young workers came home to chores that erased evening playtime. Mary Thompson juggled half days in school with regular mill work, plus washing, ironing, and milking. As for griping, "we was raised not to," she said. "Childhood," reflected Ralph Austin, "I didn't have much."[24]

The childhood Austin probably envisioned took classic shape in nonindustrial villages and small towns, where even children in modest circumstances often gained opportunities. One such boy, the son of a widowed seamstress partly supported by three older children, peddled the Detroit *Free Press* from age nine in Grayling, Michigan, and yet joined the Boy Scouts and bought a canoe with money he saved.[25] Compared with farm youth, it might seem that small-town boys gained nearly endless leisure, while household drudgery for girls continued. But arrangements were more complex. Even prosperous small-town residents often kept a milk cow, carriage horse, or both, raised large gardens, and used wood stoves. Though girls and boys both might fetch the cow, gender decorum tended to assign the heaviest outdoor tasks—chopping and hauling wood, mucking out the stable—to boys. The historian Bruce Catton, who grew up in little Benzonia, Michigan, hated "the ritual of cleaning the stable, getting hay in the manger, spreading straw for the bedding and hoisting buckets of water for the cow to drink." Inside the house, though some boys wiped dishes and scrubbed floors, girls did more. Yet a surprising number of women from small towns recall only minimal household chores. An oldest daughter could find baby minding endless and isolating, but families averaged smaller than on the farm. Except in crossroads villages where chances were scarce, town boys' big advantage over girls lay less in reduced chores than in opportunities to earn spending money, progressing from lawn mowing to a paper route, then store clerking in their teens.[26] That such jobs were optional, detached from the family economy, indicated the relative security of small-town childhoods. Except among the poor, most boys and girls had fairly sheltered childhoods with time for play.

In the view of reformers, this was emphatically untrue of immigrant working-class children in the nation's cities. Alarm about this swelling population, augmented by stories of southern mill workers and investigations of coal mining triggered by a 1902 strike, translated by the early 1900s into a sense of crisis about child labor.[27] This alarm rested on conviction that child labor was expanding rapidly and was mostly a nonfarm problem.

But was it? The Census Bureau reported impressive aggregates: 765,000 children ages 10 through 15 "gainfully employed" in 1870; 1,750,000 in 1900; 1,990,000 in 1910 (subsequently reestimated downward to 1,622,000); and 1,061,000 in 1920 (revised upward this time to 1,417,000). In the reformers' freehand summary, the U.S. had 1,000,000 more child laborers in 1900 than in 1870. Measured against the growing population ages 10 through 15, however, the increase looked less dramatic—from 13 percent in 1870 to 18 percent in 1900. Disaggregation revealed further complexities. Despite the reformers' urban focus, the majority of reported child laborers worked in agriculture: 62 percent in 1900 and 61 percent in 1920 (later reestimated as 71 percent). Reports showing two to three times as many boys as girls employed indicate that census takers excluded much work done by girls. Unsurprisingly, employment rose with age; in 1910, just 12 percent of children ages 10 through 13 reportedly worked but nearly 31 percent of those ages 14 and 15.[28]

As the radical reestimates and gender disparities suggest, census statistics gave a misleading impression of children's work, vitiated by shifting procedures and pervasive undercounting. Farm work in particular went unreported. The census counted no workers under age 10, nor did it count children who attended school, even though most spent far more time at farm work. Setting the 1900 and 1910 census dates for April, when intensive work was just beginning in the cotton South and well before the summer peak in the North, guaranteed that enumerators would fail to count many children about to embark on months of hard work. Instructions in 1900 and 1910 not to count "children working for their parents at chores, errands, or general housework" invited enumerators to dismiss girls' efforts as "housework" and boys' as "chores." Seeking to redress some of these deficiencies, 1910 instructions told enumerators never to assume "without inquiry, that a woman, or child, has no occupation." Such an embarrassing upsurge in reported farm employment among women and children resulted from this admonition that the Census Bureau changed instructions for 1920 and moved the census date to January 1, the nadir of farm work. Yet even the 1910 census understated children's farm work. A Colorado study found more child workers in beets alone than the census reported in all forms of agriculture across the state. Almost as policy, the Census Bureau was committed to underreporting children's work in farm households. Bureau officials avowed greater faith in nonfarm statistics, but many of the same factors favored underestimation: exclusion of housework and chores, of children attending school, and of any under age 10. Those who lied about their ages, most street traders, most industrial homeworkers, and many domestic servants went unreported.[29] The safest conclusion is that child labor in the sense of reasonably hard, sustained work was much more widespread than the census recognized but had not appreciably increased since 1870, since children had always worked on farms.[30] As the nonfarm population swelled, urban child labor grew more conspicuous, but no reliable evidence shows that child labor was increasing relative to the numbers of urban children.

Although workers in manufacturing constituted only 16 percent of child laborers enumerated in 1900, their plight aroused disproportionate concern because the work was frequently difficult and dangerous. In Pennsylvania's infamous glass factories, boys with the worst job, the "carrier pigeons," toted three or four red-hot bottles on an asbestos shovel to the annealing oven, 72 trips of 100 feet each hour, taken at a slow run. Young workers elsewhere breathed fumes from varnish and naphtha and absorbed phosphorous, toxic dyes, and lead. Illinois factory inspectors in 1895 found boys operating dangerous machines because their fathers had been injured by the same machines; the boys were working to save their fathers' jobs. Whereas in theory farm parents looked out for their children, industrial employers gave little heed to safety and disavowed responsibility for injuries and deaths, often blaming the children's own carelessness.[31]

Why, then, did children work in such places? Answers collected by Helen Todd in Illinois repeated those of southern millhands: family need, dislike of school, and the attractions of accomplishment. Of 800 wage-earning children she interviewed, 381 blamed their fathers' sickness or death. Perhaps rationalizing their fate, working children claimed a sense of achievement missing at school: "You never understands what they tells you in school, and you can learn right off to do things in a factory." They felt prouder giving mother a pay envelope than a report card.[32]

Store clerks and messengers were often underage. Most conspicuous were the cash boys and girls who rushed packages, sales slips, and change around large department stores. Many more children clerked and delivered orders before and after school for small stores.[33] Yet these children seemed less at risk and aroused less concern than factory hands.

More vexing to reformers were the bustling children—more boys than girls—out on city streets earning money. The very young scavenged along alleys and rail lines, in abandoned buildings, on construction sites, and around the dumps and docks, affronting middle-class ideals of the sheltered childhood. Children picked up more than scrap at construction sites and sometimes progressed from gleaning coal that fell from trains to pilfering boxcars. These activities served family needs, but not entirely. Coal and most wood went home; paper and metal went to the junk man for petty cash that might or might not reach home.[34]

Although children peddled all manner of small items on the streets, newspapers formed their classic stock in trade. Conveniently, they could sell or deliver before and after school. By the 1910s many more boys delivered morning papers to regular subscribers than sold them individually, but evening papers still depended on street sales. Boys began young; a 1903 newsboy study in Buffalo found more than one-quarter under age 10 and four-fifths under age 14. Selling did not disrupt home life or schooling, for almost all lived with two parents and most were still in school. Cute small fry could sell easily and sometimes fronted for older boys, begging every late-night passerby to buy their "last" paper so they could go home. Lacking evidence of grave physical risks, reformers decried the moral dangers of street trading. Petty frauds and the excitement of street life, they charged, readied boys for major crime and unfitted them for steady jobs. Independent access to cash would surely corrupt; New York's Child Labor Committee charged that three-quarters of newsboys who sold at night had venereal disease by age 15. Less melodramatically, investigators depicted newsboys "shooting craps, pitching pennies, trading dirty stories . . . and stuffing themselves with 'trash.' " Theirs was no cash-starved, sheltered childhood. Yet historian David Nasaw believes they handed over more to parents than they spent. Often outweighing reform diatribes, rival images romanticized the newsboy as entrepreneur, eliciting admiration that frequently stymied regulation. Dreams of a democratic brotherhood of the streets inspired several conservative reformers, notably Toledo's John Gunckel, to form ostensibly self-governing newsboys' republics to regulate the trade.[35]

In practice, the line blurred between newsboys and working-class boys in general. By 1913, the Toledo Newsboys' Association claimed 8,950 members. Though doubtless inflated, this figure suggests the frequency with which boys combined newspaper selling or delivery with other activities. For example, at age 11 or 12 a Bay City, Michigan, boy worked early mornings for the newspaper circulation department and delivered his own route, making $3 a week by 1920. After school he washed dishes at home and sometimes helped in the family bakery. Yet he also remembers swimming and skating.[36] No single activity defined such boys.

Small girls went scavenging and a few sold newspapers (they comprised 6 percent of vendors in Chicago in 1905), but safety and propriety tied most to home. Young girls contributed through industrial homework, extra housework generated by boarders, or baby-sitting for neighbors. Only the last generated independent income, but not much. An Italian immigrant girl reportedly settled for baby-sitting at five cents a day, although by around 1918 a Detroit girl's mother considered 10 cents an evening to baby-sit a neighbor's three children inadequate and forbade her daughter to continue.[37]

Industrial homework was a shadowy area of child labor. Working on very low piece rates, mothers and small children clipped, sorted, painted, pasted, strung, or sewed small items. The 1911 Immigration Commission reported only 6 percent of families involved, though turnover was high and more tried it at least briefly. A 1918 study of Providence, Rhode Island, found that almost 8 percent of children had done some industrial homework that year but that more than half had quit (usually along with their whole family) before year's end. Opportunities varied. Cigar making by Bohemian immigrant families, which exercised New York reformers in the 1890s, declined in the early 1900s. By then, clothing manufacture in New York, Chicago, and Philadelphia probably employed as many children as did southern textiles, yet cities dominated by heavy industry furnished little homework.

Stereotypes shaped discussions of homework. Although the pay slightly cushioned slack seasons that workers could not control, reformers excoriated money-hungry mothers and shiftless fathers. Men and boys purportedly dodged homework, yet 41 percent of children involved in Providence were boys. And despite charges that homework blocked schooling, most children did it before and after school. Unquestionably children worked young—46 percent below age 11 in Providence. Yet the main forms of work there—mounting snap fasteners on cardboard for sale by the dozen, stringing tags, and separating threads on lace—though mindless and ill paid were safe. Many children initially enjoyed the sense of accomplishment but tired of repetition. Others made work a social occasion, even helping friends for free. Elsewhere, a girl of 10 who crocheted slippers with three friends exulted, "We have *such* good times working together! Sometimes, we don't go to bed until eleven o'clock!" Except for earning money, the girls differed little from the endlessly stitching sisters of Louisa May Alcott's *Little Women*. The key to this child's good humor, however, was probably that her work was only intermittent. Fewer than half the family groups undertaking homework in Providence worked as many as 230 person-hours in all of 1918. For most it was only an occasional sideline.[38]

Unpaid housework and child care consumed vastly more of girls'—and even boys'—time. Yet as accepted features of family life, these chores occasioned little public comment. From an early age, lower-class girls faced heavier domestic workloads than boys. Civic Club reformers observing Pittsburgh playgrounds reported that boys were untroubled by "abnormal industriousness," whereas parents "continually asked that [girls] only six or seven years old be given sewing. They said, 'It is no good to come to play.' " A study of working-class schools around 1914 attributed one-quarter of girls' absences to household duties. Meanwhile, boys' semirural outdoor chores had mostly vanished in big cities. Yet 15 percent of boys' absences in Chicago were also for household duties; if girls were unavailable, boys stayed home to do laundry or nurse sick relatives.[39]

With a modicum of prosperity, chores often declined markedly. Having grown up in New York among "lower middle class" Jewish and Irish families,

Catharine Brody recalled, "With us, the boys were quite free, and almost the only duty that devolved upon the girls was minding the current baby." Children of the "very poor" may have "scrubbed floors, washed dishes, and helped with the family laundry to exhaustion. But except for the baby-minding . . . and sometimes the dish-washing, the mothers of the lower middle class passed over their duties reluctantly." Their reluctance stemmed, Brody speculated, occasionally from "a passion for perfection" but more often from determination to spare their daughters drudgery: "To have scrubbed a floor for one's mother was a boast." On the whole, women raised amid urban prosperity concur with Brody's memories. When pressed to remember something beyond taking her sister for buggy rides and helping with dishes, a former Detroit girl volunteered that she had swept the house steps once a week. Curiously, the skill that women most often reported having failed to learn from mother was cooking, perhaps because it took more time to teach than routine cleaning.[40]

By requiring few chores or only low-skilled ones, mothers attenuated ties of apprenticeship between themselves and daughters. These ties had broken for most nonfarm boys and were compromised by drudgery for many farm children. Although progressive educators proposed to fill the gap, home economics and vocational education largely failed as substitutes. Ironically, with middle-class children long out of the labor market, child-rearing advisers began urging parents to assign chores, not for utility but for building character. Well-to-do girls whose main duty was "producing themselves" did the traditional female stints of stitchery. "Before I went out to play," remembered a mill manager's daughter, "I had to hem a dish towel or something, and it had to be done properly."[41]

Since parents resisted making allowances entitlements, preferring to dole out small sums for treats, to have spending money that they controlled most children had to earn it. In 1896 only 7 percent of 2,000 California girls ages 7 to 16 received an allowance, whereas 69 percent sometimes earned money; 10 percent of boys enjoyed allowances, whereas 74 percent earned at least occasional money. Boys and girls mowed lawns and ran errands for neighbors; boys delivered newspapers and sold magazines, again to neighbors. Although allowances began appearing in model budgets around World War I, they probably remained uncommon. Benjamin Spock, whose father made $10,000 a year, had to earn every penny of spending money. By this time, *paid* work had come to seem valuable for character, to the point that Boy Scouts and Camp Fire Girls earned small sums for promotion.[42]

Such requirements presumed a childhood without sustained work. By the 1910s, the campaign to impose that norm on working-class whites became a centerpiece of progressive reform. Yet the crusade was narrowly conceived and had a limited effect on deeply rooted social practices.

Since child labor had long seemed worthy, initial concern was weak and spawned only ineffective state laws. In 1892, Jacob Riis mocked New York's as devices for teaching the underaged to lie and mused that children might be better off working than on the streets. But the age awareness that accompanied graded schooling was fostering a rough consensus. As early as 1889, a Pennsylvania survey found workers agreeing that children should ideally not start work until age 14 or 15. By 1900, 15 states had set 14 as the minimum age for child labor, though giant loopholes remained.[43]

In 1904 Edgar Gardner Murphy, an Episcopalian clergyman who had campaigned for an age 12 minimum for mill work in Alabama, joined conservative northern philanthropists to form the National Child Labor Committee. Initially the NCLC propagandized for state laws. Against the working-class family economy, these reformers set the child's individual needs, cautiously blaming parents more than employers. A cartoon showed the period equivalent of welfare mothers—obese immigrant parents, sodden with drink—being pulled along by their straining, emaciated children. Although settlement workers such as Jane Addams realized they were asking working-class mothers to forgo money essential to family budgets, they could offer no effective replacement. Somehow, underpaid fathers must provide all the income their families needed. In this the child labor cause resembled much progressive reform; regulatory or merely hortative in nature, it failed to secure adequate public resources. Propaganda combined detailed investigation to expose children's victimization with sermons on children's corruption in the workplace,

"One reason for the child labor problem": The *New York Herald*'s cartoonist attacks the family economy, 28 February 1903. (Ernest Poole, *Child Labor—The Street* [New York: Child Labor Committee, 1903], facing 13)

their need for play, and the danger of race degeneracy. The NCLC also directed its fire narrowly against mines, mills, and factorylike canneries, avoiding any challenge to agriculture until almost 1920.[44] Whether this policy stemmed from political prudence, since farm interests could block legislation, or from rural nostalgia and blindness to exploitation of farm children, it rendered reform irrelevant to the majority of working children.

By 1912 only nine states had reached the NCLC's standard for a model law: a minimum age of 14 for employment in manufacturing; 16 for mining; an eight-hour day for industrial workers ages 14 and 15; night work prohibited under age 16; and documentary proof of age. In a burst of enthusiasm, by 1914 some 26 more states came into substantial compliance. But southern textile interests blocked effective legislation in their states. Children there circumvented even modest age requirements, avowing that they were "just past twelve." Elsewhere, workers resisted assaults on their families' security. A twister in Lawrence, Massachusetts, recalled her dismissal for working underage as " 'a terrible blow.' News of the calamity spread rapidly; by nightfall, 'all the women came to my mother and told her not to worry. Everyone was angry and in a few days I got a new name, new papers, and a new job.' "[45]

Frustrated by spotty enforcement nationwide and southern intransigence, the NCLC turned to federal legislation. The resulting Keating-Owen Act of 1916 prohibited interstate shipment of products from mines employing children under age 16 and from factories that used children under age 14 or worked those ages 14 or 15 more than eight hours a day six days a week or after 7 P.M. Yet this law potentially affected at most 150,000 of several million child workers. Southern interests challenged the law; and after just nine months of enforcement by the Children's Bureau, in *Hammer v. Dagenhart* (1918) the U.S. Supreme Court quashed the Keating-Owen Act as an unconstitutional extension of congressional power to regulate interstate commerce. Senator Atlee Pomerene tried again, amending a revenue bill to tax profits of corporations that contravened limits on child labor similar to those in Keating-Owen. The amendment became law in 1919; but after desultory enforcement by the Treasury Department, this use of Congress's taxing power met decisive rejection by the Supreme Court in *Bailey v. Drexel* (1922).[46]

Legal restriction secured some results. State laws chipped away at child labor in mining and manufacturing. Even the Carolinas and Georgia legislated against mill work by children under age 12 and then, toward 1920, under age 14. While Keating-Owen and the Pomerene amendment were briefly in effect, although operatives resisted, many manufacturers discovered they could prosper without child labor.[47]

Overall, though, the legal campaign constituted one of progressive child-saving's failures. According to the crusade's leading historian, industrial homework "flourished as much in 1922 as in 1904." Restriction of girls' domestic service was unthinkable. Despite municipal ordinances, street traders remained essentially unregulated in most cities. And farming, which employed the majority of working children, remained immune to legal oversight.[48] Why were results so limited? The movement attracted support from philanthropic businessmen linked to large corporations, the new middle class of social workers, clergymen, and journalists, plus union leaders who spoke for upper-echelon skilled labor. But the reformers never won over their potential beneficiaries. They scorned parents of nonfarm child laborers and offered the children only compulsory schooling, which some desired but many hated. Although reforms in theory protected children against exploitive parents, the reformers did not challenge farmers or help children gain freedom to choose. In dealing with parents, child labor opponents could muster neither the power to impose their will unimpeded nor the generosity and money needed to offer benefits, such as well-funded mothers' pensions, that might have reduced child labor with less coercion.

Nonetheless, the proportion of children doing full-time or very taxing part-time work declined somewhat between 1900 and 1920, in large part because the farm population was slowly shrinking. Lower birthrates and slightly higher incomes also reduced pressures on family economies and the need for "little mothers." Reinforcing these social changes, the belief spread that children were precious beings to be schooled and sheltered. Casting about for more specific explanations but doubtful that child labor and school attendance laws had much effect, historians have looked to changes in business and technology. By the late 1910s, newspapers began squeezing out old-style newsboys by emphasizing home delivery and building all-weather booths downtown that they staffed with adults. Proliferation of automobiles imperiled street trades. In southern textile mills, managers had always considered young workers mistake prone, though cheap. A shift toward finer yarns made childish errors costly, and increasing integration of spinning and weaving required adult strength and skill. By World War I only 6 percent of textile workers in the Carolinas were under age 16. In other industries, low-skill jobs were vulnerable to mechanization. Pneumatic tubes and cash registers eliminated cash girls and boys in large department stores. Telephones displaced flocks of messenger boys.[49] Yet technology also spawned new part-time jobs. Thus telephones created demand for boys to deliver phoned-in grocery orders after school. And consumerism opened part-time employment for waitresses, soda jerks, and store clerks.

In the countryside, youth-related reform sought not to end child labor but to transform drudgery into enticing socialization for farm life. Four-H grew from diverse initiatives starting around 1904: curricular experiments in rural schools, demonstration projects for southern farmers, and corn growing contests for boys in southern and midwestern states. By 1912, these projects were coalescing around the four leaf clover symbol and claimed membership of nearly 73,000 boys and 23,000 girls. Boys' corn clubs and girls' tomato canning clubs predominated, but potato, poultry, pig and other specialty clubs were underway. Rapid growth followed, especially during World War I.[50]

Drawing on the ideals of the Country Life movement, educators who tried 4-H–style programs hoped to stem migration off the land by teaching love of nature and exciting boys about scientific farming through projects such as seed and soil testing. Success was somewhat mixed, since the state leader for Michigan reported that one-sixth of projects that failed did so because the children moved to the city after joining the club. But 4-H descended more directly from the U.S. Department of Agriculture's demonstration education and the land grant colleges' extension work. These agencies became the main sponsors, working together after the 1914 Smith-Lever Act institutionalized federal-state cooperation in agricultural extension. Consequently, the clubs' overriding purpose was to teach profitable commercial agriculture as an alternative to cotton and to less capital-intensive ways of farming. Boys and girls were to keep careful books, defining success by net profit. Using the new methods, boys would show up their cautious old man, eclipsing his corn yields per acre. Girls' tomato clubs promoted the same commercial ethos, selling canned tomatoes under club labels. Overriding safety fears, O. H. Benson of the USDA crusaded to replace glass jars with tins processed in pressure cookers—the commercial standard. Recognizing the clubs as allies, local bankers and fertilizer dealers happily assisted. Club members were to use purchased inputs—high-grade seed and purebred stock—often borrowing from supportive bankers. The much-publicized record holder of the early years, Jerry Moore of Winona, South Carolina, grew 228 3/4 bushels of corn on his acre in 1910 by applying two tons of chemical fertilizer. Admittedly, he ran up the proceeds by selling 50 bushels as seed corn, but the lesson was clear: spending brought profit.[51]

In this form, club work constituted a subtler attack on the family economy than did the NCLC's frontal assault. Beyond the obvious challenge to parental farming authority, 4-H implicitly denigrated the small-scale production for family use that enabled farm families to manage on limited cash incomes. By requiring each member to pursue an individual project entirely separate from the family's overall farming operations and then compute the profit exactly, club work created a sense of personal entitlement antagonistic to the corporate (often patriarchal and exploitive) ethos of the farm family economy. Club leaders expected children to be attracted by "prizes and . . . real money all their own." Contests encouraged children to measure their achievements against peers rather than in relation to family needs. Yet club leaders responded ambivalently to the relative flexibility of gender roles that facilitated family farm operations. Although the early corn and canning clubs enforced sex segregation, later pig, poultry, and potato clubs admitted both boys and girls. On the other hand, by 1919 club leaders de-emphasized moneymaking canning for girls in favor of cooking and garment making that

Jerry Moore, champion boy corn raiser. (William A. McKeever, *Farm Boys and Girls* [New York: Macmillan, 1912], facing 150)

served strictly domestic needs.[52] For girls, unpaid service to the family tempered commercialized self-assertion.

Many prosperous nonfarm children enjoyed prolonged, sheltered childhoods. But for most farm children and many others, no firm barrier separated childhood leisure and adult work; young people began helping early and soon took on serious tasks. Like schooling, these often amounted to drudgery that contributed little to children's sense of industry. Dull labor did little to build their confidence in growing skill, tenacity, and the respect of others. Yet like schooling at its best, early work could have opposite results. Former child workers sometimes recall with pride their growth in skill and endurance and the praise they won from grown-ups. And many who did grueling, otherwise unrewarding labor recognize the value of their contributions to their families. From the perspective of progressive reformers (and that of today), the danger was that even enthusiastic workers might prematurely form an identity around competencies that marked a developmental dead end. Unlike the schools' artificial vocational and home economics instruction, 4-H made an unusual effort to endow real work with developmental potential. Yet club work espoused ulterior commercial motives that threatened stable family farming.

A secondary goal of 4-H, as of public schooling and much else on the progressive agenda, was to challenge existing family and community ties that bound the young socially, economically, and culturally. Reformers hoped to reassemble the young in approved, adult-supervised aggregations of peers. This ambition shaped reform responses to children's play.

Play and Fantasy

As the proportion of children living on farms declined, playtime expanded. Although nonfarm children at play tended to sort themselves by age and sex, in style of activity the progressive era saw a modest convergence as girls' play drew closer to boys'. In genteel culture, children's literature presented a parallel but more exciting realm of free play and adventure, although that freedom was compromised for girls. By 1920 juvenile literature had become a separate specialty, sheltered from the new realism of adult fiction. To the dismay of reformers, however, commercial popular culture—first dime novels, then movies—kept breaching the dikes.

Compared with others, farm children lacked time for play and choice of companions. A minority whose families were reasonably prosperous and not too work obsessed recall evenings reading together and playing games with their father or siblings. But most farmers had only modest access to books, and few could afford many magazines. Board games seemed costly luxuries, and many pious parents shunned standard playing cards. A child labor investigator found many West Virginia farmers hostile to play by children: "There's plenty of work for 'em and no time for foolishness." Others objected on principle: "I don't believe in them things. All my children have 'professed' and they go to church and Sunday school." Strict Protestants forbade play on Sunday, to the point that two southern girls remember being allowed to sit on a swing but forbidden to move. Although the majority of children did not face such strict rules, farm work easily crowded play out of weekday routines. Broader contacts came on family occasions, as children accompanied parents to dances, church suppers, and Grange meetings. Farm families often visited for Sunday dinner; if religious values permitted, the visitors' children became playmates for the day.[53]

Because playmates and playtime were scarce, the school yard looms large in memories of rural play. Occasionally the children divided, with the older playing baseball and the younger ones tag. The NCLC agent complained of West Virginia playgrounds where "the boys scuffled with one another, while the girls strolled about in pairs or small groups." More frequently, though, boys and girls of all ages stayed together. They often played baseball in versions adapted to odd numbers and primitive equipment, but rural school yards also formed the last stronghold of traditional large-group games beloved by folklorists and recreation experts. Many West Virginia schools played prisoner's base every day, "boys and girls and small and large children together." Such games did not demand specialized skills that might bar beginners. In one universal favorite, duck on a rock, players threw stones at a larger rock (the duck) balanced on a boulder. The player guarding the duck had to replace it if dislodged and tag players running to retrieve their stones. Another widely played game, ante over, began with one team throwing a ball over the schoolhouse; if someone on the far side caught the ball, he or she ran around the building and tried to hit the first team's members with the ball. One former farm girl recalls with pride getting hit on the head and knocked down.[54]

Though inconvenienced by chores, small-town boys escaped their farm cousins' heavy labor. From ages 7 to 12 or 13, they traditionally poured surplus energy into sledding, swimming, fishing, and foraging in the woods. Nineteenth-century writers called these boys "wild," "primitive savages" who perpetrated petty thefts and pranks and fought among themselves; it was a ruthlessly competitive subculture of males jostling for mastery. As cities mushroomed and upper-middle-class men began to fear effete overcivilization, they applauded nostalgic evocations of this small-town boyhood. Starting with Thomas Bailey Aldrich's *Story of a Bad Boy* (1869) and Mark Twain's *Adventures of Tom Sawyer* (1876), "boy-books" retained great popularity through the early 1900s. Theodore Roosevelt urged every boy to read Aldrich's *Story of a Bad Boy*. Advice writers also found a related market. Starting with his *American Boy's Handy Book* (1882), Daniel Carter Beard made a career describing outdoor stunts and structures of the sort requiring 40 poles and 2 trees spaced just right. Crammed with directions for Indian-style camping, Ernest Thompson Seton's *Two Little Savages* (1903) enjoyed huge success.[55]

This style of play survived outside guidebooks. Young B. F. Skinner lived a sheltered version in Susquehanna, Pennsylvania. Though his friends wrestled, they never threw punches; yet on Halloween these respectable boys played prankster, running trip wires across the sidewalk. They built a hut in the woods, but their tinkering drifted toward modern devices: a telegraph, a steam cannon made from a discarded boiler. In smaller numbers, city boys carried on the tradition, swimming amid sewage and fishing for whatever survived the water. But gang fights alarmed authorities, pranks were redefined as vandalism, and bonfires brought the police. Besides, woodsy play came to seem a bit old fashioned and juvenile. With ever-increasing intensity, modern boys focused their enthusiasm on team sports.[56]

Baseball had taken firm hold of American boys by the 1890s. Every survey of play from then through 1920 found it ranked first among boys' recreations. And ball games rose in popularity with age; they enjoyed a prestige that woodsy roaming could not match. In 1900, 68 percent of boys across South Carolina named baseball among things they liked best to do, followed by football at 56 percent. Swimming came a distant third at 24 percent, then marbles at 15 percent. Without sponsorship, children improvised. Boys and girls produced baseballs by winding string or cord around a rubber ball; woodcutters kept watch for likely branches to use as bats. In rural areas boys and girls played together; but separation increased with population, as boys grew numerous enough to play apart.[57]

Boosted by the prestige of college teams, football spread through the high schools, appealing most to older nonfarm boys. Theodore Roosevelt's famous advice to American boys, "Hit the line hard; don't foul and don't shirk, but hit the line hard!" made football a metaphor for manliness. In the era of the flying wedge and piling on, however, football earned a reputation for brutality. Each year's fatalities included high-school-age boys, although rules changes were reducing the toll by the 1910s. Basketball, invented in 1891, spread rapidly until by 1920 as many city boys played it as football.[58] But baseball remained preeminent among younger and rural boys.

Boys' play rarely anticipated workaday adult roles. At least until World War I, few American boys even played soldier, although football inspired a lively debate over whether it prepared boys for war.[59] The balance between team player and star would eventually become a metaphor for careerism in bureaucratic settings; but progressive Americans mistrusted big firms, and any such gloss applied better to high school sports than to the scrappy play of younger boys.

Enthusiasm for sports divided some boys from their fathers. Native Americans accustomed to play that imitated adult activities wondered how games like baseball taught anything of value, yet government schools produced exceptional athletes—not merely Jim Thorpe but all-Indian professional baseball teams. Work-oriented immigrants were aghast when their sons' enthusiasm for American team sports increased with age. "When I was a boy," complained a Jewish father, "we played rabbit, chasing each other, hide-and-seek. Later we stopped." But not in America, where even adults "run after a leather ball like children."[60]

Girls' play spurred less such concern; more than boys, they rehearsed their duties as adults, stayed close to home, and favored clearly childish games that they would abandon by their teens. Girls' imitative play peaked at primary school age, when as future housekeepers and teachers they played house and school. From about age six onward, girls treated their dolls as babies, although most lost interest before their teens. A 1902 study of children's friendships asserted that play at "being 'grown up folks' " led girls to start pairing off with best friends substantially younger than boys (6 or 7 rather than 8 or 10). Whereas boys could play games in throngs, sustained play at mothering dolls both fostered and required a more "intimate relationship." Since women typically bore more responsibility than men for managing social relationships within and outside the family, girls practiced. Although older boys did form close friendships, they had to train for a more impersonal, frankly competitive world in adulthood. Even quarrels took gendered forms. Whereas boys had fistfights, Catharine Brody recalls more elaborate rituals among girls. When two girls were not speaking, perhaps because one had failed to walk the other home, intermediaries would choreograph a reconciliation meeting: so that neither had to speak first, on a given signal both girls would speak at once.[61]

As dutiful daughters, girls in large numbers took music lessons on the piano or parlor organ. Convention prescribed that women attend to religion and the arts, so girls trained to play hymns and secular music. Boys were not immune, but being less compliant and dreading the sissy label, only half as many studied music. Learning an instrument was not precisely recreation, since instructional dogma required piano students to build technique and finger strength by playing endless "studies, scales, and exercises 'with power and energy.' " In Ethel Spencer's recollection, practice consisted mostly of checking the clock. Dropout rates were high, observers agreeing that the majority quit before achieving facility. For families that could afford them, player pianos (from about 1900 onward) and eventually phonographs offered entertainment with less effort.[62] Although music lessons offered some children opportunities for self-expression, more often they degenerated into drudgery that cannot have strengthened indifferent pupils' sense of industry.

Even at play, girls frequently compromised with practicality and duty. Thus a study of New England and California children in the 1890s found that boys formed clubs primarily for sports, whereas girls most often assembled "industrial" groups such as sewing circles. Many girls had to combine recreation with baby minding, choosing relatively stationary games such as hopscotch and skipping rope. When free, girls favored the wider-ranging games

Girls (and one boy) rollerskate behind a grocery wagon, Brooklyn, New York, c. 1900. (From the Collections of Henry Ford Museum & Greenfield Village, 32.351.115, photograph by Jenny Chandler)

of early childhood, with tag and hide-and-seek their favorites. Roller-skating, an adult fad that passed to children in the 1890s, extended girls' range—but only within limits, since skates required fairly smooth pavement, whereas boys, who more often had bicycles, could ride almost anywhere. Encumbered by flannel dresses and bloomers, far fewer girls than boys learned to swim. Though moderately vigorous, girls' outdoor play was more constrained than boys'. Furthermore, girls more or less accepted, as one self-described mischief maker wrote in 1897, that "when we are older it is time to settle down." Another girl opined that after age 13 "a lady should not climb trees unless to get away from a dog."[63]

Girls did not necessarily shun team sports. Because of their earlier growth spurt, those of grammar school age could excel in open competition. And farm girls commonly played baseball. Yet rural boys also harassed girls on occasion; a Missouri farm girl complained that boys threw snowballs ("big and hard") at girls heading for the outhouse. And the boys sometimes played apart, while the girls, one recalled, "would just get in little clusters and talk and giggle and laugh." Conversely, in some towns girls played ball with the boys; but in general, exclusion from sports in which players had to hone skills meant that city girls more often joined boys at relatively unspecialized games such as prisoner's base. A 1912 survey of Milwaukee concluded that whereas boys played sports, girls had little to do beyond attending movies, reading, "walking on the streets and visiting their friends."[64]

For nonfarm girls, the turn of the century brought somewhat greater acceptance of athleticism beyond the tomboy phase. The upper-class young woman idealized in 1890 by Charles Dana Gibson as the "Gibson Girl"—tall, slim, and vigorous—excelled at tennis, archery, and golf. Less athletic than these sports but even more openly competitive, croquet—whose name derives from the aggressive act of smacking (croqueting) other players' balls out of position—enjoyed huge popularity among girls around 1900. Yet the combination of physical exertion and competition troubled gender conservatives. New York City's Public Schools Athletic League, organized in 1903 by Luther Gulick, sponsored team sports and citywide track meets for elementary school boys. But because Gulick believed competitive athletics unsuitable for girls, the Girls' Branch of the PSAL offered no elementary track program and forbade individual or interschool competition. Instead, girls assembled for folk-dancing "fetes" in Central Park. Similarly, municipal playgrounds in New York and Pittsburgh had folk dancing and no competitive athletics for girls. As the first intensely competitive team sport for women, basketball challenged these limitations. Within two decades of the sport's invention, basketball for women spread through elite colleges and into high schools. Early teams played mostly by men's rules and tussled aggressively for the ball. Although specialists in women's physical education eventually hobbled the girls with restrictive rules, some high schools in the Midwest and West still tolerated highly competitive girls' basketball in the 1910s. Perhaps reflecting this regional support for girls' sports, playgrounds in Los Angeles sponsored girls' basketball, plus volleyball and modified baseball. Fragmentary evidence from play surveys suggests that girls' interest in team sports increased somewhat between the 1890s and the 1920s. But a major transformation would have required school-sponsored sports below high school age, and younger girls were mostly on their own.[65]

Recreation specialists worried more about boys' play. Then as always, children spent much of their playtime deciding what to do, talking, and engaging in desultory activities that critics dismissed as worthless loafing. A "play census" of Cleveland on June 23, 1913, reported that 9 percent of the children counted were working, 50 percent playing, and the rest "doing nothing." Even among those reported playing, nearly half had been "fighting, teasing, pitching pennies, shooting craps, stealing apples, 'roughing a peddler,' chasing chickens," or mostly " 'just fooling'—not playing anything in particular." Recreation organizers had learned to regard play as the *active* expression of instincts vital to a child's development; failure to exercise these

"What shall we play?" Stereograph, c. 1890s. (From the Collections of Henry Ford Museum & Greenfield Village, 88.0.1251.1)

capacities would prove disastrous. "The boy without play," pronounced George Johnson, reporting on the Cleveland survey, "is father to the man without a job."[66] Johnson's choice of gender was not accidental, as 62 percent of the children counted were boys. They outnumbered girls more than two to one on streets and three to one in alleys and vacant lots. On playgrounds the numbers were equal, and in private yards the girls outnumbered boys five to four. So girls were less likely to be outdoors and, if they were, more likely to be where adults could supervise them. In the minds of reformers, uncontrolled boys posed the main problem.

One response, spurred by distaste for commercial recreation, was to revive (or invent) an Anglo-American "play heritage," purportedly dating back to "Merrie England." Folk dancing and Maypole ceremonies at playgrounds and settlement houses, reformers believed, would Americanize immigrants and counter the socialists' May Day. These exercises in ethnocentric anachronism conscripted mostly girls, however, and died out after World War I.[67]

More enduring was the vogue of supervised athletics, which many agencies began between the 1890s and 1910s. For men worried that middle-class boys were turning soft, organized sport promised to build strength, courage, and persistence. But control was the paramount objective, especially in programs for lower-class boys. Mistrustful of boys' self-directed play, recreation specialists emphasized that supervised team sports would teach obedience to rules and to coaches, cooperation, and self-sacrifice. YMCAs and Sunday school athletic leagues sponsored basketball and baseball for middle-class boys, boys' clubs and settlement houses did the same for working-class boys, and municipal playgrounds served varied classes.[68]

As social control, however, supervised sports proved relatively ineffective. Outside New York City, few school systems organized athletics below the high school grades, even though elementary school pupils far outnumbered high schoolers. Gangs turned some playgrounds into fiefdoms or battle zones. Private agencies had limited reach within the middle class and little influence outside it. Far from meekly accepting cultural imposition, lower-class players turned genteel character building to their own purposes. Thus a boys' club coach reported that the boys showed no interest in maintaining "the strict amateur standing of the amateur sportsman. They desired always to play for some stake . . . [but] were easily dissuaded from playing for money and perfectly satisfied to play for a prize instead."[69] Except to a degree among high school students, adults did not gain control of youthful sports in the progressive era. Little League was still in the future.

Much as opinion leaders had accepted that children needed play, so they agreed by the late nineteenth century that children's literature should not be glumly didactic. Fictional adventure, even frivolity and fantasy, seemed vital food for children's imaginations. The problem for reformers was to wall off a realm sheltered from commercial exploitation. Meticulous separation by age would have struck readers of the late nineteenth century as anomalous. To an extent unimagined today, adults read novels about children. *The Adventures of Huckleberry Finn* (1884), *Little Lord Fauntleroy* (1886), *Rebecca of Sunnybrook Farm* (1903), and *Penrod* (1914) all were bestsellers. Conversely, children read or heard books written mainly for adults. Many rural schoolhouses contained remarkably disparate little libraries, built around donations. Children recall fathers on the school board who bought the few books purchased annually and favored items they wanted to read themselves, including current novels. Reading aloud was a fairly common family entertainment, not merely a bedtime ritual for small children. Mother or an older sister would read classic novels by Dickens or Scott and sometimes more contemporary fare.[70] Genteel culture assumed broad understanding by different age groups. Yet shared readership did not preclude portrayal of childhood as radically different from adulthood. Stories in small-town and country settings traded on urban adults' escapism and nostalgia, while romanticized images of childish innocence and energy played upon notions of children as the hope of the future. As overt didacticism faded, novelists portrayed children unburdened by work or even moral responsibility.[71]

This separation of childhood from adult values was conspicuous in books about boys. Mischievous "bad" boys virtually escaped conventional moral judgment. Taken to vulgar extremes, comic writing invited readers to regard boyish foibles, even cruelty, with tolerant amusement. In *Peck's Red-Headed Boy* (1903), boys cheerfully killed a friendly dog. Reckoning that poison would be "too uneventful," they tied dynamite to its tail, and "the sky rained dog." Although Tom Sawyer was never so nasty and could summon bursts of heroism, his normal behavior glorified playful irresponsibility. Booth Tarkington's Penrod, a later, suburbanized incarnation of the type, got into endless scrapes, which Tarkington burlesqued with sympathetic facetiousness. These fictional boys did not grow in wisdom and stature and in favor with God and man. Rather they remained, like Tom, preserved in the amber of eternal boyhood or, if they took on new responsibilities they did so unprepared, and grew up in one arbitrary leap. In romantic nostalgia, boyhood became the high point of life. Similarly, adventure stories evaded adulthood. "Boys defeated black-armored knights and rescued girls from burning buildings; . . . over and over they won crucial football games and made the clinching baseball play." As historian Daniel T. Rodgers notes, such stories no longer celebrated "the character-building reward of effort; rather, they made a romance of victory," achieved in one heroic act.[72]

Fictional girls had less autonomy, since classic novels of girlhood commonly centered on their struggle to learn and accept the constraints and responsibilities of growing up. Typically near or in their teens, the protagonists were somewhat older than boy-book boys and less able to ignore the approach of adulthood. Through 1920, Louisa May Alcott remained the favorite author of American girls. Jo, the central character in Alcott's *Little Women* (1868–1869), was physically boisterous and an aspiring writer. She chafed against the loss of girlhood and, unlike Tom Sawyer and his kin, learned to curb and expiate her faults, one by one. As the years passed, two March sisters married and one died; Jo then married an unromantic Professor Bhaer and settled down to run a school. A long generation later, *Rebecca of Sunnybrook Farm* (1903) and her near-clone, *Anne of Green Gables* (1908) bore fewer moral burdens, but they too grew up to responsibility. In each case a poor girl went off to live with an aged couple, one person emotionally inhibited and the other flinty. Imaginative and voluble but radically innocent and generous hearted, the girls had no grave faults to conquer but did have to learn restraint and decorum. Though each triumphed academically at school and won the respect and love of classmates, the emotional core of each novel was a story of youth enlivening staid households and opening their guardians' frozen hearts to love. In the end each girl renounced (or at least postponed) further education in order to care for an aged loved one. After celebrating spunk, each author romanticized female renunciation.[73]

Below the level of genteel literature surged a flood of westerns and crime stories. Jacob Riis blamed "flash literature and penny-dreadfuls" for the "rank and morbid growth" of criminal fantasies among tenement-house boys. Similarly, recreation experts attributed the exploits of "knickerbockered bandits" in Springfield, Illinois, to their reading of 10-cent paperbacks "in the recesses of some livery stable or lumber yard."[74] Promoters of public libraries and wholesome children's literature played heavily on adults' fear of dime novels. These initially appealed to men and boys alike but by 1900 were losing their adult readers to pulp magazines and becoming a purely juvenile form. Late-nineteenth-century publishers had already been producing slightly sanitized adventure stories for boys. From 1900 onward, series books with boy heroes poured onto the market, featuring adventures with radio, airplanes, motor cars, and motorcycles. Stories of school life and sports proliferated, then boys followed the action to World War I. Although they avoided the lurid criminality of many dime novels, series books infuriated educators with fantasies of effortless triumph by know-it-all youngsters. Franklin K. Mathiews, chief librarian for the Boy Scouts of America, railed that publishers were "blowing out the boy's brains" with tales of young upstarts who moved about "in airplanes as easily as though on bicycles" and lectured their elders on submarine technology.[75]

Series for girls followed toward 1910, equally juvenile in their assumption that no adults would read them. Motor Boys and Radio Boys were succeeded by Motor Girls, Radio Girls, Flying Girls, Outdoor Girls, and Moving Picture Girls. Slightly older heroines carried their college class to victory in basketball. Though girls' stories followed the same adventure formula as boys', they eschewed fistfights and gunplay, focusing, in addition to accidents and natural disasters, on issues (however trivialized) of social standing and responsibility. Stolen letters, forged examinations, and betrayals of family secrets challenged the heroine to discover "her true friends" or to save "her dear friend's reputation." The result, comments critic Jane Smith, resembled Jane Austen rewritten by Zane Grey. Unlike the boys of fiction, moreover, these girls had not found the secret of perennial childhood, for they kept getting older, and eventually married.[76] In popular as well as genteel fiction, unending youthful freedom was for boys.

As cheap fiction divided by age, with series books for young readers only, a parallel fissure opened within genteel culture. Amid heightened awareness of childhood's distinctiveness, the old world of common reading was splitting. Separate children's libraries and literature gained prominence between 1900 and 1920. As late as 1893, 70 percent of public libraries barred children under 12. But as libraries shifted from treasure houses to public amenities, children's rooms came to seem essential. In the early 1900s, when millionaire

Andrew Carnegie offered a free library building to any municipality that promised a specified operating budget, proponents of accepting his offer emphasized children's needs. Over time, children's rooms grew more clearly juvenile, as standard rectangular library tables with high, sit-up-straight chairs gave way to low, round tables and smaller chairs. Although not all children responded, public libraries served many girls and some boys.[77]

By the 1910s children's and adult literature were parting company. The custom of reading aloud at home was waning. Adult narration survived artificially in library story hours, but literary classics figured only in simplified form. Some of the division reflected growing realism in adult fiction, which threatened to soil a sheltered childhood. But children who read by themselves preferred large type and lots of pictures. Librarians and educators specializing in children's reading began to issue age-graded reading lists that eliminated not merely morally unsuitable books but also long or complex ones. Recognizing a market, publishers formed profitable children's divisions, and in 1919 Mathiews organized National Children's Book Week.[78] Directed by professionals, children's reading would be safely juvenile. The impact of these developments, however, was muted by children's uncertain appetite for reading. In 1896, when Worcester, Massachusetts, schoolchildren listed their amusements, just 83 of 1,000 boys and 108 of 1,000 girls mentioned reading, although another study in settings less immigrant than Worcester reported that boys read a good deal and girls often read favorite books to each other.[79]

In any case, just when children's books seemed to be growing safer and more available, a new medium assaulted the barriers erected to shelter children's imaginations. Tickets to live drama cost too much for working-class children; middle-class boys and girls averaged only one outing monthly. Even vaudeville was a rare treat on workers' incomes. So working-class young people were thrilled when, starting about 1905, storefront movie theaters sprang up throughout their neighborhoods. Charging five cents for half an hour of short films, these nickelodeons opened a world of wonders, close at hand and quick to visit. By 1908, 8,000 to 10,000 were operating nationwide. Movie theaters spread downtown, eventually showing longer films and raising ticket prices slightly—but without losing their mass audience. Soon they reached every little town. In 1920, Children's Bureau agents studying 11 isolated West Virginia mining villages found only one regular church and one playground but six movie houses. The core audience was young. Those in their teens and twenties predominated in the evening, but younger children formed the next-largest market, especially on afternoons and weekends. In Cleveland in 1915, 78 percent of elementary-school boys and 84 percent of girls attended movies, averaging one and a half times a week. Jammed together in nearly total darkness, children yelled, threw wrappers, and jumped on chairs. "They were called silent pictures," Sam Levenson recalled, "but the audience certainly wasn't."[80]

Like dime novels, movies alarmed progressive child savers. Anticipating today's media critics, they feared that portrayal of adult sexuality would breach children's wholesome ignorance, though bits of nudity and plots involving extramarital sexuality were mild by today's standards. Echoing attacks on dime novels, moralists worried about copycat crimes. Jane Addams charged that three young moviegoers, ages 9 through 13, bought a revolver and tried to imitate a stagecoach holdup by robbing and murdering the local milkman. (Fortunately, their lasso spooked the milkman's horse and the young gunman missed.) In *The Spirit of Youth and the City Streets* (1909), Addams denounced commercial recreation as "vice deliberately disguised as pleasure." Memorably describing theater as "the house of dreams" for working-class children, she was fascinated and appalled by the new nickelodeons. Attempting to disguise virtue as pleasure, Hull House opened its own nickel theater, but Cinderella and travel films could not compete with cowboys and pirates down the street. In 1909, Addams's colleagues in the Juvenile Protective Association turned to censorship and secured enforcement of a city ordinance under which police excised scenes of robbery or murder and sometimes banned entire movies.[81]

Although the U.S. Supreme Court in 1915 upheld local and state censorship, the flood of movies forced compromise. Moviemakers mostly avoided explicit sex and insured that screen criminals got punished, yet matinee shows still included lots of crime melodramas alongside slapstick comedies. In David Nasaw's words, the industry "walked the fine line between offending the reformers and boring the children." On the whole, recreation specialists calmed down surprisingly, perhaps because movies did not engulf children's time the way television later did. A weekend play census in Cleveland found that children spent slightly more time reading (106 minutes) than at movies (84 minutes) and vastly more time on the street.[82]

Still, the compromise was unstable and would breed recurrent controversy in later decades, for it ran counter to progressive policy concerning children. Whether dealing with child labor, street play, children's reading, or juvenile delinquency, reformers sought to separate children from adult activities, shield them from contamination, and bring their formation under the guidance of experts in child welfare. The arrangement regarding movies was different. Although the industry made gestures toward protecting children's morals, it weighed these against the need to excite both children and older customers. Most children saw the same movies that adults did, and although some watched with parents, many were on their own.

Values and Roles

Children of elementary school age were too young to form identities such as Erik Erikson associates with later adolescence, but they were learning formulaic values and conventional social roles. Adult inculcation of religious and patriotic values secured ritual assent. Children learned specific social roles more specifically and vividly, for the progressive era saw sharp social differentiation. By their preteens, children had learned roles they would be expected or allowed to play in terms of race, ethnicity, and gender.

Religious education responded conservatively to new developmental ideas about childhood. Christian churches used two slightly different approaches. One method, often combined with parochial schooling among Catholics and Lutherans, emphasized instruction in catechism, liturgy, and the meanings embodied in the church year, leading eventually to confirmation. British-origin Protestants favored Sunday schools focused on Biblical instruction, followed by religious conversion or a simple decision to seek full church membership. Neither approach changed fundamentally in the progressive era. By the late nineteenth century, Sunday school rhetoric depicted children as innocent sunbeams. The assurance "Jesus Loves Me" (the era's most popular Sunday school hymn) dispelled fear of hell, especially in churches of the northern middle class. Terror of hellfire still tormented many children, however. Southern evangelicals, Holiness preachers, and spiritual directors in Catholic convent schools all stoked the flames of imagination, especially at revivals, camp meetings, and retreats.[83]

Whatever the theology, children memorized authoritative texts that were often unadapted to their age and occasionally written in languages they did not understand. Catholic altar boys learned responses in Latin; a Protestant Dutch farmer's son learned his catechism and psalms phonetically in Dutch, which his generation no longer spoke. Most English-speaking Sunday schools used the International Sunday School Convention's uniform lessons, under which all ages studied the same Scripture passage and all memorized the same Golden Text. Large Sunday schools sorted children by age for teaching but did not vary the curriculum. Consequently, even the youngest pupils began 1906 discussing whose wife a woman would be in heaven if widowed seven times on earth. Explanation of texts depended on the individual teacher, but in 1921 Indiana Sunday school teachers reported spending a median of just 67 minutes weekly in lesson preparation. Since respectable young women were virtually drafted into teaching, instruction invited Henry Seidel Canby's dismissive summary of it as "Bible stories parroted by misses doing their duty." Results could be quirky. One elderly lady remembers best two items from Sunday school: the story of a woman pounding a tent peg through an Assyrian's head and her teacher's inability to explain how Jesus sat on a roof (since Michigan roofs were peaked). Adults who expected reliable theological outcomes risked disappointment. When a child-study investigator quizzed children ages 8 to 15 (mostly United Brethren, Lutheran, Methodist, and Presbyterian), she found their answers distressingly "stereotyped." A majority wrote that good people go to heaven and bad to hell, but barely half understood Christ as a savior, though older children more often proclaimed that hell is fiery and Christ saves sinners.[84] Many more boys than girls professed ignorance. The lay volunteers who ran Sunday schools resisted professionals who criticized their "prescientific pedagogy" and "simplistic theology." In 1903 William Rainey Harper, president of the University of Chicago, spearheaded organization of the Religious Education Association to popularize the fruits of recent Biblical scholarship and child psychology. But when the reformers designed graded lessons keyed to children's developmental stages, these offended conservative lay piety, and most Sunday schools stuck with the uniform lessons through 1920.[85]

Sunday school loomed especially large because home worship was dwindling. Religious writers agreed that by 1920 only the most fervent Protestant parents did much more than say grace at meals and listen to their children's bedtime prayers. Of course religious and moral education continued less formally; but not all families communicated readily.[86]

A surprising number of children determined their own Sunday school attendance. Because Sunday was a slow day, even children of unchurched parents often tagged along with friends. Although a majority of Sunday school pupils attended at their parents' church, roughly one-third were children of parents affiliated with some other church or none at all. Sunday school appealed especially to isolated farm children, who came for company, and the overworked, who came to relax. An elderly domestic from North Carolina reflected, "For us children it was just a place to play and play. Nobody wanted you to do no chores, like at home. And I know it was the only place you could go and not feel somebody was going to make you do something other than sit down and sit still."[87]

Judged by total attendance, which rose steadily from year to year, turn-of-the-century Sunday schools were thriving. To the disappointment of enthusiasts who wanted to hold older youths and adults, however, Sunday school remained quintessentially a children's institution; between ages 12 and 16 attendance fell by half.[88] As their ignorance of doctrine suggested, boys were less compliant religiously than girls, who outnumbered them in Sunday school approximately five to four from ages 6 to 12 and four to three or even two to one in the teens. Southern males associated conversion with unmanly submission, and northern writers assumed that boys disliked Sunday school. No less a pillar of respectability than Senator Henry Cabot Lodge proclaimed that boys were "young heathens" with a "wholesome dislike" of any "religious prig."[89] Against the humility and restraint expected of young churchgoers, other codes bid powerfully for older boys' allegiance: the obligation to fight, the need to win.

Boys seemed more receptive to American civil religion. Still, school authorities feared social unrest and immigrant disloyalty. Starting around 1890, more assertive patriotic indoctrination, supported by flag rituals, spread through northern urban schools. Increasingly, children saluted and recited the formula first published by the *Youth's Companion* in 1892: "I pledge allegiance to my Flag and the Republic for which it stands: one Nation indivisible, with Liberty and Justice for All." At the level of ritual affirmation, the authorities secured striking results. Several turn-of-the-century studies asked American elementary-school children whom they would most like to resemble. Although at most 6 percent named religious exemplars, the number selecting men from American history rose rapidly with age. More than 70 percent of white boys in Nashville picked historic Americans; boys in their early teens particularly favored American military heroes. In conformity to the schoolroom cult of admiration for George Washington, more than one-quarter of children surveyed claimed him as their ideal. No doubt children often wrote to please their elders; yet comparative studies, which should have suffered the same flaw, indicate that progressive-era American children, especially boys, identified more strongly with national heroes than did English and German children of the period.[90]

Girls named more varied ideals than boys. Larger numbers picked acquaintances (even teachers), fictional characters, authors, musicians, and women renowned for service. Yet in two of three studies a majority of girls named male ideals. Estelle Darrah, the pioneer researcher in the field, blamed history in schools for presenting "only male characters" and dealing "almost entirely with conquest and war."[91]

Theoretically inclusive patriotism existed in precarious balance with growing awareness of invidious distinctions based on wealth, ethnicity, race, gender, and age. Even before their teens, children learned to judge others and to play (or cope with or resist) roles prescribed according to their social status. Henry Sheldon, who studied children's group affiliations in the 1890s, believed that girls formed smaller, more intimate groups than boys and drew lines by social exclusion. White boys formed looser, more competitive relationships; they would play sports with any ethnic group, Sheldon wrote, "even negroes," but drew lines more violently than girls.[92]

American ideology obscured children's awareness of social class. Countervailing efforts failed, as pedestrian Socialist Sunday schools never enrolled one child in a thousand. Tacitly, children learned to feel class superiority. Sheldon concluded that although very young children made no distinctions, they learned a strong "feeling of caste" by age 10: "Girls, if so told by their mothers, think themselves too good to play with girls of the working classes or of alien nationalities."[93] But American culture offered a rich array of surrogates for explicit recognition of social class.

Town children learned to scorn country folk, noting, as one southern girl did, the boys' "misfit 'store pants' " and the girls' faded dresses. A Michigan farm boy remembers the mortification of going to town with hair cut at home that "looked like the beavers had abused it."[94]

Ethnicity, often reinforced by religion, divided children. In a community where they predominated, German Lutherans who attended parochial school would "holler things" at non-Germans heading to public school. A Slovak boy remembers "being called 'Hunky' all the time at school. I guess that's why I was always getting beat up." But most ethnoreligious prejudices were milder than the anti-Semitism that greeted Jewish children. At age 11, Harry Golden was "cockalized" by Irish boys in New York City, an ordeal he considered common in his generation: "The enemy kids threw the Jew to the ground, opened his pants, and spat and urinated on his circumcised penis while they shouted, 'Christ killer.' "[95] Early movies reinforced stereotypes with sketches of slow-witted Irish domestics initiating comic disasters and grasping Jewish merchants cheating purchasers. Yet second-generation children could distance themselves by laughing at the unassimilated travesties on-screen.

No such dual perspective mitigated the denigration of African Americans. Since storefront theaters were too cramped for segregation, most barred black patrons. White children of all backgrounds came together in a carnival of racism. Movies such as *Dancing Nig* and *How Rastus Got His Pork Chops* mocked African Americans as stupid creatures of impulse.[96] In milder forms, racism pervaded children's culture, popping up in stories, rehearsed in the ubiquitous "Eeny, meeny, miney, moe / Catch a nigger by his toe. . . ." Even in remote North Dakota, young Era Bell Thompson had to steel herself to feign indifference from time to time when someone yelled, "Nigger!"[97]

Racism intensified between 1890 and 1920, as southern governments codified segregation. Sadie and Elizabeth Delany first encountered these Jim Crow rules around 1896, when they were seven and five. As they boarded a trolley in Raleigh, North Carolina, the driver told them to move back. "We children objected loudly because we always liked to sit in front, where the breeze would blow your hair," the sisters recalled. "But Mama and Papa just gently told us to hush." The park where they were heading had changed too. The spring now bore a sign: "white" on one side, "colored" on the other. "We may have been little children," Sadie Delany commented, "but, honey, we got the message loud and clear. But when nobody was looking, Bessie took the dipper from the white side and drank from it." As the girls grew older, their father, an Episcopal priest, enforced strict chaperonage. They would not speak to white men, fearful that mistreatment would force their father to protest and endanger his life.[98] Though northern cities were more open, when Boston newsies elected an African-American boy to their newsboys' court, the new judge shrank from active participation because, a white colleague explained, "you see, some people don't like niggers." The late 1910s, when hundreds of thousands of southern blacks moved to northern cities, made white racism there more salient and violent. In July of 1919, an African-American teenager drifted too close to a "white" beach in Chicago. His murder triggered street battles that left 23 blacks and 15 whites dead.[99]

Despite severe exploitation, rural black parents could shield their children somewhat through isolation, although any child with white playmates was bound to notice when they headed off to better-equipped schools. Even very young children were hard to shelter in cities. In New York, Mary White Ovington saw a file of kindergartners set upon by Irish boys throwing sticks and yelling "nigger." The four-year-old in the lead had already learned not to react. "Don't notice them," she told the child beside her. "Walk straight ahead." Reminiscences suggest that most African-American children had a troubling awareness of racism by age six or so.[100]

Aggressive racism took time to develop. Investigations after Chicago's 1919 riot concluded that children got on fairly well in the lower grades. But tensions increased with age, "and graduations from elementary schools usually brought requests from white parents and children that whites and blacks march separately." By that age many white children had learned a moral double standard. In a North Carolina mill village, white boys enjoyed "rocking" black boys, one time inflicting serious injuries. "But there were limits," former residents recalled. "Stealing was not tolerated." Most children learned the gospel of love in segregated Sunday schools. A New England boy reported that when "two half colored children" joined his Christian Endeavor Society, the members "continually teased and taunted" them.[101]

Potentially, gender roles functioned like racism, differentiating for deprivation. Although many progressive-era writers favored sharper gender divisions, social and cultural trends were inconsistent, and children received mixed messages. Boys' and girls' farm work fairly often overlapped, and the need for players drew country girls into coed sports. In some ways, therefore, declining rural populations meant more constricted roles for average girls. But urbanization affected gender socialization in varied ways. Children's chores grew more sex segregated, yet town life fostered extended education. Despite policy talk of differentiation, elementary-school boys and girls received the same formal schooling, with girls on average advancing ahead of boys. Although boys and girls drew apart on urban playgrounds, older girls gained modest opportunities in sports. Possibilities broadened enough that turn-of-the-century researchers attributed girls' frequent choice of male ideals to their "reaching out after the larger life lived by men." A modern historian, Victoria Bissell Brown, argues that progressive-era socialization, though ostensibly directed to raising wives and mothers, taught middle-class girls to measure themselves against male criteria and classmates, cutting them off from the values of women's culture while holding out a promise of opportunity unlikely to be realized in adulthood.[102] Entertainment taught compromised goals. The movies provided models of female assertiveness and stardom, but embedded in a framework of heterosexual romance. Girls' series books gave their readers vicarious athletic triumphs and independent adventures, yet as time passed the heroines married and took second place to husbands.

Girls knew that adults expected them to be more self-abnegating than boys. When asked in 1897 what "John" might plant in a garden, a 13-year-old girl replied warily that if she were a boy she would plant "vegetables or something that would be of profit." As a girl, she proposed flowers to give away. Organizers of the Boy Scouts of America and Camp Fire Girls wrote a similar distinction into promotion requirements: whereas Boy Scouts were to earn money and save it, Camp Fire Girls were to give their earnings away. Wiggin's Rebecca of Sunnybrook Farm laments, "Boys always do the nice splendid things, and girls can only do the nasty dull ones that get left over." Individual girls resisted, but without the license that fiction gave boys for mischief and unabashed self-interest.[103]

In real life, when asked to name the meanest child they knew, seven of eight New York children chose a boy. Girls complained mainly of other girls' "slander and backbiting," whereas nasty boys stood accused of bullying, fighting, and stealing. Unsurprisingly, progressive educators and youth workers found boys more problematic than girls. Even middle-class boys got mixed messages about compliance and concern for others. Too much academic or religious effort exposed them to scorn from peers and sometimes adults. In fiction, pranksters thrived. And although nobody loved a bully, victims won contempt.[104] Sports promised to make compliance respectable, as boys would become team players and obey their manly coach; but not all boys had talent, and mere compliance seldom led to stardom.

Age grading was less invidious than other forms of stratification, since all children advanced. But age ranges were becoming prescriptive, although less so than reformers desired. Child study popularizers spread the belief that normal development should be measured against age. Bureaucracy and psychology combined to foster stricter age grading in urban schools and to make "retardation" seem wrong. Although age distinctions remained more fluid in rural schools, by the 1910s most had formal promotion from grade to grade. Children ranked games by age. Thus Catharine Brody recalled, "Ring games and 'London Bridge Is Falling Down' were all very well for little children, but potsies [a New York variant of hopscotch] could be played well on to the eleventh year, for it was a game at once of chance and of skill and strength."[105] The new team sports fostered age awareness, since the specialized skills and strength required to excel took years to develop.

Children sorted themselves to a degree. In a 1902 survey of urban and middle-class children, virtually all named as their closest friend someone the same sex and very close in age. YMCA men considered three years the maximum age difference tolerated by young teenagers; beyond that, the older ones complained of associating with "kids." At the same time, younger boys sought to impress older ones. Marquis James took lifelong pride in a switching from his first-grade teacher in Enid, Oklahoma. The boy before him "bawled," but young Marquis "didn't let out a peep . . . though crying when licked was not considered altogether disgraceful for a small boy." Big boys, he knew, never cried. And they approved: "When school let out that evening larger boys I didn't know very well took notice of me." Age norms set a minimum, but children often looked ahead, reading stories about older children and tagging along with older siblings. As a result, considerable age mixing survived, especially among working-class children.[106]

Adult-sponsored prescriptive age grading had more potential for conflict, since these norms operated less as gradations leading upward than as barriers to what adults considered precocious. Knickers with knee socks were the uniform of nonfarm boyhood; only at around age 12 to 15 did boys finally graduate to long pants. Less dramatically, girls' dresses were short until their teens.[107] More seriously, child labor laws set minimum ages for leaving dependent childhood, although indifferent enforcement weakened their effect. In general, children pressed upward, whereas adults demanded a measured pace. This disagreement became evident as reformers tried to institutionalize an adult-sponsored adolescence that would extend the shelter of childhood to the teens.

Of all candidates for adolescence, middle-class schoolchildren lived lives most closely calibrated by age, uncompromised by demands of the family economy. Yet even they encountered settings such as movies and theater where age separation broke down. Other children did not necessarily have a sheltered childhood as they entered their teens. Central to progressive reformers' anxieties were immigrant boys. Looking back on his final years of grade school, Leonard Covello, who became a renowned New York educator, remembered juggling a multiplicity of roles. He had immigrated from Avigliano in Italy, done well in school, been deeply influenced by a Protestant mission called the Home Garden, and yet dutifully helped support his family: "Now I was living what seemed like fragmentary existences in different worlds. There was my life with my family and Aviglianese neighbors. My life on the streets of East Harlem. My life at the Home Garden with Miss Ruddy. Life at the local public school. Life at whatever job I happened to have. Life in the wonder-world of books. There seemed to be no connection, one with the other; it was like turning different faucets on and off. Yet I was happy."[108]

5

Adolescence as Extended Childhood

Defined broadly enough—as a transitional stage between childhood and adulthood—adolescence is virtually universal. Even defined more narrowly, adolescence as modern Americans know it has many antecedents. "Youths" in eighteenth-century New England experienced protracted "marginality and dependence," during which their sensuality and frolicking with peers drew rebukes from the pulpit. Among the nineteenth-century urban middle class, major features of modern adolescence came to seem right and proper. Increasingly, a respectable nonfarm father's children lived at home for much of their teens, received extended schooling, and did not contribute earnings or prolonged labor to the family economy.[1] For such teenagers, youth was becoming an extension of the sheltered childhood. What the progressive era added—besides a new label, adolescence—was heightened adult concern to control teenagers outside the family setting and explicit effort to keep them safely juvenile. Reformers and youth workers campaigned to institutionalize the dependence of urban adolescents and make their status more childlike.

The term *adolescence,* which gained wide currency soon after 1900, gave reform concerns a scientific-sounding name. Popularized by the psychologist G. Stanley Hall and his disciples, the concept of adolescence as a developmental crisis particularly impressed Protestant youth workers but influenced educators and child welfare workers as well. Unlike educational theorists such as E. L. Thorndike, who emphasized continuity between childhood and adolescence, Hall dramatized adolescence as a virtual new birth, when new instincts poured in upon the young. Teenagers must sublimate their sexuality into idealistic enthusiasm and religious faith, he warned, as masturbation would trigger degeneracy. Hall's romantic portrait of adolescence as "a stormy period of great agitation, when the very worst and best impulses in the human soul struggle against each other for its possession," argued powerfully for adult control. Idealizing adolescence as "the infancy of man's higher nature," Hall urged delaying the responsibilities of adulthood.[2]

Alarm about adolescents drew on contemporary anxieties about children on the streets and commercial entertainment. Church workers and public educators worried that urban culture tainted even middle-class school pupils, that boys quit Sunday school and might also grow impatient with high school. At the same time, shifting dependency ratios made prolonged adult support and supervision of teenagers more feasible. Because of declining birthrates, the ratio of young people from birth through age 18 to adults in the American population was no larger in 1920 than the ratio in 1870 of children under age 12 to adults. If control of children had seemed possible earlier, so did control of teenagers by 1920. And yet as adults sought to prolong social childhood, physiological maturity came ever younger. Since at least 1870, the age at which girls began menstruating had been declining. North American boys of 1920 averaged some 2 inches taller and 15 pounds heavier at age 15 than their counterparts of 1880, as richer diets, better health, and reduced exercise brought them close to adult size much younger.[3]

In reaction, hostility to "precocity"—physical, social, economic, even intellectual—marked progressive-era discussions of adolescents. Praising high school boys, two prominent settlement workers asserted that "the economic dependence of children between fourteen and seventeen years of age is far more normal than the precocious worldliness of the employed boy." Similarly, a high school principal complained, "Children are becoming men and women too early." He urged prolonging "infancy" into adolescence by keeping children in school past age 14. Although much advice merely prescribed that teenagers follow a middle-class timetable, writers also began referring to adolescents as children and demanding that they remain as economically and socially dependent as children.[4]

Adult efforts to reinforce adolescent dependence and tighten adult supervision outside the family took many forms. Crusaders against child labor sought to delay full-time paid employment. Juvenile court promoters bolstered officialdom's discretionary powers to chastise the young. Youth workers tried to co-opt and guide the recreational life of middle-class teenagers, either delaying adolescence altogether or channeling and attenuating adolescent instincts. And high school spokesmen broadened their claims to socialize students. In sketching these adult initiatives, this chapter does not attempt a comprehensive account of progressive-era adolescence. Youth remained a transitional stage leading toward adulthood, not simply an extension of childhood. From the start, campaigns to make adolescence childlike enjoyed very limited success. But they bequeathed to the twentieth century an impressive residue of institutions.

Juvenile Delinquency

Progressives lauded juvenile courts as one of the era's foremost innovations in child saving. Ideally, these courts extended dependency to age 16 or beyond by taking young people, mostly poor, whose parents could or would not exert proper control and substituting the courts' authority to decide what was best for the child. In Judge Ben Lindsey's words, courts would defend "the sacred period of adolescence." Ideally, in fully organized juvenile courts, probation officers first investigated misbehaving or neglected children, while holding them in detention facilities carefully separated from adult prisoners. Untrammeled by the formalities and rules of evidence required in adult criminal trials, juvenile judges then prescribed treatment based on each youth's condition and needs. A majority ended up on probation—the outcome publicized by juvenile court proponents—but the new courts still committed a substantial minority to reform institutions.[5]

As recent scholars have emphasized, juvenile courts mainly extended familiar techniques. Many states had experimented with probation, and nineteenth-century legislatures had granted broad discretionary authority for confinement of dependent, delinquent, and "predelinquent" children in reformatories. By the 1890s, however, reports of cold water hosing and brutal beatings exposed juvenile reformatories as nasty prisons. Fearful of punishing too cruelly, officials sometimes let petty offenders escape discipline altogether. The juvenile court provided a middle path. In harmony with the anti-institutional consensus of the 1909 White House conference, probation officers would permit minor offenders to live at home. Thus juvenile courts promised to foster a sheltered childhood for troubled youth through regulatory adjustment of the child's environment, without expensive long-term confinement or family assistance.[6]

The first juvenile court with all the standard features began operation in Chicago in 1899. In Denver, Colorado, Judge Ben Lindsey improvised a juvenile court in 1901 and emerged by 1904 as the nation's leading evangelist for empathetic, informal juvenile justice. Women's clubs lobbied for state legislation, and juvenile courts modeled in some measure on Chicago's and Denver's spread widely. Ten states passed juvenile court laws by 1905; 46 did so by 1915.[7]

Young people got an offer they could not refuse: they would forgo the rights of adult criminal defendants; in return, judges would prescribe wise treatment, like a father or a doctor. Taking the juvenile courts' benevolent professions as evidence of accomplishment, progressive-era higher courts repeatedly ruled that children needed no protection in courts that acted for the children's own benefit. Enabling legislation often supplied vague, catchall definitions of delinquency. Illinois's initial 1899 law required violation of a law or ordinance; amendments in 1901 added anyone under age 16 who was "growing up in idleness" or seemed "incorrigible." Some states required a specific offense; others passed laws more sweeping than that of Illinois. By 1914, California law permitted arrest of anyone under age 21 who appeared "in danger of growing up to lead an idle, dissolute or immoral life." Procedural informality gave the courts further latitude, with hearsay routinely accepted as evidence.[8]

These legal nets caught many small fish. A 1913 study of an Irish and German neighborhood in New York attributed more than half the juvenile arrests to "noncrimes," including "begging, bonfires, gambling, jumping on [street]cars, . . . playing shinney, playing with water pistol, putting out lights, selling papers, shooting craps, snowballing, subway disturbances, and throwing stones."[9] Such arrests represented ongoing police efforts to clear the streets, but court officers also furnished neighbors, teachers, and parents a new avenue for complaint. Trivial offenses seldom drew severe penalties. Still, a list of all charges brought in the Chicago juvenile court's first 10 years included many minor and vaguely defined offenses. Of 11,413 boys, 51 percent faced charges of theft, 22 percent incorrigibility, and 16 percent disorderly conduct. Among 2,770 girls, 43 percent confronted claims of incorrigibility, 31 percent immorality, and 15 percent stealing. Almost half the boys' theft charges stemmed from foraging along railroad tracks and in empty buildings, where the line blurred between scavenging and stealing. As the compilers of the Chicago data observed, taking small items resembled "the long tolerated privilege which the country boy enjoys of 'swiping' melons and pumpkins in neighboring gardens."[10] Although progressive-era writers seldom granted female delinquents equal tolerance, most faced only gender-biased morals charges and were innocent of theft or violence.

A significant minority of children before the juvenile courts were dependent rather than delinquent in any remotely criminal sense. Desperate parents sought court intervention—often hoping for help in controlling recalcitrant sons and daughters, but sometimes so overtaxed or destitute that they simply wanted the authorities to take a child. Other children faced neglect or abuse so extreme that officials had to remove them from home. And some nominal delinquents were actually acting out their protest against adult mistreatment. Under these circumstances, judges committed a far larger proportion of dependent than delinquent children to institutions. Yet few states prohibited consigning dependent children to juvenile reformatories. The more dire the underlying family problems, the less progressive reform through regulation had to offer. A Boston juvenile judge, Frederick Cabot, summed up his helplessness to aid a small boy: "His chief crime being the crime of poverty, the authorities do not know what to do with him."[11]

Granted broad discretion, judges disposed of children impulsively. Ben Lindsey dismissed boys outright for fighting but consigned others, ostensibly on probation, to contract labor camps on beet farms. Using dated hearsay evidence, Boston's Harvey Baker placed an African-American boy on probation merely for being thought shiftless. In Milwaukee, suspicion of masturbation sufficed to brand a girl delinquent, and a 12-year-old boy, originally collared for smoking, faced escalating charges and landed in a reformatory. Confronting such arbitrary authority, prudent youths feigned repentance and childlike submissiveness.[12]

Rather than extending flexible, quasi-parental control of young people, juvenile court practice replicated the old choice between doing little and punishing severely. Full-time probation officers were scarce everywhere and almost unknown outside large cities. With caseloads in the hundreds, they managed only superficial surveillance. In Boston, delinquents visited their officer 10 minutes a week; only one-third remained on probation more than six months. Some courts required only a monthly postcard from probationers. The alternative to superficial probation was, however, dire—confinement in a reformatory (commonly renamed reform school by the 1890s). By redirecting attention to the commitment process, juvenile courts renewed the reform schools' legitimacy and assured regular placements. Even Chicago, with the nation's largest probation force, committed 26 percent of delinquents to institutions in 1918; smaller Illinois cities committed 47 percent.[13]

Juvenile court officials justified broad discretion as necessary to cure underlying causes of delinquency. But a later study found that "50 percent of the children who had passed through the Chicago juvenile court between 1909 and 1914 had adult court records." A smaller group—boys referred for psychological evaluation by Boston's juvenile court between 1917 and 1922—learned even less about staying out of trouble. Within five years, 61 percent committed felonies and another 27 percent lesser delinquencies.[14] Juvenile courts, it appeared, neither sheltered nor cured.

Sheltering readily turned punitive when juvenile courts dealt with girls. Late-nineteenth-century purity reformers had campaigned successfully to raise the age of consent from 10 or 12 into the teens. By 1920, 26 states set it at 16 and 21 states at 18. Although reformers spun lurid tales of working girls coerced by older employers, statutory rape prosecutions almost exclusively targeted consensual (albeit frequently exploitive) relations between teenage girls and older boys or young men. Threatened by the relative freedom of American youth and needing the girls' pay, poor immigrant parents invoked the courts to curb their daughters' sexuality and prevent abused or restless girls from fleeing the family. By 1910, reformers' victimization narratives had shifted to white slavers drugging and kidnapping girls for prostitution. The more realistic threat of incest and other sexual assaults in household settings went unmentioned, as if too risky for female reformers to broach. But reformers saw lower-class girls as sexual agents, not just victims. Stirred by anxiety about adolescence and outrage against prostitution, moral crusaders of the 1910s stigmatized the sexuality of working-class girls. Contemporary investigators reported that most prostitutes said their first—usually noncommercial—sexual experience occurred between ages 15 and 18, but the possibility that many were past victims of sexual abuse now acting out or fleeing their families went unexplored.[15]

Although vague charges of "incorrigibility" often obscured the situation, the majority of girls found delinquent were condemned for sexual activity. In Los Angeles juvenile court in 1920, 63 percent of girls faced charges of "sex delinquency" and another 18 percent were accused of morals offenses, such as drinking or staying out late, that officials believed presaged sexual activity. Overall, fewer girls than boys appeared in juvenile court, but the double standard insured that almost all juveniles charged with morals offenses would be girls. Even girls arrested for nonsexual offenses underwent degrading pelvic examinations. On the presumption that they needed protection and quarantine, female delinquents suffered incarceration at two to three times the rate of male delinquents. During the 1910s, states rushed to build and expand reform schools for girls.[16]

In subjecting lower-class youths to the juvenile courts' ersatz parental control, reformers sought to prolong dependency for both sexes. Illinois in 1907 extended juvenile court jurisdiction from age 16 to 17 for boys and 18 for girls. California subsequently went all the way to 21. But courts, like parents, tried to keep girls dependent longer. In the Chicago juvenile court's first 10 years, 33 percent of the boys who appeared before the court but only 10 percent of the girls were 12 or younger. Conversely, 39 percent of the girls but only 10 percent of the boys were 16 or older. In Los Angeles in 1920, the court sided with a 17-year-old boy whose stepmother "treated him as a little child" but showed no compunction about taking control of girls the same age.[17]

We should not exaggerate the juvenile courts' influence in children's lives, however, since the vast majority passed through childhood untouched and even oblivious. The Children's Bureau estimated a total of 175,000 children's court cases in 1918, approximately one for every 100 children of the ages at risk. Of course children of the urban lower class encountered court officers more frequently, yet overworked probation officers could not really control them. Only those committed to an institution felt the full force of progressive child control. Their numbers are uncertain, since federal statistics aggregated orphans, dependent children, and delinquents. Benevolent institutions reported 112,000 juvenile inmates in 1910, by no means all delinquents. Stays were short, with 86,000 newcomers that year, 15,000 placed in families, and 57,000 discharged. Meanwhile, the U.S. had almost 20,000,000 young people ages 10 through 19.[18]

Juvenile courts left rural youths virtually untouched, though country justices sometimes institutionalized dependent children. Rural pride suggested a ready explanation: country children behaved better. A part-time county probation officer in West Virginia explained complacently: "Farm boys have to work so hard they are too tired at night to cut up deviltry." Contemporary investigators reported trivial offenses such as writing obscenities on outhouse walls and disrupting church by "giggling, and running in and out with scuffling feet." But much that passed for delinquency in town was equally inconsequential, and rural offenses included costly vandalism, beatings, and shootings. Basically, there was less juvenile delinquency in the countryside because there was less juvenile court activity there to identify and label misbehavior as delinquency. A Children's Bureau investigator complained, "Cases of rural delinquency are constantly escaping the hand of the law which, had they occurred within the city, would have received the immediate attention of the court." Country storekeepers, farmers, and justices of the peace hesitated to offend customers and neighbors by pursuing legal action and settled for urging the miscreant's parents to give him a thrashing. Rather than file formal complaints, West Virginia parents cooperated in requiring children "to work after school and on Saturdays in order to make full recompense for damage." Like the Children's Bureau agent quoted earlier, the investigator for the National Child Labor Committee who reported these practices condemned such informality. This hostility is revealing. Progressive child welfare specialists mistrusted people outside the urban middle class. When faced with more or less self-regulating communities, reformers called for formal legal controls.[19]

Rural self-regulation had severe shortcomings. Abusive parents, thieves, and bullies often went unchecked, but trivialities were not exaggerated either. Little evidence suggests that the juvenile courts' erratic interventions into young people's lives worked better. Neither system provided the sheltered childhood and adolescence of the nonfarm middle class.

Youth Work

Hall found eager disciples among Protestant youth workers. As experts on adolescence, they hoped to inspire youthful enthusiasm while keeping middle-class children supervised through the dangerous teenage years.

Club leaders seeking the lower class aimed younger, however. The mass boys' clubs that sprang from Protestant missions and social settlements during the 1880s and 1890s sought to get lower-class boys off the streets. Finding the full grown dangerous, and convinced that most except delinquents were fully employed by age 14 or so, club founders concentrated on boys 9 through 13, the peak years for street trading. After 1910, most clubs let boys stay past 14; yet club leaders continued to profess primary concern for younger lads. For their part, youth workers serving the middle class considered employed boys dangerously precocious. The "working boy" had no adolescence, a writer complained, because he "short-circuits from childhood to manhood."[20]

For older middle-class and small-town youths, Protestant churches already furnished young people's societies. In the 1880s these coalesced into the interdenominational Christian Endeavor Society, the Baptist Young People's Union, and the Methodist Epworth Society. As mainstream Sunday schools attenuated conversion into card signing at annual decision days, young church members faced no serious challenges and drifted toward an extended childhood of "perpetual becoming." Young people's societies espoused functionless earnestness, with "endeavor" focused on pledge taking and busywork. Recruiting church-oriented girls and young men who wanted to meet them, the societies had evolved by the early 1900s into social organizations for the late teens and early twenties.[21]

This left a gap for younger teens, especially boys. By puberty or soon after, most boys quit Sunday school. In response, church athletic leagues and church-sponsored Scout troops (often with the minister as coach or scoutmaster) proliferated to keep boys loyal. Meanwhile, youth workers voiced panic that middle-class boys were turning unmanly, coddled by protective mothers, corrupted by city life, enfeebled by "self-abuse" (masturbation), and mistaught by women teachers. Edgar M. Robinson, who headed YMCA boys' work in the U.S., railed against "the boy who has been . . . so carefully wrapped up in the 'pink cotton wool' of an overindulgent home [that] he is more effeminate than his sister." Other YMCA and Boy Scout writers blamed overpressured, sedentary schoolwork "for the highly nervous and passionate adolescents." Summing up the fear that boys were both unmanly and uncontrolled, the Boy Scouts of America's Chief Scout, Ernest Thompson Seton, lamented that farm boys had been "strong, self-reliant," yet "respectful to . . . superiors [and] obedient to parents." Industrialization and passive entertainment had turned boys into "flat-chested cigarette smokers with shaky nerves and doubtful vitality." As a remedy, boys' workers proposed supervised, strenuous recreation to keep boys dependent yet energetic.[22]

Although the earliest Young Men's Christian Associations accepted full members as young as 14, in the 1880s YMCAs began relegating schoolboys 10 through 15 to separate junior departments. After 1900, spurred by Robinson to make adolescence their professional specialty, YMCA boys' workers set age limits at 12 to 16, later 18. YMCAs offered gymnastics, basketball, swimming, summer camps, and hobby clubs; for the minority willing to go further, carefully guided self-government, Bible study, and religious evangelism invited fuller commitment. The choice of programs proved reasonably attractive to older middle-class boys; YMCA junior membership rose from 31,000 in 1900 to 219,000 by early 1920, about half age 15 or older. Hi-Y clubs also gained prominence in some high schools, although they lacked the prestige of independent fraternities.[23]

Boy Scouting grew even faster but had less success holding older boys. Founded by a British general, Robert S. S. Baden-Powell, Scouting came to the U.S. in 1910. Under YMCA influence, the Boy Scouts of America limited admission to boys 12 and older and defined its task as forestalling adolescent problems. Chief Scout Executive James West explained that Scouting "takes the boy . . . when he is beset with the new and bewildering experience of adolescence and diverts his thoughts therefrom to wholesome and worthwhile activities." In effect, BSA leaders hoped to prolong energetic, asexual, preadolescent boyhood. They also offered churches and schools help in keeping boys loyal, and churches sponsored half of all troops. Although Baden-Powell proclaimed patrols under boy leaders the essential units for Scouting, American scoutmasters ran almost all activities in larger troop-sized aggregations under close adult control. Thus the BSA proposed a trade: schoolboys should accept close adult direction in return for outdoor recreation and assurances that they were manly fellows. The Scout uniform, modeled on the U.S. Army's, advertised this combination of submission to discipline and demonstrative masculinity. Although attractive to small boys, it embarrassed high schoolers. Woodsy rambles also struck older boys as childish in comparison with team sports. And Boy Scout leaders resisted signs of adolescence, discussing "girlitis" and the "girl-struck boy" with distaste. Scouting appealed hugely to young boys, who often tried to join underage; by 1920, membership totaled 377,000. But most boys quit around the age of puberty; nationwide, Boy Scouts' median age in 1919 was just 13.8 and fewer than 10 percent were 16 or older. Even the middle-class schoolboys who typically joined Scout troops resisted prolonging childhood into adolescence.[24]

Middle-class girls initially spurred less organized concern than their brothers. They seemed more compliant: girls stayed longer on average in high school and Sunday school and joined young people's societies in much larger numbers. Girls of all classes roamed the streets less freely than boys. In consequence, by one 1912 count, 20 times as many youth work programs served boys as girls. As new schemes for girls expanded thereafter, their spokespersons voiced concern not that girls were escaping adult control but rather that they were diffusely unhappy within their allotted roles, "liable to moods of irritability, depression, and excitement" according to a YWCA leader. A Girl Scout official urged that "the homemaker of tomorrow . . . must be made efficient in her task and happy in it," and the Camp Fire Girls' final law was "Be happy."[25]

Although "little girls" organized separately within local Young Women's Christian Associations as early as the 1880s, nationally it was not until 1909 that YWCA professionals focused directly on "the adolescent girl." At first enrolling ages 10 through 15, they soon shifted "girlhood" upward to encompass ages 12 to 18 and set about organizing high school girls.[26]

The largest new organization, Camp Fire Girls, reacted explicitly against the broadening of women's roles. Hoping to forestall Girl Scouting, Boy Scout leaders helped Luther Gulick and his wife, Charlotte Vetter Gulick, design a program to recapture girls for domesticity; Luther Gulick declared that for girls "to copy the Boy Scout movement would be utterly and fundamentally evil." While urging that girls prepare for social service (described in contemporary terms as "municipal housekeeping" and "universal motherhood"), the Gulicks strove above all to put "romance" into housework. Centering the program on pretended Indian rituals around the campfire, they sought to recapitulate "the first grand division of labor" when "the woman stayed at home and kept the fire burning."[27] Although the Gulicks initially set no age limits, they aimed for the teens, hoping to manage the "adolescent crisis." Yet dressing up as an "Indian maiden" in a "ceremonial gown" decorated with honor beads for soup making and baby care must have struck some girls as childish. Perhaps actual practice was simpler; a former Camp Fire Girl from Michigan remembers only that "the mothers would give us cookies [and we would] just talk about whatever." Incorporated in 1912, Camp Fire grew rapidly; membership totaled 94,000 in 1917.[28]

Although Girl Scouting welcomed girls up to age 18, they could join at 10, young enough to be socially acceptable as tomboys. In prolonging aspects of the tomboy phase into the teens, the Girl Scouts' founder, Juliette Low, challenged the strictures under which southern ladies like herself (and northern ones too) had grown up. Girl Scouting combined requirements for proficiency in homemaking with many outdoor requirements borrowed directly from Boy Scouting. In attenuated form, Girl Scouting echoed the new series books in which intrepid girls courted outdoor adventure. Like the Boy Scouts, Girl Scouts wore uniforms imitating the U.S. Army's. Low started the first troops in 1912, but growth was slow until World War I, when her uniformed girls paraded and sold war bonds. Riding a wave of patriotism, Girl Scouting reached 50,000 members by 1920.[29]

Tacitly admitting difficulty holding adolescents, in the 1930s Camp Fire Girls lowered the age of entry to 10, and the Boy Scouts launched Cub Scouting for younger boys. Ironically, the most successful legacy of the progressive-era campaign to guide middle-class adolescents was the subsequent development of immensely popular organized recreation for preadolescent and younger children.[30]

High Schools

Between 1890 and 1920, public high schools began moving toward the central role they now occupy in adolescence. According to the U.S. Commissioner of

Education, enrollment approximately doubled every decade, from 203,000 in 1890 (underreported by 50,000 to 100,000) to 2,187,000 in 1920. Private high schools gained students more slowly, from 95,000 in 1890 (also underreported) to 184,000 in 1920. Total secondary school enrollment equaled only 7 percent of the population ages 14 through 17 in 1890 but reached 32 percent by 1920. Thus the experience of attending high school at least briefly grew fairly common. High school graduation also increased but remained less frequent, equal to 3.5 percent of 17-year-olds in 1890, 6 percent in 1900, 9 percent in 1910, and 16 percent in 1920. Fifty-seven percent of the 1890 graduates were girls and 60 percent were girls the other years. For girls in particular, high school furnished a sheltered "moratorium," rich in culture and friendship.[31]

Yet one should not exaggerate these changes. Even by 1920, only one child in six graduated from high school. Farm children any distance from town had trouble attending, though some did. African-American youths lacked high schools in southern states and nationwide comprised fewer than 1.3 percent of all high school students. In northern cities, class differences skewed high school attendance through 1920. Most (though not all) studies reported a clear majority of students from families of white-collar workers.[32]

For many students, high schooling did not extend a sheltered childhood. Most farm children worked long hours, many city boys had part-time jobs, and girls helped at home. High schooling was not just a holding pattern; students and their families saw it as a route to careers. This aspect of secondary education, which the present discussion will not consider, marked it as a ladder to adulthood rather than an extension of childhood. Hall's vision of adolescence as a sheltered moratorium for personal development, which met the needs of recreational youth workers, was less appealing to educators. Yet high school students, as they anticipated graduation and the struggles of adult life, recognized that high school was a relatively protected interlude of freedom and irresponsibility.[33] More importantly—and more by force of circumstance than by design—school authorities took steps that reduced high school students toward more childlike status.

Some changes stemmed from the city schools' growth in size, which highlighted their custodial functions. Nostalgia for an imagined early golden age when high school students were self-disciplined scholars is misguided. But expansion did change the tone. Thomas Gutowski has shown how, as Chicago high school teachers lost assurance that they were preparing a small elite, they began treating the masses "as old children rather than young adults." Faculty-only washrooms started appearing in the 1890s; teachers ceased addressing students as "Mr." or "Miss" around 1907; compulsory lunchrooms, hall passes, and similar surveillance rules multiplied. In small-town and village high schools, however, teacher-student relations remained closer. Pupils and teachers encountered each other on village streets and often played sports together. Although familiarity did not presume full equality, it curbed tendencies to treat teenagers as mere children.[34]

Policy talk about curriculum followed the big schools' lead. The National Education Association's Committee of Ten report, published in 1894, recommended courses of study centered on English, Latin, modern languages, science, mathematics, and history. These subjects would discipline students' mental faculties, preparing them for college or, more commonly, for "life" and white-collar occupations. But as high school enrollments mushroomed, educators lost confidence that academic studies would equip students to be responsible citizens. Instead, professionals decided the new masses should be trained for "social efficiency" by teaching them directly how to perform in all areas of life. Thus the landmark report *Cardinal Principles of Secondary Education*, published in 1918 for the NEA, recommended the following "main objectives of education: 1. Health. 2. Command of fundamental processes. 3. Worthy home-membership. 4. Vocation. 5. Citizenship. 6. Worthy use of leisure. 7. Ethical character." Though unstated, the implication was clear: high school pupils were still children who must be told exactly what to believe and do.[35]

In practice, change was less pronounced. Although smaller proportions of students studied history and science, other academic fields declined less, and subjects introduced to foster social efficiency initially secured only modest enrollments. Although by 1949 nearly twice as many girls studied home economics as algebra, as late as 1922 algebra was still ahead. Industrial courses remained technologically laggard holding operations, although commercial classes taught usable skills. Meanwhile, the many small high schools perforce confined instruction to a short list of academic subjects.[36]

More significant for the extension of childhood was the school authorities' takeover of extracurricular activities. The idea of secondary education as a sheltering environment was not new; convent schools had long sequestered girls. And boarding schools for sons of the wealthy, which proliferated from the 1880s onward, sought to protect "childhood innocence," burning off energy in sports. On the other hand, village high schools loosened adult surveillance, as farm children often had to board in town during the week (one reason relatively few attended); parents even let some girls "batch" in rented rooms. City high school officials initially took little responsibility for student life outside the classroom and dismissed sports and clubs as impediments to study; but gradually, between the 1890s and 1920s, they began to regulate elements of students' social lives.[37]

Recent historians have portrayed this takeover of student activities as a reaction to immediate problems rather than a premeditated drive for administrative control. In the 1880s and 1890s, high school students formed their own football, baseball, and debating teams for interschool competition, mostly without faculty control or school financing. Some also published uncensored student newspapers. But publications and athletic associations went broke; complaints of bad officiating and botched schedules were legion; and interschool sports, especially football, earned notoriety as private backers hired semiprofessional ringers who trounced and terrified genuine student athletes. Starting in the 1890s, principals and superintendents responded defensively to protect their schools' reputations. High school athletic associations began to limit eligibility to students in good standing; by the early 1920s, almost all states had statewide athletic associations. Principals and teachers censored publications, coached debaters, and made sure bills got paid. Students mostly approved, since leagues now played full seasons and publications stayed in business. Above all, students were relieved to play opponents of their own caliber. On the other hand, the older system with all its mishaps had required initiative and responsibility. Participants in teacher-led extracurricular activities were in the position of children, playing games that others controlled. It was mostly at this point, mainly in the 1910s, that educators in large numbers began to expatiate about the virtues of sports and other activities for building school spirit.[38]

School control of student social life spread only gradually and incompletely. Among large high schools, football was the only activity controlled by a clear majority of schools before 1910, followed by baseball and basketball around 1910, then publications, debating, and dramatics during the 1910s, and musical groups about 1920. Although clubs proliferated after 1920, small high schools sponsored relatively few activities even then. Girls' basketball caught on early, but other women's sports were limited. School-sponsored social life had to compete with commercial entertainment: movies, which nearly every high school student attended by the 1910s; theater and vaudeville, which many students could afford occasionally; and social dancing, which blossomed in popularity in between 1910 and 1920. Some high schools sponsored a few dances, but young people danced more at dance halls, dancing academies, and private parties. In Springfield, Illinois, where school officials discouraged school dances, high school sororities scandalized recreation experts by holding dances at a hotel.[39]

The most direct challenge to school control of student life came from independent fraternities and sororities, which operated in nearly half the larger high schools by 1904. Imposing status systems based on wealth and social popularity and dominating or sabotaging school activities, they enraged school authorities. Educators charged fraternities with fostering smoking, drinking, and ribaldry, discouraging academic achievement, and disrupting school unity. And yet, although 13 states legislated against high school secret societies between 1907 and 1913, school officials could only drive fraternities and sororities underground, not eradicate them.[40]

Other invidious distinctions evoked little resistance from school authorities. Some Chicago high schools fielded integrated athletic teams, but except where African-American students comprised a tiny minority, social activities were restricted to whites. At Wendell Phillips High School, where black students formed the majority by 1920, social events and clubs were by invitation, for whites only. Excluded from the school glee club, African-American students refused the principal's suggestion that they form their own Jim Crow choir.[41]

One educational enthusiasm of the 1910s, the junior high school, ran partly counter to the extension of childhood. Junior high schools generally combined grades seven and eight and sometimes nine. By providing more specialized instruction and differentiated curricula, proponents hoped to ready pupils for high school and expand vocational training for lower-class boys. Starting at or before puberty, junior highs could institute sex segregation and purportedly ease the transition to adolescence. Differentiation and vocationalism meant, however, removing children from the relatively protective atmosphere of elementary school and hustling the lower class toward adult work in lowly occupations. By 1919 to 1920, 181,000 pupils attended junior high schools.[42]

Overall, progressive-era efforts to extend a sheltered, fully dependent childhood into the teens secured modest results. These were not entirely trivial, since adults invested real resources, especially after 1910, through youth work and high schools. Yet outcomes resembled those of other reforms directed toward younger children.

To change a condition as general as childhood, to make the urban, middle-class model universal, demanded massive investments of adult time and effort, huge commitments of economic and social resources, and willingness to abandon racial and class prejudices. Resources *were* flowing toward children in the progressive era, but mainly by way of rising average incomes, smaller families, rural-urban migration, and extended schooling. By comparison, much contemporary reform was mere tinkering—though well publicized at the time and duly chronicled by historians. The relatively inexpensive, ostensibly efficient progressive approach of passing new laws and regulations, revising curricula, reforming administration, and strengthening professional guidance addressed neither the massive inertia of existing practices nor the need for huge investments to make change affordable for families. These reform techniques worked feebly then. They work little better now.

Chronology

1890   Gross National Product per capita: $208. Average school attendance per enrolled pupil: 86 days. Average school spending per pupil per day in attendance: 12.8 cents.

1891   Basketball invented at YMCA Training School in Springfield, Massachusetts.

1892   *Youth's Companion* publishes Pledge of Allegiance.

1893   Joseph Rice publishes *The Public School System of the United States,* based on 1892 magazine articles exposing mechanical teaching and praising progressive educators.

1894   Luther Emmett Holt publishes the first of many editions of *The Care and Feeding of Children.* The National Education Association's Committee of Ten recommends high school curricula centered on modern academic subjects.

1896   John Dewey and Alice Chipman Dewey open the Laboratory School at the University of Chicago.

1899   Chicago establishes the country's first juvenile court.

1900   The Census Bureau establishes a limited Death Registration Area, improving child mortality statistics; the Area expands over the next 20 years. Births per 1,000 population: 32. Deaths under age one (Death Registration Area only): 162 per 1,000 children under age one. Deaths ages one through 14 (DRA only): 24 per 1,000 children ages one through 14. Gross National Product per capita: $252 (1890 prices). School enrollment per 1,000 population ages 5 to 20: 536 white, 311 African American and other. Average school attendance per enrolled pupil: 99 days. Average school spending per pupil per day in attendance: 15.1 cents (1890 prices).

1901   The Southern Education Board forms. Ben Lindsey starts a juvenile court in Denver.

1903   Luther Gulick organizes New York City's Public Schools Athletic League. Kate Douglas Wiggin publishes *Rebecca of Sunnybrook Farm*. The Religious Education Association is founded.

1904   Founding of the National Child Labor Committee. G. Stanley Hall publishes *Adolescence*.

1906   John Spargo publishes *The Bitter Cry of the Children*. The Playground Association of America is organized.

1908   Theodore Roosevelt appoints a Commission on Country Life.

1909   White House Conference on the Care of Dependent Children enunciates preference for family or family-style care rather than institutional placement. Leonard Ayres publishes *Laggards in Our Schools*. Jane Addams publishes *The Spirit of Youth and the City Streets*.

1910   Boy Scouts of America incorporated. Births per 1,000 population: 30. Deaths under age one (Death Registration Area only): 132 per 1,000 children under age one. Deaths ages one through 14 (DRA only): 17 per 1,000 children ages one through 14. Gross National Product per capita: $323 (1890 prices). School enrollment per 1,000 population ages 5 to 20: 613 white, 448 African American and other. Average school attendance per enrolled pupil: 113 days. Average school spending per pupil per day in attendance: 20.2 cents (1890 prices).

1911   The General Federation of Women's Clubs and the National Congress of Mothers begin a campaign for pensions for mothers of dependent children (40 states pass enabling legislation by 1920).

1912   Congress establishes the U.S. Children's Bureau to investigate child welfare issues. Camp Fire Girls is incorporated and launched publicly. The first Girl Scout troops are organized.

1914   The Children's Bureau publishes its widely distributed manual, *Infant Care*. President Wilson proclaims Mother's Day.

1915   The Census Bureau establishes a Birth Registration Area, improving child-related statistics.

1916   Congress passes the first federal child labor law, the Keating-Owen Act (declared unconstitutional by the U.S. Supreme Court in *Hammer v. Dagenhart*, 1918).

1918   *Cardinal Principles of Secondary Education,* prepared for the National Education Association, recommends education for social efficiency.

1919   Congress amends a revenue bill to tax products of child labor (declared unconstitutional by the U.S. Supreme Court in *Bailey v. Drexel*, 1922). Lewis Terman and Robert Yerkes revise army intelligence tests for school use. Franklin Mathiews organizes National Children's Book Week. Murder of an African-American teenager triggers Chicago race riots.

1920   Births per 1,000 population: 28. Deaths under age one (Death Registration Area only): 92 per 1,000 children under age one. Deaths ages one through 14 (DRA only): 12.5 per 1,000 children ages one through 14. Gross National Product per capita: $327 (1890 prices). School enrollment per 1,000 population ages 5–20: 657 white, 535 African American and other. Average school attendance per enrolled pupil: 121 days. Average school spending per pupil per day in attendance: 18.0 cents (1890 prices).

Notes

CY   *Children and Youth in America: A Documentary History*, vol. 2: *1866–1932*, ed. Robert H. Bremner et al. (Cambridge, Mass.: Harvard University Press, 1971)

GPO   Washington, D.C.: Government Printing Office

HS   U.S. Bureau of the Census, *Historical Statistics of the United States, Colonial Times to 1970* (GPO, 1975).

NSSE   National Society for the Study of Education, *Yearbook*

OHC   Oral History of Childhood: interview transcripts (cited by interviewee's initials) at the Clarke Historical Library, Central Michigan University. Two-letter abbreviations followed by "OHC" are the initials of individuals interviewed for the Oral History of Childhood Collection.

Chapter 1

1. Hal S. Barron, "Staying Down on the Farm," in *The Countryside in the Age of the Capitalist Transformation: Essays in the Social History of Rural America*, ed. Steven Hahn and Jonathan Prude (Chapel Hill: University of North Carolina Press, 1985), 330–31; *HS*, 457.

2. Jacob A. Riis, *How the Other Half Lives: Studies among the Tenements of New York* (1890; reprint, New York: Hill and Wang, 1957); Sanborn in *CY*, 9.

3. *HS*, 11–12, 457.

4. *HS*, 49; Ansley J. Coale and Melvin Zelnik, *New Estimates of Fertility and Population in the United States* (Princeton: Princeton University Press, 1963), 22, 36; Ansley J. Coale and Norfleet W. Rives Jr., "A Statistical Reconstruction of the Black Population of the United States, 1880–1970," *Population Index* 39 (1973): 26.

5. *HS*, 15–16; Coale and Zelnik, *New Estimates*, 181–82; Coale and Rives, "Statistical Reconstruction," 21.

6. U.S. Bureau of the Census, *Farm Population of the United States* (GPO, 1926), 68.
7. Id., *Indian Population in the United States and Alaska: 1910* (GPO, 1915), 53–54; id., *Fourteenth Census of the United States Taken in the Year 1920*, volume 2, *Population, 1920: General Report and Analytical Tables* (GPO, 1922), 157; Roger Daniels, *Coming to America: A History of Immigration and Ethnicity in American Life* (New York: HarperCollins, 1990), 240–55; S. Ryan Johansson, "The Demographic History of the Native Peoples of North America: A Selective Bibliography," *Yearbook of Physical Anthropology* 25 (1982): 139–43.
8. U.S. Census Office, *Compendium of the Eleventh Census: 1890*, part 3 (GPO, 1897), 251; id., *Report on Population of the United States at the Eleventh Census: 1890*, part 2 (GPO, 1895), 2–3; Bureau of the Census, *Fourteenth Census*, volume 2, 158–59, 171–86, 288–304; id., *Farm Population*, 68; *HS*, 242; Coale and Rives, "Statistical Reconstruction," 21; Coale and Zelnik, *New Estimates*, 181–82.
9. *HS*, 224.
10. "The Rich Get Richer, But Never the Same Way Twice," *New York Times* (16 August 1992): E3; Jeffrey G. Williamson and Peter H. Lindert, *American Inequality: A Macroeconomic History* (New York: Academic Press, 1980), 81 (quotation), 68–81.
11. *HS*, 168; Daniel Horowitz, *The Morality of Spending: Attitudes toward the Consumer Society in America, 1875–1940* (Baltimore: Johns Hopkins University Press, 1985), 71–94; John J. McCusker, "How Much Is That in Real Money? A Historical Price Index," *Proceedings of the American Antiquarian Society* 101 (1991): 330–32.
12. Juergen Kocka, *White Collar Workers in America, 1890–1940: A Social Political History in International Perspective* (London: Sage Publications, 1980), 77; *HS*, 168.
13. Peter R. Shergold, *Working-Class Life: The "American Standard" in Comparative Perspective, 1899–1913* (Pittsburgh: University of Pittsburgh Press, 1982), 45–51; Steven Dubnoff, "A Method for Estimating the Economic Welfare of Families of Any Composition: 1860–1909," *Historical Methods* 13 (1980): 171–80; *HS*, 168; Williamson and Lindert, *American Inequality*, 105.
14. David B. Danbom, *The Resisted Revolution: Urban America and the Industrialization of Agriculture, 1900–1930* (Ames: Iowa State University Press, 1979), 7 (quotation); Gilbert C. Fite, *Cotton Fields No More: Southern Agriculture, 1865–1980* (Lexington: University Press of Kentucky, 1984), 15, 21, 34; *Plain Folk: The Life Stories of Undistinguished Americans*, ed. David M. Katzman and William M. Tuttle Jr. (Urbana: University of Illinois Press, 1983), 77.
15. Danbom, *Resisted Revolution*, 6 (quotation); PF, JV, OHC.

16. John Bodnar, *The Transplanted: A History of Immigrants in Urban America* (Bloomington: Indiana University Press, 1985), 76–77; Robert Hunter, *Poverty* (1904; reprint, New York: Harper Torchbooks, 1965), 56–58.

17. Bodnar, *Transplanted,* 73; James R. Barrett, *Work and Community in the Jungle: Chicago's Packinghouse Workers, 1894–1922* (Urbana: University of Illinois Press, 1987), 94–95; Tamara K. Hareven, *Family Time and Industrial Time: The Relationship between the Family and Work in a New England Industrial Community* (Cambridge: Cambridge University Press, 1982), 189, 211–17; Jacqueline Jones, *Labor of Love, Labor of Sorrow: Black Women, Work, and the Family, from Slavery to the Present* (New York: Basic Books, 1985), 163.

18. Judith E. Smith, *Family Connections: A History of Italian and Jewish Immigrant Lives in Providence, Rhode Island, 1900–1940* (Albany: State University of New York Press, 1985), 23; Rose Cohen, *Out of the Shadow* (New York: George H. Doran and Co., 1918), 94–95; Edward L. Ayers, *The Promise of the New South: Life After Reconstruction* (New York: Oxford University Press, 1992), 68 (quotation); Jacqueline Dowd Hall et al., *Like A Family: The Making of a Southern Cotton Mill World* (New York: W. W. Norton & Co., 1989), 52 (quotation); Virginia Yans-McLaughlin, *Family and Community: Italian Immigrants in Buffalo, 1880–1930* (Urbana: University of Illinois Press, 1982), 171–94.

19. Linda Gordon, *Heroes of Their Own Lives: The Politics and History of Family Violence, Boston 1880–1960* (New York: Penguin Books, 1989), 57; Marilyn Dell Brady, "The New Model Middle-Class Family (1815–1930)," in *American Families: A Research Guide and Historical Handbook,* ed. Joseph M. Hawes and Elizabeth I. Nybakken (New York: Greenwood Press, 1991), 83–123.

20. Margaret Marsh, *Suburban Lives* (New Brunswick, N.J.: Rutgers University Press, 1990), 76–82; David I. Macleod, *Building Character in the American Boy: The Boy Scouts, YMCA, and Their Forerunners, 1870–1920* (Madison: University of Wisconsin Press, 1983), 8; Robert L. Griswold, " 'Ties That Bind and Bonds That Break': Children's Attitudes toward Fathers, 1900–1930," in *Small Worlds: Children and Adolescents in America, 1850–1950,* ed. Elliott West and Paula Petrick (Lawrence: University Press of Kansas, 1992), 255–74.

21. Stewart E. Tolnay, "Family Economy and the Black American Fertility Transition," *Journal of Family History* 11 (1986): 268; Jenny Bourne Wahl, "New Results on the Decline in Household Fertility in the United States from 1750 to 1900," in *Long-Term Factors in American Economic Growth,* ed. Stanley L. Engerman and Robert E. Gallman (Chicago: University of Chicago Press, 1986), 413–18; Frank W.

Notestein, "The Decrease in Size of Families from 1890 to 1910," *Milbank Memorial Fund Quarterly* 9 (1931): 183.

22. Theodore Roosevelt, "Twisted Eugenics," *Outlook* 106 (1904): 32; Riis, *Other Half*, 134; Miriam King and Steven Ruggles, "American Immigration, Fertility, and Race Suicide at the Turn of the Century," *Journal of Interdisciplinary History* 20 (1990): 347–69.

23. Vern L. Bullough, "A Brief Note on Rubber Technology and Contraception: The Diaphragm and the Condom," *Technology and Culture* 22 (1981): 104–11; Paul A. David and Warren C. Sanderson, "Rudimentary Contraceptive Methods and the American Transition to Marital Fertility Control, 1855–1915," in *Long-Term Factors,* ed. Engerman and Gallman, 313–66.

24. Michael R. Haines, "Western Fertility in Mid-Transition: Fertility and Nuptiality in the United States and Selected Nations at the Turn of the Century," *Journal of Family History* 15 (1990): 24–36.

25. Richard A. Easterlin, "Factors in the Decline of Farm Family Fertility in the United States: Some Preliminary Research Results," *Journal of American History* 63 (1976): 600–614.

26. Leigh Eric Schmidt, *Consumer Rites: The Buying and Selling of American Holidays* (Princeton, N.J.: Princeton University Press, 1995), 246–54; Donald H. Parkerson and Jo Ann Parkerson, " 'Fewer Children of Greater Spiritual Quality': Religion and the Decline of Fertility in Nineteenth-Century America," *Social Science History* 12 (1988): 60–62; Sara M. Evans, *Born for Liberty: A History of Women in America* (New York: Free Press, 1989), 147–52, 160–63; "Why I Have No Family," *The Independent* 58 (1905): 654–59.

27. Tolnay, "Family Economy," 267–83; Deborah Fink and Alicia Carriquiry, "Having Babies or Not: Household Composition and Fertility in Rural Iowa and Nebraska, 1900–1910," *Great Plains Quarterly* 12 (1992): 159–64.

28. John F. McClymer, "The 'American Standard' of Living: Family Expectations and Strategies for Getting and Spending in the Gilded Age," *Hayes Historical Journal* 9 (Spring 1990): 20–43; Michael R. Haines, "The Life Cycle, Savings, and Demographic Adaptation: Some Historical Evidence for the United States and Europe," in *Gender and the Life Course,* ed. Alice S. Rossi (New York: Aldine Publishing Co., 1985), 45–54.

29. Jenny Bourne Wahl, "Trading Quantity for Quality: Explaining the Decline in American Fertility in the Nineteenth Century," in *Strategic Factors in Nineteenth Century American Economic History,* ed. Claudia Goldin and Hugh Rockoff (Chicago: University of Chicago Press, 1992), 375–97; Mary P. Ryan, *Cradle of the Middle Class: The Family in Oneida County, New York, 1790–1865* (Cambridge: Cambridge Uni-

versity Press, 1981), 184; Mark J. Stern, *Society and Family Strategy: Erie County, New York, 1850–1920* (Albany: State University of New York Press, 1987), 113; John Modell, "An Ecology of Family Decisions: Suburbanization, Schooling, and Fertility in Philadelphia, 1880–1920," *Journal of Urban History* 6 (1980): 407.

30. Lydia Kingsmill Commander, "Why Do Americans Prefer Small Families?" *The Independent* 57 (1904): 849–50.

31. Viviana A. Zelizer, *Pricing the Priceless Child: The Changing Social Value of Children* (New York: Basic Books, 1985), 3, 26, 131, 150.

32. Phillips Cutright and Edward Shorter, "The Effects of Health on the Completed Fertility of Nonwhite and White U.S. Women Born between 1867 and 1935," *Journal of Social History* 13 (1979): 209–10; Peter Uhlenberg, "Changing Configurations of the Life Course," in *Transitions: The Family and the Life Course in Historical Perspective,* ed. Tamara K. Hareven (New York: Academic Press, 1978), 77–79; Notestein, "Decrease," 183.

33. Linda Gordon and Sara McLanahan, "Single Parenthood in 1900," *Journal of Family History* 16 (1991): 98, 104; Elizabeth Hafkin Pleck, *Black Migration and Poverty: Boston 1865–1900* (New York: Academic Press, 1979), 162–86; Donna L. Franklin, *Ensuring Inequality: The Structural Transformation of the African-American Family* (New York: Oxford University Press, 1997), 37–39.

34. S. Philip Morgan et al., "Racial Differences in Household and Family Structure at the Turn of the Century," *American Journal of Sociology* 98 (1993): 815; Peter Uhlenberg, "Death and the Family," *Journal of Family History* 5 (1980): 315; Samuel H. Preston and John McDonald, "The Incidence of Divorce within Cohorts of American Marriages Contracted since the Civil War," *Demography* 16 (1979), 3–4, 13; Bureau of the Census, *Marriage and Divorce, 1867–1906,* part 1 (1909; reprint, Westport, Conn.: Greenwood Press, 1978), 126; Reena Sigman Friedman, " 'Send Me My Husband Who Is in New York City': Husband Desertion in the American Jewish Immigrant Community, 1900–1926," *Jewish Social Studies* 44 (1982): 1–4.

35. GC, JR, OHC.

36. Claudia Goldin, *Understanding the Gender Gap: An Economic History of American Women* (New York: Oxford University Press, 1990), 64, 100.

37. James T. Patterson, *America's Struggle Against Poverty, 1900–1980* (Cambridge, Mass.: Harvard University Press, 1981), 28; Michael B. Katz, *In the Shadow of the Poorhouse: A Social History of Welfare in America* (New York: Basic Books, 1986), 81, 91–93, 103–4; Martha May, "The 'Problem of Duty': Family Desertion in the Progressive Era," *Social Service Review* 62 (1988), 46–51; Mary E. Richmond and

Fred S. Hall, *A Study of Nine Hundred and Eighty-Five Widows Known to Certain Charity Organizations in 1910* (1913; reprint, New York: Arno Press, 1974), 50–51; Mary Ann Mason, *From Father's Property to Children's Rights: The History of Child Custody in the United States* (New York: Columbia University Press, 1994), 96–100.

38. Theda Skocpol, *Protecting Soldiers and Mothers: The Political Origins of Social Policy in the United States* (Cambridge, Mass.: Harvard University Press, 1992), 424–77; Joanne L. Goodwin, "An American Experiment in Paid Motherhood: The Implementation of Mothers' Pensions in Early-Twentieth-Century Chicago," *Gender and History* 4 (1992): 324–38; CY, 392–94; Molly Ladd-Taylor, *Mother-Work: Women, Child Welfare, and the State, 1890–1930* (Urbana: University of Illinois Press, 1994), 147–59; IF, OHC; Andrew Billingsley and Jeanne M. Giovanni, *Children of the Storm: Black Children and American Child Welfare* (New York: Harcourt Brace Jovanovich, 1972), 49–59.

39. LH, WD, OHC (quotations); William A. Owens, *This Stubborn Soil: A Frontier Boyhood* (New York: Vintage Books, 1989), 44; Gordon, *Heroes*, 110–11, 201.

40. *Proceedings of the Conference on the Care of Dependent Children Held at Washington, D.C., January 25, 26, 1909* (New York: Arno Press, 1971), 98; Nurith Zmora, *Orphanages Reconsidered: Child Care Institutions in Progressive Era Baltimore* (Philadelphia: Temple University Press, 1994), 48–49; Susan Tiffin, *In Whose Best Interest? Child Welfare Reform in the Progressive Era* (Westport, Conn.: Greenwood Press, 1982), 42; LeRoy Ashby, *Saving the Waifs: Reformers and Dependent Children, 1890–1917* (Philadelphia: Temple University Press, 1984), 232–33.

41. Hyman Bogen, *The Luckiest Orphans: A History of the Hebrew Orphan Asylum of New York* (Urbana: University of Illinois Press, 1992), 101, 109; Tiffin, *In Whose Best Interest*, 67–74, 80–82; Ashby, *Saving*, 18–31, 133–205; Jack M. Holl, *Juvenile Reform in the Progressive Era: William R. George and the Junior Republic Movement* (Ithaca: Cornell University Press, 1971), 4–9; Kenneth Cmiel, *A Home of Another Kind: One Chicago Orphanage and the Tangle of Child Welfare* (Chicago: University of Chicago Press, 1995), 38–63.

42. Zelizer, *Pricing*, 178 (quotation), 175; Marilyn Irvin Holt, *The Orphan Trains: Placing Out in America* (Lincoln: University of Nebraska Press, 1992), 53–79, 130, 159; *Proceedings . . . 1909*, 9–10.

43. Peter C. Holloran, *Boston's Wayward Children: Social Services for Homeless Children, 1830–1930* (Rutherford: Fairleigh Dickinson University Press, 1989), 101 (quotation); Tiffin, *In Whose Best Interest*, 105 (quotation); Holt, *Orphan Trains*, 138–41, 174.

44. Andrew Billingsley, *Black Families in White America* (Englewood Cliffs: Prentice-Hall, 1968), 102 (quotation); McClymer, "American Standard," 23–25; Horowitz, *Morality,* 89–105.

45. *The Culture of Consumption: Critical Essays in American History, 1880–1980,* ed. Richard Wightman Fox and T. J. Jackson Lears (New York: Pantheon, 1983), x, xi, xiii.

46. Ethel Spencer, *The Spencers of Amberson Avenue: A Turn-of-the-Century Memoir,* ed. Michael P. Weber and Peter N. Stearns (Pittsburgh: University of Pittsburgh Press, 1984), 21; *Plain Folk,* ed. Katzman and Tuttle, 84, 88; Margaret F. Byington, *Homestead: The Households of a Mill Town* (1910; reprint, Pittsburgh: University Center for International Studies, 1974), 64; Harvey A. Levenstein, *Revolution at the Table: The Transformation of the American Diet* (New York: Oxford University Press, 1988), 104–5, 149–50; RF, BS, HM, LD, LA, OHC; I. A. Newby, *Plain Folk in the New South: Social Change and Cultural Persistence* (Baton Rouge: Louisiana State University Press, 1989), 365–66; Fite, *Cotton Fields,* 37–38.

47. Levenstein, *Revolution,* 30–31, 137–55.

48. Spencer, *Spencers,* 42 (quotation), 38; OHC interviews.

49. HM, RB, JR, RJ, OHC; Fite, *Cotton Fields,* 38.

50. Neil M. Cowan and Ruth Schwartz Cowan, *Our Parents' Lives: The Americanization of Eastern European Jews* (New York: Basic Books, 1989), 45–46; John Modell and Tamara K. Hareven, "Urbanization and the Malleable Household: An Examination of Boarding and Lodging in American Families," *Journal of Marriage and the Family* 35 (1973): 467–79.

51. BS, OHC (quotation); Robert Barrows, "Beyond the Tenement: Patterns of American Urban Housing, 1870–1930," *Journal of Urban History* 9 (1983): 395–420; Shergold, *Working-Class Lives,* 151–53.

52. Sally McMurry, *Families and Farmhouses in Nineteenth-Century America: Vernacular Design and Social Change* (New York: Oxford University Press, 1988), 178–83, 192–200, 218; Karin Calvert, "Children in the House, 1890 to 1930," in *American Home Life, 1880–1930: A Social History of Spaces and Services,* ed. Jessica H. Foy and Thomas J. Schlereth (Knoxville: University of Tennessee Press, 1992), 75–86; Elizabeth Collins Cromley, "A History of American Beds and Bedrooms, 1890–1930," in ibid., 126–29.

53. Fred W. Peterson, *Homes in the Heartland: Balloon Frame Farmhouses of the Upper Midwest, 1850–1920* (Lawrence: University Press of Kansas, 1992), 80 (quotation), 92, 154; W. E. Burghardt Du Bois, *The Negro American Family* (1909; reprint, Cambridge, Mass.: M.I.T. Press, 1970), 52–53 (quotations).

54. Ayers, *Promise,* 210 (quotation); Bureau of Labor Statistics, *Cost of Living in the United States* (GPO, 1924), 1 (quotation), 333; McClymer, "American Standard," 42.

55. Richard L. Bushman and Claudia L. Bushman, "The Early History of Cleanliness in America," *Journal of American History* 74 (1988): 1231 (quotation); Bureau of Labor Statistics, *Cost,* 333; Peterson, *Homes,* 211; JS, JJ, JK, HM, OHC.

56. Horowitz, *Morality,* 54, 94–106; OHC interviews.

57. Zelizer, *Pricing,* 103; David Nasaw, "Children and Commercial Culture: Moving Pictures in the Early Twentieth Century," in *Small Worlds,* ed. West and Petrick, 17–19; JF, OHC.

58. Lawrence Frederic Greenfield, "Toys, Children, and the Toy Industry in a Culture of Consumption, 1890–1991" (Ph.D. diss., Ohio State University, 1991), 89–162; Bernard Mergen, "Made, Bought, and Stolen: Toys and the Culture of Childhood," in *Small Worlds,* ed. West and Petrick, 102–3.

59. Ayers, *Promise,* 66 (quotation), 103; JW, VP, RJ, RB, HB, OHC.

60. The title of a book by Swedish feminist and eugenicist Ellen Key, published in the U.S. in 1909, this phrase became an American commonplace. Tiffin, *In Whose Best Interest,* 14. "The race" sometimes meant all humanity but more often presupposed a hierarchy of races.

61. "Ode: Intimations of Immortality from Recollections of Early Childhood," in *The Poetical Works of Wordsworth* (Boston: Houghton Mifflin, 1982), 354; W. E . Burghardt Du Bois, *The Souls of Black Folk* (1903; reprint, Greenwich, Conn.: Fawcett Publications, 1961), 153; Bernard Wishy, *The Child and the Republic: The Dawn of Modern American Child Nurture* (Philadelphia: University of Pennsylvania Press, 1968), 126, 109, 160–62; T. J. Jackson Lears, *No Place of Grace: Antimodernism and the Transformation of American Culture, 1880–1920* (New York: Pantheon, 1981), 144–49.

62. Kate Douglas Wiggin, *Children's Rights: A Book of Nursery Logic* (Boston: Houghton, Mifflin, 1892), 21.

63. William A. Link, *The Paradox of Southern Progressivism, 1880–1930* (Chapel Hill: University of North Carolina Press, 1992), 39–40 (quotation); Booker T. Washington, *Up from Slavery* (1901), in *Three Negro Classics* (New York: Avon Books, 1965), 31.

64. CY, 559 (quotation), 555–64; Hamilton Cravens, "Child-Saving in the Age of Professionalism, 1915–1930," in *American Childhood: A Research Guide and Historical Handbook,* ed. Joseph M. Hawes and N. Ray Hiner (Westport, Conn.: Greenwood Press, 1985), 416 (quotation), 425–27, 438; Gordon, *Heroes,* 15 (quotation).

65. John Spargo, *The Bitter Cry of the Children* (New York: Macmillan, 1906), 264–65, xiv; Florence Kelley, "The Sordid Waste of Genius," *Charities* 12 (1904): 454.

66. Dorothy Ross, *G. Stanley Hall: The Psychologist as Prophet* (Chicago: University of Chicago Press, 1972), 279–91, 314; G. Stanley Hall, *Adolescence: Its Psychology and Its Relations to Physiology, Anthropology,*

Sociology, Sex, Crime, Religion, and Education, volume 1 (New York: D. Appleton, 1904), ix–xv.

67. Quotations: Ross, *Hall,* 308; Hall, *Adolescence,* volume 2, 72; Hall, "Some Defects of the Kindergarten in America," *Forum* 28 (1900): 581; John Dewey, *The School and Society* (Chicago: University of Chicago Press, 1907), 71.

68. Hall, *Adolescence,* volume 1, viii; Howard P. Chudacoff, *How Old Are You? Age Consciousness in American Culture* (Princeton, N.J.: Princeton University Press, 1989), 81.

69. Chudacoff, *How Old,* 51–53, 86–87, 95, 126–33; OHC interviews.

70. Ross, *Hall,* 284–86, 341–45; Steven L. Schlossman, "Before Home Start: Notes toward a History of Parent Education in America, 1897–1929," *Harvard Educational Review* 46 (1976): 443–45; Macleod, *Building Character,* 109–14.

71. Joseph F. Kett, "Curing the Disease of Precocity," in *Turning Points: Historical and Sociological Essays on the Family,* ed. John Demos and Sarane Spence Boocock (Chicago: University of Chicago Press, 1978), 183–211.

72. U.S. Children's Bureau, *Infant Care,* by Mrs. Max West (GPO, 1914), 63.

73. Peter G. Filene, "An Obituary for 'The Progressive Movement,' " *American Quarterly* 22 (1970): 20–34; Jane Addams, *Twenty Years at Hull House* (1910; reprint, New York: New American Library, 1961), 20; Link, *Paradox,* 124–241. For concise guides to the vast literature on progressive reform, see Daniel T. Rodgers, "In Search of Progressivism," *Reviews in American History* 10 (December 1982): 113–32; Richard L. McCormick, "Public Life in Industrial America," in *The New American History,* ed. Eric Foner (Philadelphia: Temple University Press, 1990), 93–117.

74. Rodgers, "Progressivism," 124–26; Richard Wightman Fox, "The Culture of Liberal Protestant Progressivism," *Journal of Interdisciplinary History* 23 (1993): 644–45; Gordon, *Heroes,* 77–78; Robert M. Crunden, *Ministers of Reform: The Progressives' Achievement in American Civilization, 1889–1920* (Urbana: University of Illinois Press, 1984), 3–38; Mina Carson, *Settlement Folk: Social Thought and the American Settlement Movement, 1885–1930* (Chicago: University of Chicago Press, 1990), 22–25, 49.

75. Ashby, *Saving,* 125–26.

76. McCormick, "Public Life," 107; Carson, *Settlement Folk,* 139–45.

77. Robyn Muncy, *Creating a Female Dominion in American Reform, 1890–1935* (New York: Oxford University Press, 1991), 68; Katz, *Shadow,* 165; Gordon, *Heroes,* 13, 15, 27–28, 64–76.

78. Anne Firor Scott, *Natural Allies: Women's Associations in American History* (Urbana: University of Illinois Press, 1991), 142, 147 (quotations), 88, 96, 111–25, 141–52; Ladd-Taylor, *Mother-Work,* 61 (quota-

tion), 55–98; "Introduction," in *Gender, Class, Race, and Reform in the Progressive Era,* ed. Noralee Frankel and Nancy S. Dye (Lexington: University Press of Kentucky, 1991), 3–4; Peter G. Filene, *Him/Her/Self: Sex Roles in Modern America,* 2nd ed. (Baltimore: Johns Hopkins University Press, 1986), 38; Muncy, *Female Dominion,* 38–65.

79. Allen F. Davis, *Spearheads for Reform: The Social Settlements and the Progressive Movement, 1890–1914* (New York: Oxford University Press, 1967), 3–38, 61; Carson, *Settlement Folk,* 22–25, 52, 61; Muncy, *Female Dominion,* 3–11, 25–27, 35.

80. Maren Stange, *Symbols of Ideal Life: Social Documentary Photography in America, 1890–1950* (Cambridge: Cambridge University Press, 1989), 13, 24–28; Linda Gordon, "Social Insurance and Public Assistance: The Influence of Gender in Welfare Thought in the United States, 1890–1935," *American Historical Review* 97 (1992): 38–41; Seth Koven and Sonya Michel, "Womanly Duties: Maternalist Politics and the Origins of Welfare States in France, Germany, Great Britain, and the United States, 1880–1920," ibid., 95 (1990): 1077.

81. Muncy, *Female Dominion,* xv, 47 (quotations), 38–102. For a more favorable view, see Kriste Lindenmeyer, *"A Right to Childhood": The U.S. Children's Bureau and Child Welfare, 1912–1946* (Urbana: University of Illinois Press, 1997), 1–162.

82. For summaries of progressive child saving, see Ronald N. Cohen, "Child-Saving and Progressivism, 1885–1915," in *American Childhood,* ed. Hawes and Hiner, 273–309; Katz, *Shadow,* 113–45; Joseph M. Hawes, *The Children's Rights Movement: A History of Advocacy and Protection* (Boston: Twayne Publishers, 1991), 26–53.

83. Link, *Paradox,* 163 (quotation); Martha Minow, "We, the Family: Constitutional Rights and American Families," *Journal of American History* 74 (1987): 976 (quotations); Andrew J. Polsky, *The Rise of the Therapeutic State* (Princeton: Princeton University Press, 1991), 65–80.

84. Crunden, *Ministers,* 196 (quotation), 165; Link, *Paradox,* 124–59; Polsky, *Therapeutic State,* 91–97.

85. Rivka Shpak Lissak, *Pluralism and Progressives: Hull House and the New Immigrants, 1890–1919* (Chicago: University of Chicago Press, 1989), 103 (quotation), 35–53, 80–122; Link, *Paradox,* 245.

86. Koven and Michel, "Womanly Duties," 1079–80, 1094–103; Peter H. Lindert, *Fertility and Scarcity in America* (Princeton: Princeton University Press, 1978), 212.

Chapter 2

1. Samuel H. Preston and Michael R. Haines, *Fatal Years: Child Mortality in Late Nineteenth-Century America* (Princeton: Princeton University Press, 1991), 86.

2. Judith Walzer Leavitt, *Brought to Bed: Childbearing in America, 1750 to 1950* (New York: Oxford University Press, 1986), 25, 161–62; *HS*, 57; Robert Morse Woodbury, *Causal Factors in Infant Mortality: A Statistical Study Based on Investigations in Eight Cities* (GPO, 1925), 17, 169, 191.

3. EB, ML, OHC; Emma Duke, *Infant Mortality: Results of a Field Study in Johnstown, Pa.* (GPO, 1913), 43; Frances Sage Bradley and Margaretta A. Williamson, *Rural Children in Selected Counties of North Carolina* (GPO, 1918), 34; Howard V. Meredith, "Change in the Stature and Body Weight of North American Boys During the Last 80 Years," in *Advances in Child Development and Behavior,* ed. Lewis P. Lipsitt and Charles C. Spiker, vol. 1 (New York: Academic Press, 1963), 71, 89; W. Peter Ward, *Birth Weight and Economic Growth: Women's Living Standards in the Industrializing West* (Chicago: University of Chicago Press, 1993), 92–96.

4. *CY*, 986 (quotation); Richard R. Wertz and Dorothy C. Wertz, *Lying-In: A History of Childbirth in America* (expanded ed., New Haven: Yale University Press, 1989), 211; Duke, *Infant Mortality*, 32; Molly Ladd-Taylor, *Raising a Baby the Government Way: Mothers' Letters to the Children's Bureau, 1915–1932* (New Brunswick, N.J.: Rutgers University Press, 1986), 15.

5. Eugene R. Declercq, "The Nature and Style of Practice of Immigrant Midwives in Early Twentieth Century Massachusetts," *Journal of Social History* 19 (1985): 118 (quotation), 121–24; Neal Devitt, "The Statistical Case for Elimination of the Midwife: Fact versus Prejudice, 1890–1935," *Women and Health* 4 (1979): 81–87, 170–75; Wertz and Wertz, *Lying-In*, 50–55, 127, 206; *CY*, 874–77; Leavitt, *Brought to Bed*, 47, 78, 119–28, 210.

6. *CY*, 986 (quotation); Devitt, "Statistical Case," 181.

7. Wertz and Wertz, *Lying-In*, 103–4; J. Jill Suitor, "Husbands' Participation in Childbirth: A Nineteenth-Century Phenomenon," *Journal of Family History* 6 (1981): 278–93.

8. Wertz and Wertz, *Lying-In*, 133, 150–57.

9. Elizabeth Moore, *Maternity and Infant Care in Kansas* (GPO, 1917), 26, 31; Duke, *Infant Mortality*, 45; Bradley and Williamson, *Rural Children*, 35, 71.

10. Bradley and Williamson, *Rural Children*, 42 (quotation), 38–39, 75; Moore, *Maternity*, 42–44; Florence Brown Sherbon and Elizabeth Moore, *Maternity and Infant Care in Two Rural Counties in Wisconsin* (GPO, 1919), 53, 70; Helen M. Dart, *Maternity and Child Care in Selected Rural Areas of Mississippi* (GPO, 1920), 42–43; *A Home-Concealed Woman: The Diaries of Magnolia Wynn Le Guin, 1901–1913*, ed. Charles A. Le Guin (Athens, Ga.: University of Georgia Press, 1990), 42, 56, 60.

11. Moore, *Maternity*, 42; Bradley and Williamson, *Rural Children*, 39; John Knodel and Hallie Kintner, "The Impact of Breast Feeding Patterns on the Biometric Analysis of Infant Mortality," *Demography* 14 (1977): 395.

12. Woodbury, *Causal Factors*, 88, 216–18; Rima D. Apple, *Mothers and Medicine: A Social History of Infant Feeding, 1890–1950* (Madison: University of Wisconsin Press, 1987), 171.

13. Apple, *Mothers*, 8–13, 140–42; Harvey A. Levenstein, *Revolution at the Table: The Transformation of the American Diet* (New York: Oxford University Press, 1988), 124.

14. Kathleen W. Jones, "Sentiment and Science: The Late Nineteenth Century Pediatrician as Mother's Advisor," *Journal of Social History* 17 (1983): 85 (quotation), 80–89; Richard A. Meckel, *Save the Babies: American Public Health Reform and the Prevention of Infant Mortality, 1850–1929* (Baltimore: Johns Hopkins University Press, 1990), 56–58.

15. L. Emmett Holt, *The Care and Feeding of Children: A Catechism for the Use of Mothers and Children's Nurses*, 9th ed. (New York: D. Appleton, 1918), 190, 191 (quotations), 58–104; ibid. (New York: D. Appleton, 1894), 34–35, 55–56; Mrs. Max [Mary] West, *Infant Care* (GPO, 1914), 64.

16. Apple, *Mothers*, 149 (quotations), 109, 147; Holt, *Care and Feeding* (1894), 19; (1918), 31, 50; West, *Infant Care*, 14, 33, 37, 55; Laura E. Berk, *Child Development*, 2nd ed. (Boston: Allyn and Bacon, 1991), 200; Mrs. Max West, *Prenatal Care*, 4th ed. (GPO, 1915), 35; CY, 965.

17. Holt, *Care and Feeding* (1918), 125 (quotation), 108, 131–43; (1894), 38, 43; West, *Infant Care*, 49; Dorothy Ruth Mendenhall, *Milk: The Indispensable Food for Children* (GPO, 1918), 10–14; Levenstein, *Revolution*, 30–31, 155.

18. Jones, "Sentiment," 80–89; Benjamin Spock and Mary Morgan, *Spock on Spock: A Memoir of Growing Up with the Century* (Franklin Center, Pa.: The Franklin Library, 1989), 7, 25.

19. Kenneth J. Carpenter, *The History of Scurvy and Vitamin C* (Cambridge: Cambridge University Press, 1987), 163 (quotation), 161, 181; Holt, *Care and Feeding* (1918), 136 (quotation), 108; Levenstein, *Revolution*, 149; Thomas E. Cone Jr., *History of American Pediatrics* (Boston: Little, Brown and Co., 1979), 120–24, 166–69; CY, 844.

20. Meredith, "Change," 75, 91–94.

21. Stuart Galishoff, *Safeguarding the Public Health: Newark, 1895–1918* (Westport, Conn.: Greenwood Press, 1975), 107; Meckel, *Save the Babies*, 5–6.

22. U.S. Public Health Service, *Vital Statistics Rates in the United States, 1900–1940* (GPO, 1947), 95–98, 150; Preston and Haines, *Fatal Years*, 74, 86, 129–30; U.S. Bureau of the Census, *United States Life Tables, 1890, 1901, 1910, and 1901–1910* (GPO, 1921), 52.

23. Ibid., 64–86; U.S. Bureau of the Census, *United States Abridged Life Tables, 1919–1920* (GPO, 1923), 12–14; Public Health Service, *Vital Statistics,* 175.

24. Preston and Haines, *Fatal Years,* 97, 150–53; Public Health Service, *Vital Statistics,* 578; Bradley and Williamson, *Rural Children,* 66, 73; Woodbury, *Causal Factors,* 54.

25. Preston and Haines, *Fatal Years,* 100–102; Samuel H. Preston et al., "Child Mortality Differences by Ethnicity and Race in the United States: 1900–1910," in *After Ellis Island: Newcomers and Natives in the 1910 Census,* ed. Susan Cotts Watkins (New York: Russell Sage Foundation, 1994), 32–74.

26. Preston and Haines, *Fatal Years,* 86, 146, 159.

27. Ibid., 119–210; Woodbury, *Causal Factors,* 128, 148–50.

28. Ladd-Taylor, *Raising a Baby,* 42.

29. CY, 966 (quotation); Meckel, *Save the Babies,* 42 (quotation), 118; Preston and Haines, *Fatal Years,* 4–5; Woodbury, *Causal Factors,* 14; Duke, *Infant Mortality,* 37. On diphtheria, see Elliott West, *Growing Up in Twentieth-Century America: A History and Reference Guide* (Westport, Conn.: Greenwood Press, 1996), 55–57.

30. W. E. Burghardt Du Bois, *The Souls of Black Folk* (1903; reprint, Greenwich, Conn.: Fawcett Publications, 1961), 154.

31. Sydney A. Halpern, *American Pediatrics: The Social Dynamics of Professionalism, 1880–1980* (Berkeley: University of California Press, 1988), 1–82; Charles R. King, *Children's Health in America: A History* (New York: Twayne Publishers, 1993), 78–79; Preston and Haines, *Fatal Years,* 4–20; Meckel, *Save the Babies,* 42; Cone, *History,* 206–8; William A. Owens, *This Stubborn Soil: A Frontier Boyhood* (New York: Vintage Books, 1986), 16; VS, EK, JJ, OHC.

32. Preston and Haines, *Fatal Years,* 22–25; Holt, *Care and Feeding* (1918), 25; Meckel, *Save the Babies,* 39; Gretchen A. Condran and Eileen Crimmins-Gardner, "Public Health Measures and Mortality in U.S. Cities in the Late Nineteenth Century," *Human Ecology* 6 (1978): 41; K. Celeste Gaspari and Arthur G. Woolf, "Income, Public Works, and Mortality in Early Twentieth-Century American Cities," *Journal of Economic History* 45 (1985): 355–59.

33. Galishoff, *Safeguarding,* 30–33; Michael E. Teller, *The Tuberculosis Movement: A Public Health Campaign in the Progressive Era* (New York: Greenwood Press, 1988), 110–11; William A. Link, *The Paradox of Southern Progressivism, 1880–1930* (Chapel Hill: University of North Carolina Press, 1992), 205–6.

34. Woodbury, *Causal Factors,* 90–102.

35. Meckel, *Save the Babies,* 89 (quotation), 65–90; Judith Walzer Leavitt, *The Healthiest City: Milwaukee and the Politics of Health Reform* (Princeton: Princeton University Press, 1982), 157–58; Susan Turnbull

Shoemaker, "The Philadelphia Pediatric Society and Its Milk Commission, 1896–1917," *Pennsylvania History* 53 (1986): 275, 282; Sears, Roebuck and Co., *Catalog* 115 (1906): 395–96; 118 (1909): 541; 134 (1917): 682. Tube bottles disappeared by 1917.

36. Meckel, *Save the Babies*, 92–95, 123–56; Alisa Klaus, *Every Child a Lion: The Origins of Maternal and Infant Health Policy in the United States and France, 1890–1920* (Ithaca, N.Y.: Cornell University Press, 1993), 290.

37. Klaus, *Every Child*, 162–68, 259, 288; Meckel, *Save the Babies*, 146–49, 201; Robyn Muncy, *Creating a Female Dominion in American Reform, 1890–1935* (New York: Oxford University Press, 1991), 100.

38. Public Health Service, *Vital Statistics*, 254–55, 296–97; Gretchen A. Condran and Rose A. Cheney, "Mortality Trends in Philadelphia: Age- and Cause-Specific Death Rates, 1870–1930," *Demography* 19 (1982): 115; Galishoff, *Safeguarding*, 112–16; Douglas Ewbank and Samuel H. Preston, "Personal Health Behaviour and the Decline in Infant and Child Mortality: The United States, 1900–1930," *Proceedings of the Health Transition Workshop* (Canberra: n.p., 1989), 116–49; West, *Growing Up*, 63–64.

39. Ida B. Wells, *Crusade for Justice: The Autobiography of Ida B. Wells*, ed. Alfreda M. Duster (Chicago: University of Chicago Press, 1970), 250; Jan Lewis, "Mother's Love: The Construction of an Emotion in Nineteenth-Century America," in *Social History and Issues in Human Consciousness*, ed. Andrew E. Barnes and Peter N. Stearns (New York: New York University Press, 1989), 213–22.

40. Robert L. Griswold, *Fatherhood in America: A History* (New York: Basic Books, 1993), 13–17, 42–45, 69–77; Deborah Fink, *Agrarian Women: Wives and Mothers in Rural Nebraska, 1880–1940* (Chapel Hill: University of North Carolina Press, 1992), 141.

41. West, *Infant Care*, 59; Kate Douglass Wiggin, *Children's Rights: A Book of Nursery Logic* (Boston: Houghton, Mifflin, 1892), 18 (quotation); Griswold, *Fatherhood*, 6; Margaret Marsh, *Suburban Lives* (New Brunswick, N.J.: Rutgers University Press, 1990), 74–83.

42. Margaret O'Brien Steinfels, *Who's Minding the Children? The History and Politics of Day Care in America* (New York: Simon and Schuster, 1973), 54 (quotation), 34, 40–49; Leslie Woodcock Tentler, *Wage-Earning Women: Industrial Work and Family Life in the United States, 1900–1930* (New York: Oxford University Press, 1979), 63 (quotation), 161–64; Emily D. Cahan, *Past Caring: A History of U.S. Preschool Care and Education for the Poor, 1820–1965* (New York: National Center for Children in Poverty, 1989), 17–28.

43. Elizabeth H. Pleck, "A Mother's Wages: Income Earning among Married Italian and Black Women, 1896–1911," in *A Heritage of Her Own: Toward a New Social History of American Women*, ed. Nancy F. Cott

and Elizabeth H. Pleck (New York: Simon and Schuster, 1979), 367–82.

44. Mary White Ovington, *Half a Man: The Status of the Negro in New York* (1911; reprint, New York: Hill and Wang, 1969), 32 (quotation), 39; Tentler, *Wage-Earning Women*, 155–56.

45. Jane Addams, *Twenty Years at Hull House* (1910; reprint, New York: Signet, 1981), 130; Alice Kessler-Harris, *Out to Work: A History of Wage-Earning Women in the United States* (New York: Oxford University Press, 1982), 188–92.

46. Owens, *Stubborn Soil*, 11–12, 21; Jacqueline Jones, *Labor of Love, Labor of Sorrow: Black Women, Work, and the Family, from Slavery to the Present* (New York: Vintage Books, 1986), 88.

47. JA, OHC (quotation); Addams, *Twenty Years,* 127; Dart, *Maternity,* 46; Bradley and Williamson, *Rural Children,* 40.

48. Catharine Brody, "A New York Childhood," *American Mercury* 14 (1928): 60 (quotation); David Nasaw, *Children of the City: At Work and At Play* (New York: Oxford University Press, 1986), 108 (quotation), 107; Spock, *Spock,* 5; John Spargo, *The Bitter Cry of the Children* (New York: Macmillan, 1906), 38–39; Tentler, *Wage-Earning Women,* 158–59; JS, LH, OHC.

49. Spencer, *Spencers,* 31, 32; David M. Katzman, *Seven Days a Week: Women and Domestic Service in Industrializing America* (Urbana: University of Illinois Press, 1981), 118, 138, 185–87, 268; HS, 41, 139; *Plain Folk: The Life Stories of Undistinguished Americans,* ed. David M. Katzman and William R. Tuttle Jr. (Urbana: University of Illinois Press, 1982), 179.

50. Daniel E. Sutherland, *Americans and Their Servants: Domestic Service in the United States from 1800 to 1920* (Baton Rouge: Louisiana State University Press, 1981), 58, 183; Peter G. Filene, *Him/Her/Self: Sex Roles in Modern America,* 2nd ed. (Baltimore: Johns Hopkins University Press, 1986), 9, 255.

51. Mary Cable, *The Little Darlings: A History of Child Rearing in America* (New York: Charles Scribner's Sons, 1975), 102 (quotation); Wishy, *Child and the Republic,* 22–23, 94–101.

52. Holt, *Care and Feeding* (1894), 66, 65 (quotations); (1918), 192–95; West, *Infant Care,* 58 (quotation), 60, 62.

53. West, *Infant Care,* 36, 47 (quotations), 37, 57.

54. Holt, *Care and Feeding* (1894), 50 (quotation); (1918), 25, 160–62, 193; West, *Infant Care,* 51 (quotation), 30, 65–66.

55. Holt, *Care and Feeding* (1918), 26, 163; West, *Infant Care,* 23, 56–57; Berk, *Child Development,* 125.

56. Holt, *Care and Feeding* (1918), 172 (quotation), 175; West, *Infant Care,* 59, 60 (quotations).

57. Quotations: Holt, *Care and Feeding* (1918), 167, 169; West, *Infant Care*, 60.

58. Elizabeth Ewen, *Immigrant Women in the Land of Dollars: Life and Culture on the Lower East Side, 1890–1925* (New York: Monthly Review Press, 1985), 138 (quotation), 139; Elsa G. Herzfeld, "Superstitions and Customs of the Tenement-House Mother," *Charities* 14 (1905): 985–86; Karin Calvert, *Children in the House: The Material Culture of Early Childhood, 1600–1900* (Boston: Northeastern University Press, 1992), 123–24; David F. Musto, *The American Disease: Origins of Narcotic Control* (New Haven: Yale University Press, 1973), 94.

59. Ibid., 59 (quotation); Sears, *Catalog* 104 (1897): 660; 134 (1917): 1134.

60. Julia Wrigley, "Do Young Children Need Intellectual Stimulation? Experts' Advice to Parents, 1900–1985," *History of Education Quarterly* 29 (1989): 57 (quotation), 46–57; Celia B. Stendler, "Sixty Years of Child Training Practices," *The Journal of Pediatrics* 36 (1950): 126.

61. West, *Infant Care*, 59 (quotation), 13–14; West in Ladd-Taylor, *Raising a Baby*, 131; Mrs. Max West, *Child Care: Part 1, the Preschool Age* (GPO, 1918), 37 (quotation).

62. West, *Infant Care*, 61; Wrigley, "Do Young Children," 46, 71–72.

63. West, *Child Care*, 53 (quotation), 7–9, 37, 47, 55–60.

64. Ibid., 47, 46 (quotations); Ellen Key, *The Century of the Child* (New York: G. P. Putnam's Sons, 1909), 183.

65. West, *Child Care*, 49; Key, *Century*, 140–41; Daniel R. Miller and Guy E. Swanson, *The Changing American Parent* (New York: John Wiley & Sons, 1958), 13.

66. Peter N. Stearns, "Girls, Boys, and Emotions: Redefinitions and Historical Change," *Journal of American History* 80 (1993): 37–62; Carol Zisowitz Stearns and Peter N. Stearns, *Anger: The Struggle for Emotional Control in America's History* (Chicago: University of Chicago Press, 1986), 73, 96; Peter N. Stearns and Timothy Haggerty, "The Role of Fear: Transitions in American Emotional Standards for Children, 1850–1950," *American Historical Review* 96 (1991): 74–79.

67. Gelett Burgess, *Goop Tales: Alphabetically Told* (1904; reprint, New York: Dover Publications, 1973), title page, 61.

68. Jay Mechling, "Advice to Historians on Advice to Mothers," *Journal of Social History* 9 (1975): 44–63; Neil Sutherland, "When You Listen to the Winds of Childhood, How Much Can You Believe?" *Curriculum Inquiry* 22 (1992): 235–45.

69. Ladd-Taylor, *Raising a Baby*, 103 (quotation); Le Guin, *Home-Concealed Woman*, 53 (quotation), 15, 23, 31, 93, 100, 163, 283.

70. Ladd-Taylor, *Raising a Baby*, 84 (quotation); Barbara Ehrenreich and Deirdre English, *For Her Own Good: 150 Years of the Experts' Advice*

to Women (Garden City, N.Y.: Anchor Press, 1978), 182 (quotation); Emily Henderson Grant, "The Unskilled Profession," *Woman's Home Companion* 38 (May 1911): 4 (quotation); Margaret Mead, *Blackberry Winter: My Earlier Years* (New York: William Morrow & Co., 1972), 25–26 (quotation), 60.

71. Anna B. Noyes, *How I Kept My Baby Well* (Baltimore: Warwick and York, 1913), 14, 141–42, 177 (quotations), 31, 37, 99, 180.

72. Philip Greven, *Spare the Child: The Religious Roots of Punishment and the Psychological Impact of Physical Abuse* (New York: Vintage Books, 1992), 5–90; Gordon, *Heroes,* 180; Elizabeth Pleck, *Domestic Tyranny: The Making of Social Policy against Family Violence from Colonial Times to the Present* (New York: Oxford University Press, 1987), 46; Link, *Paradox,* 88–89; OHC interviews.

73. Theodore Rosengarten, *All God's Dangers: The Life of Nate Shaw* [Ned Cobb] (New York: Alfred A. Knopf, 1975), 22; N. Ray Hiner, "Children's Rights, Corporal Punishment, and Child Abuse: Changing American Attitudes, 1870–1920," *Bulletin of the Menninger Clinic* 43 (1979): 233–48; Gordon, *Heroes,* 69–72; Pleck, *Domestic Tyranny,* 69–84, 127–31.

74. Margaret Connell Szasz, "Native American Children," in *American Childhood,* ed. Hawes and Hiner, 319; Spencer, *Spencers,* 121.

75. Le Guin, *Home-Concealed Woman,* 68–69 (quotation), 165; CD, HW, OHC (quotations).

76. Earl Barnes, "Punishment as Seen by Children," *Pedagogical Seminary* 3 (1894): 241 (quotation), 239–45.

77. Pleck, *Domestic Tyranny,* 243n. (quotation), 122 ff.; Anita Schorsch, *Images of Childhood: An Illustrated Social History* (New York: Mayflower Books, 1979), 162.

78. Jane Addams, *Democracy and Social Ethics* (1902; reprint, Cambridge, Mass.: The Belknap Press, 1964), 45 (quotation); Stearns and Stearns, *Anger,* 98; Howard S. Erlanger, "Social Class and Corporal Punishment in Childrearing: A Reassessment," *American Sociological Review* 39 (1974): 68–85; Ralph Ellison, *Shadow and Act* (New York: Random House, 1964), 85; Elizabeth Hampsten, "The Nehers and the Martins in North Dakota, 1909–1911," in Lillian Schlissel et al., *Far From Home: Families of the Westward Journey* (New York: Schocken Books, 1989), 189, 209; Gordon, *Heroes,* 179; OHC interviews.

79. Pleck, *Domestic Tyranny,* 46, 205–11; Erlanger, "Social Class," 80.

80. N=96. See OHC. Many interviews did not discuss discipline.

81. PF, OHC.

82. Hampsten, "Nehers," 218; RK, LH, MH, OHC.

83. Reproduced in Jerome M. Clubb et al., *The Process of Historical Inquiry: Everyday Lives of Working Americans* (New York: Columbia University Press, 1989), 95.

84. Owens, *Stubborn Soil*, 23–25; Spencer, *Spencers*, 73; ML, OHC.

85. Spencer, *Spencers*, 122; MW, RL, HW, OHC; Le Guin, *Home-Concealed Woman*, 56; *Plain Folk*, ed. Katzman and Tuttle, 85; Marsh, *Suburban Lives*, 74–83 (quotation).

86. Wanda C. Bronson et al., "Patterns of Authority and Affection in Two Generations," *Journal of Abnormal and Social Psychology* 58 (1959): 146.

87. Sears, *Catalog*, 104 (1897), 278, 309, 692–96; 115 (1906): 1079; 118 (1909): 761; 134 (1917): 179–204; Calvert, *Children*, 97, 127, 144–46; Spencer, *Spencers*, 68–70.

88. Jo B. Paoletti and Carol L. Kregloh, "The Children's Department," in *Men and Women: Dressing the Part,* ed. Claudia Brush Kidwell and Valerie Steele (Washington: Smithsonian Institution Press, 1989), 26–33; Calvert, *Children*, 96–119; Berk, *Child Development*, 517.

89. Le Guin, *Home-Concealed Woman*, 33; Doris Kearns, *Lyndon Johnson and the American Dream* (New York: Harper & Row, 1976), 22–23; Sears, *Catalog* 104 (1897): 182–85, 278, 304–5; 118 (1909): 959, 983; 134 (1917): 187, 432–36; Calvert, *Children*, 110; Paoletti and Kregloh, "Children's Department," 33.

90. Paoletti and Kregloh, "Children's Department," 34; Sears, *Catalog* 134 (1917): 52–55, 185–90, 400.

91. Calvert, *Children*, 125–28; Noyes, *How I Kept My Baby Well*, 63, 73, 80.

92. JW (quotation), MH, AM, OHC; Dorothy Howard, *Dorothy's World: Childhood in Sabine Bottom, 1902–1910* (Englewood Cliffs, N.J.: Prentice-Hall, 1977), 103–4, 186, 196; Mildred A. Renaud, "Rattlesnakes and Tumbleweeds: A Memoir of South Dakota," *American Heritage* 26.3 (April 1975): 56.

93. West, *Child Care*, 39 (quotation); RP, OHC.

94. Amanda Dargan and Steven Zeitlin, *City Play* (New Brunswick, N.J.: Rutgers University Press, 1990), 19, 54–55, 75–79, 86, 155; Nasaw, *Children*, 18–19, 28–29; HH, OHC; Viviana A. Zelizer, *Pricing the Priceless Child: The Changing Social Value of Children* (New York: Basic Books, 1985), 38.

95. Clarence D. Rainwater, *The Play Movement in the United States* (Chicago: University of Chicago Press, 1922), 20–25, 43, 211; Jacob A. Riis, *The Children of the Poor* (1892; reprint, New York: Charles Scribner's Sons, 1923), 183–86.

96. Rainwater, *Play Movement*, 246 (quotation); Dominick Cavallo, *Muscles and Morals: Organized Playgrounds and Urban Reform, 1880–1920* (Philadelphia: University of Pennsylvania Press, 1981), 32–38.

97. Rainwater, *Play Movement*, 62, 219–22, 235; Cavallo, *Muscles*, 47.

98. Nasaw, *Children*, 36–38; Cavallo, *Muscles*, 46.

99. West, *Child Care*, 40; JA, OHC.

100. G. L. Freeman and R. S. Freeman, *Yesterday's Toys* (Watkins Glen, N.Y.: Century House, 1962), 11–12, 44, 85, 96, 106–9, 115, 121–27;

Bernard Mergen, *Play and Playthings: A Reference Guide* (Westport, Conn.: Greenwood Press, 1982), 153 (stereograph), 107–8; AB, LD, JK, CB, OHC; Spock, *Spock*, 6, 34; West, *Child Care*, 42–44.

101. Le Guin, *Home-Concealed Woman*, 64 (quotation), 28; ML, DB, OHC; A. Caswell Ellis and G. Stanley Hall, "A Study of Dolls," *Pedagogical Seminary* 1 (December 1896): 152–55.

102. Miriam Formanek-Brunell, *Made to Play House: Dolls and the Commercialization of American Girlhood, 1830–1930* (New Haven: Yale University Press, 1993), 8–11, 71, 100–106; Ellis and Hall, "Study," 136, 155.

103. LC (quotation), LS, HD, OHC.

104. Ellis and Hall, "Study," 136, 149 (quotations), 138–47; Formanek-Brunell, *Made to Play House*, 25–33.

105. Formanek-Brunell, *Made to Play House*, 109–12; Nasaw, *Children*, 109; Eileen Boris, "Reconstructing the 'Family': Women, Progressive Reform, and the Problem of Social Control," in *Gender, Class*, ed. Frankel and Dye, 80–81.

106. E.g., WT, VR, OHC.

107. Howard, *Dorothy's World*, 98 (quotation), 69–71, 99, 181; ML (quotation), LS, BB, LA, EF, WD, OHC.

108. Bradley and Williamson, *Rural Children*, 85, 50, 52 (quotations), 51; Le Guin, *Home-Concealed Woman*, 49.

109. Italics in original. Hiner, "Children's Rights," 240.

110. Evelyn Weber, *The Kindergarten: Its Encounter with Educational Thought in America* (New York: Teachers College Press, 1969), 12–17; Dominick Cavallo, "The Politics of Latency: Kindergarten Pedagogy, 1860–1930," in *Regulated Children/Liberated Children: Education in Psychohistorical Perspective*, ed. Barbara Finkelstein (New York: Psychohistory Press, 1979), 166.

111. Michael Steven Shapiro, *Child's Garden: The Kindergarten Movement from Froebel to Dewey* (University Park: Pennsylvania State University Press, 1983), 30–44, 97; Elizabeth Dale Ross, *The Kindergarten Crusade: The Establishment of Preschool Education in the United States* (Athens, Ohio: Ohio University Press, 1976), 30, 129, 142–44; Wells, *Crusade*, 249–50; Wiggin, *Children's Rights*, 35, 109–38; Marvin Lazerson, *Origins of the Urban School: Public Education in Massachusetts, 1870–1915* (Cambridge, Mass.: Harvard University Press, 1971), 42–44.

112. Shapiro, *Child's Garden*, 136–38; Bureau of Education, *Kindergartens in the United States: Statistics and Present Problems* (GPO, 1914), 17; Lazerson, *Origins*, 56, 65–72; Cavallo, "Politics," 162–76.

113. Bureau of Education, *Kindergartens*, 98, 99 (quotations); William Issel, "Americanization, Acculturation and Social Control: School Reform

Ideology in Industrial Pennsylvania, 1880–1910," *Journal of Social History* 12 (1979): 580 (quotation); David John Hogan, *Class and Reform: School and Society in Chicago, 1880–1930* (Philadelphia: University of Pennsylvania Press, 1985), 82 (quotation); Shapiro, *Child's Garden,* 133–35.

114. Bureau of Education, *Kindergartens,* 95, 11 (quotations); Barbara Beatty, *Preschool Education in America: The Culture of Young Children from the Colonial Era to the Present* (New Haven: Yale University Press, 1995), 126–29; Weber, *Kindergarten,* 95–96; Ross, *Kindergarten Crusade,* 92–98.

115. Ross, *Kindergarten Crusade,* 60 (quotation), 62, 71; Weber, *Kindergarten,* 35–62, 127–29.

116. Wiggin, *Children's Rights,* 121; CS, OHC.

117. Weber, *Kindergarten,* 90–92; Ross, *Kindergarten Crusade,* 91–95; Bureau of Education, *Kindergartens,* 94–95.

118. Bureau of Education, *Kindergartens,* 7, 16–17, 96–103; *HS,* 368; Weber, *Kindergartens,* 95.

119. ET (quotation), HM, IH, AK, VP, OHC; Owens, *Stubborn Soil,* 49.

Chapter 3

1. Laura E. Berk, *Child Development,* 2nd ed. (Boston: Allyn and Bacon, 1991), 234–37; Erik H. Erikson, *Childhood and Society,* 2nd ed. (New York: W. W. Norton, 1963), 258–60.

2. Paul C. Violas, *The Training of the Urban Working Class: A History of Twentieth Century American Education* (Chicago: Rand McNally, 1978), 19; Frances Sage Bradley and Margaretta A. Williamson, *Rural Children in Selected Counties of North Carolina* (GPO, 1918), 43; William M. Landes and Lewis C. Solmon, "Compulsory Schooling Legislation: An Economic Analysis of Law and Social Change in the Nineteenth Century," *Journal of Economic History* 32 (1972): 54–91.

3. John L. Rury, "American School Enrolment in the Progressive Era: An Interpretive Inquiry," *History of Education* 14 (1985): 58; Bureau of Education, *Statistics of State School Systems, 1919–20* (GPO, 1922), 68; *HS,* 368–69.

4. Robert A. Margo, *Race and Schooling in the South, 1880–1950: An Economic History* (Chicago: University of Chicago Press, 1990), 10, 26; *HS,* 375–76; *Report of the Commissioner of Education for the Year Ended June 30, 1911* (GPO, 1912), volume 2, xxix; Bureau of Education, *Statistics,* 16.

5. CY, 1102.

6. CY, 1103, 1227–28; William A. Link, *The Paradox of Southern Progressivism, 1880–1930* (Chapel Hill: University of North Carolina Press, 1992), 128–33; Margo, *Race,* 22, 35–37; J. Morgan Kousser, "Progres-

sivism—for Middle-Class Whites Only: North Carolina Education, 1880–1910," *Journal of Southern History* 46 (1980): 177–90; Bradley and Williamson, *Rural Children*, 83.

7. Margo, *Race*, 21–22; Bradley and Williamson, *Rural Children*, 46–47; James D. Anderson, *The Education of Blacks in the South, 1860–1935* (Chapel Hill: University of North Carolina Press, 1988), 34–36, 72–184.

8. James Grossman, *Land of Hope: Chicago, Black Southerners, and the Great Migration* (Chicago: University of Chicago Press, 1989), 248–55; David B. Tyack, *The One Best System: A History of American Urban Education* (Cambridge, Mass.: Harvard University Press, 1974), 117, 120; CY, 1305–6; John Bodnar et al., *Lives of Their Own: Blacks, Italians, and Poles in Pittsburgh, 1900–1960* (Urbana: University of Illinois Press, 1982), 35–37.

9. HM, OHC; Patricia Albjerg Graham, *Community and Class in American Education, 1865–1918* (New York: John Wiley & Sons, 1974), 49; James W. Sanders, *The Education of an Urban Minority: Catholics in Chicago, 1833–1965* (New York: Oxford University Press, 1977), 35–38.

10. Timothy Walch, *Parish School: American Catholic Parochial Education from Colonial Times to the Present* (New York: Crossroad Publishing Co., 1996), 68–82; BS, OHC; Sanders, *Education*, 44–50, 61–71, 115–19, 150, 247; Morgan M. Sheedy, "The Catholic Parochial Schools of the United States," *Report of the Commissioner of Education for the Year 1903* (GPO, 1905), 1089; HS, 377; Walter H. Beck, *Lutheran Elementary Schools in the United States*, 2nd ed. (St. Louis: Concordia Publishing House [c. 1965]), 224, 355–58, 402.

11. Michael C. Coleman, *American Indian Children at School, 1850–1930* (Jackson: University Press of Mississippi, 1993), 16–18, 44; Frederick E. Hoxie, *A Final Promise: The Campaign to Assimilate the Indians, 1880–1920* (Cambridge: Cambridge University Press, 1989), 53–54, 202–43; CY, 1355; Wilma A. Daddario, " 'They Get Milk Practically Every Day': The Genoa Indian Industrial School, 1884–1934," *Nebraska History* 73 (Spring 1992): 6–7.

12. Barbara Finkelstein, *Governing the Young: Teacher Behavior in Popular Primary Schools in Nineteenth-Century United States* (New York: Falmer Press, 1989), 44–45.

13. Willard S. Elsbree, *The American Teacher: Evolution of a Profession in a Democracy* (New York: American Book Co., 1939), 554; Wayne E. Fuller, *The Old Country School: The Story of Rural Education in the Middle West* (Chicago: University of Chicago Press, 1982), 177–81; Nancy Hoffman, *Woman's "True" Profession: Voices from the History of Teaching* (New York: Feminist Press, 1981), 212.

14. Adele Marie Shaw, "Backward Country Schools Near Big Cities," *World's Work* 8 (1904): 5253 (quotation); Cordier, *Schoolwomen*, 111, 127; LH, VS, BW, AB, JW, VP, OHC; Fuller, *Old Country School*, 13.

15. J. M. Rice, *The Public-School System of the United States* (New York: Century Co., 1893), 31 (quotations), 31–33, 56–59.

16. Ibid., 41, 220–29; Lawrence A. Cremin, *The Transformation of the School: Progressivism in American Education, 1876–1957* (New York: Vintage Books, 1961), 22 (quotations); William J. Reese, *Power and the Promise of School Reform: Grassroots Movements During the Progressive Era* (Boston: Routledge and Kegan Paul, 1986), 50 (quotations).

17. Reese, *Power*, 118 (quotation); Rice, *Public-School System*, 6–27, 44–53, 184–86; Tyack, *One Best System*, 7, 95–104, 127.

18. William James, *Talks to Teachers on Psychology and to Students on Some of Life's Ideals* (1899; reprint, New York: Dover Publications, 1962), 17, 34 (his italics); G. Stanley Hall, "The Ideal School as Based on Child Study," in National Education Association, *Proceedings* 40 (1901): 478; CY, 1134; Cremin, *Transformation*, 113–14; Joseph M. Hawes, *The Children's Rights Movement: A History of Advocacy and Protection* (Boston: Twayne Publishers, 1991), 31.

19. John Dewey, *The School and Society* (Chicago: University of Chicago Press, 1907), 44; Herbert M. Kliebard, *The Struggle for the American Curriculum, 1893–1958* (Boston: Routledge & Kegan Paul, 1986), 71–73.

20. Ellen Condliffe Lagemann, "The Plural Worlds of Educational Research," *History of Education Quarterly* 29 (1989): 210, 212 (quotations), 201–12; William H. Kilpatrick, "The Project Method," *Teachers College Record* 19 (1918): 320, 329; Kliebard, *Struggle*, 30–31; Cremin, *Transformation*, 135, 277–83; Larry Cuban, *How Teachers Taught: Constancy and Change in American Classrooms, 1890–1980* (New York: Longman, 1984), 37.

21. Leonard P. Ayres, *Laggards in Our Schools: A Study of Retardation and Elimination in City School Systems* (New York: Charities Publication Committee, 1909), 5, 6, 220, 7 (quotations; his italics in both cases); David Tyack and Elisabeth Hansot, *Learning Together: A History of Coeducation in American Public Schools* (New Haven: Yale University Press, 1990), 166 (quotation); Julia Wrigley, *Class Politics and Public Schools: Chicago, 1900–1950* (New Brunswick, N.J.: Rutgers University Press, 1982), 52–54.

22. Cremin, *Transformation*, 181 (quotation); Ellwood P. Cubberley, editor's introduction to Walter Scott Monroe, *Measuring the Results of Teaching* (Boston: Houghton Mifflin, 1918), vi; Walter Scott Monroe et al., *Educational Tests and Measurements* (Boston: Houghton Mifflin, 1917), 48.

23. Monroe, *Measuring*, 19 (quotation), 1–36, 175–202, 245–66; Edward L. Thorndike, "Handwriting," *Teachers College Record* 11 (March 1910): 5 (quotation); id., "The Nature, Purposes, and General Methods of Measurements of Educational Products," *NSSE* 17 (1918): 20 (quotation); Franz Samelson, "Was Early Mental Testing . . . ," in *Psychological Testing and American Society, 1890–1930*, ed. Michael M. Sokal (New Brunswick: Rutgers University Press, 1987), 116–21.

24. Paul Davis Chapman, *Schools as Sorters: Lewis M. Terman, Applied Psychology, and the Intelligence Testing Movement, 1890–1930* (New York: New York University Press, 1988), 27–82.

25. Ibid., 35; Nicholas Lemann, "The Great Sorting," *Atlantic Monthly* 276 (September 1995): 83–88; Walter S. Monroe, "Existing Tests and Standards," *NSSE* 17 (1918): 71.

26. William S. Gray, "The Relation of Silent Reading to Economy in Education," *NSSE* 16 (1917): 17, 18 (quotations); Edward L. Thorndike, "Reading as Reasoning: A Study of Mistakes in Paragraph Reading," *Journal of Educational Psychology* 8 (1917): 321–32.

27. Walter A. Jessup, "Current Practices and Standards in Arithmetic," *NSSE* 14 (1915): 118, 117 (quotations), 129; Mary Hurlbut Cordier, *Schoolwomen of the Prairies and Plains: Personal Narratives from Iowa, Kansas, and Nebraska, 1860s–1920s* (Albuquerque: University of New Mexico Press, 1992), 127 (quotation); Monroe, *Measuring*, 175–93.

28. Arnold Gesell and Beatrice Chandler Gesell, *The Normal Child and Primary Education* (Boston: Ginn and Co., 1912), 208, 305; Edmund Burke Huey, *The Psychology and Pedagogy of Reading* (1908; reprint, Cambridge, Mass.: M.I.T. Press, 1968), 266–89; Neil M. Cowan and Ruth Schwartz Cowan, *Our Parents' Lives: The Americanization of Eastern European Jews* (New York: Basic Books, 1989), 87; Rice, *Public-School System*, 75, 100, 213; Adele Marie Shaw, "The Public Schools about New York," *World's Work* 7 (1904): 4319.

29. "Theodore Roosevelt on the New Nationalism," in *Major Problems in the Gilded Age and Progressive Era*, ed. Leon Fink (Lexington, Mass.: D. C. Heath and Co., 1993), 346; "Playing with Fire," *Dial* 20 (1896): 294 (quotation); B. F. Skinner, *Particulars of My Life* (New York: Alfred Knopf, 1976), 70; Marvin Lazerson, *Origins of the Urban School: Public Education in Massachusetts, 1870–1915* (Cambridge, Mass.: Harvard University Press, 1971), 80, 102–9, 132, 180–89; Kliebard, *Struggle*, 16–18, 35–36; Henry W. Holmes, "Time Distributions by Subjects and Grades in Representative Cities," *NSSE* 14 (1915): 25.

30. Vincent P. Franklin, *The Education of Black Philadelphia: The Social and Educational History of a Minority Community, 1900–1950* (Philadelphia: University of Pennsylvania Press, 1979), 57 (quotations),

53–57; Alice Littlefield, "Learning to Labor: Native American Education in the United States, 1880–1930," in *The Political Economy of North American Indians,* ed. John H. Moore (Norman: University of Oklahoma Press, 1993), 43–59; Daddario, " 'They Get Milk,' " 3–5; Jacqueline A. Rouse, "Atlanta's African-American Women's Attack on Segregation, 1900–1920," in *Gender, Class, Race, and Reform in the Progressive Era,* ed. Noralee Frankel and Nancy S. Dye (Lexington: University of Kentucky Press, 1991), 14–19; Bradley and Williamson, *Rural Children,* 48.

31. Reese, *Power,* 222 (quotation), 53–62, 148–53, 177–208, 221, 235; Violas, *Training,* 31–32; William R. Hood, "Recent Progress in City Schools," *Report of the Commissioner of Education for the Year Ended June 30, 1911* (GPO, 1912), volume 1, 141–53.

32. Their italics. Gesell and Gesell, *Normal Child,* 283–84; Baker in CY, 929; Ayres, *Laggards,* 6, 121–30; Tyack, *One Best System,* 179.

33. Bourne in CY, 1140; Ronald D. Cohen, *Children of the Mill: Schooling and Society in Gary, Indiana, 1906–1960* (Bloomington: Indiana University Press, 1990), 8–71.

34. Cremin, *Transformation,* 159 (quotation); Diane Ravitch, *The Great School Wars: A History of the New York City Public Schools* (New York: Basic Books, 1988), 197–228; Cohen, *Children,* 43, 57.

35. *Report of the Commissioner of Education for the Year 1896–97* (GPO, 1898), 398–99 (quotations); Stuart A. Rosenfeld and Jonathan P. Sher, "The Urbanization of Rural Schools, 1840–1970," in *Education in Rural America: A Reassessment of Conventional Wisdom,* ed. Jonathan P. Sher (Boulder, Colo.: Westview Press, 1977), 27–32.

36. James L. Leloudis, *Schooling in the New South: Pedagogy, Self, and Society in North Carolina, 1880–1920* (Chapel Hill: University of North Carolina Press, 1996), 166 (quotation), 155–75; William A. Link, *A Hard Country and a Lonely Place: Schooling, Society, and Reform in Rural Virginia, 1870–1920* (Chapel Hill: University of North Carolina Press, 1986), 150–54; Link, *Paradox,* 211.

37. David B. Danbom, "Rural Education Reform and the Country Life Movement, 1900–1920," *Agricultural History* 53 (1979): 465–71; id., *Resisted Revolution: Urban America and the Industrialization of Agriculture, 1900–1930* (Ames: Iowa State University Press, 1979), 53–59; William L. Bowers, *The Country Life Movement in America, 1900–1920* (Port Washington, N.Y.: Kennikat Press, 1974), 13–16, 57–59.

38. Danbom, *Resisted Revolution,* 79 (quotation); Ruth Warner Towne, "Marie Turner Harvey and the Rural Life Movement," *Missouri Historical Review* 84 (1990): 392–98; Cordier, *Schoolwomen,* 220–25.

39. Dorothy Canfield Fisher, *Understood Betsy* (New York: Dell Publishing, 1993).

40. Fuller, *Old Country School*, 225 (quotation), 221, 235–38; Danbom, *Resisted Revolution*, 77, 78 (quotations), 77–79; Tyack, *One Best System*, 15; Elizabeth Hampsten, *Settlers' Children: Growing Up on the Great Plains* (Norman: University of Oklahoma Press, 1991), 40; RB, HM, OHC; Bowers, *Country Life*, 108–10.

41. Ayres, *Laggards*, 188–89; Edith Abbott and Sophonisba P. Breckenridge, *Truancy and Non-Attendance in the Chicago Schools* (Chicago: University of Chicago Press, 1917), 119–48.

42. Harriette Simpson Arnow, *Old Burnside* (Lexington: University Press of Kentucky, 1977), 89–90; Bureau of Education, *Statistics*, 56.

43. JS (quotation), RK, JK, OHC; Marie Jastrow, *A Time to Remember: Growing Up in New York before the Great War* (New York: W. W. Norton & Co., 1979), 80.

44. Mary Antin, *The Promised Land* (Boston: Houghton Mifflin, 1925), 209; Cowan, *Our Parents' Lives*, 102; Harry Golden, *The Right Time: An Autobiography* (New York: G. P. Putnam's Sons, 1969), 48.

45. Stephan F. Brumberg, *Going to America, Going to School: The Jewish Immigrant Public School Encounter in Turn-of-the-Century New York City* (New York: Praeger, 1986), 132 (quotation); Selma Cantor Berrol, *Growing Up American: Immigrant Children in America, Then and Now* (New York: Twayne Publishers, 1995), 44 (quotation); RB, OHC.

46. Hampsten, *Settlers' Children*, 35–36; Lowe in *Growing Up Asian American: An Anthology*, ed. Maria Hong (New York: William Morrow and Co., 1993), 178; Cowan, *Our Parents' Lives*, 96, 98 (quotations), 94.

47. Coleman, *American Indian Children*, 16–31, 60–71; Polingaysi Qoyawayma, *No Turning Back* (Albuquerque: University of New Mexico Press, 1964), 20–25.

48. CY, 1358 (quotation), 1357.

49. John Fire/Lame Deer and Richard Erdoes, *Lame Deer: Seeker of Visions* (New York: Simon and Schuster, 1972), 34 (quotation); Coleman, *American Indian Children*, 83, 105, 158–59; Robert A. Trennert Jr., *The Phoenix Indian School: Forced Assimilation in Arizona, 1891–1935* (Norman: University of Oklahoma Press, 1988), 46, 113, 121–26; Daddario, "They Get Milk," 7; Twenty-two Navajo Men and Women, *Stories of Traditional Navajo Life and Culture* (Tsaile, Ariz.: Navajo Community College Press, 1977), 121, 131.

50. Twenty-two Navajo, *Stories*, 136 (quotation), 59–61, 129, 153–55; Carol Devens, " 'If We Get the Girls, We Get the Race': Missionary Education of Native American Girls," *Journal of World History* 3 (1992): 234–37.

51. Julia Richman quoted in Selma Berrol, "Immigrant Working-Class Families," in *American Families: A Research Guide and Historical Handbook*, eds. Joseph M. Hawes and Elizabeth I. Nybakken (New

York: Greenwood Press, 1991), 335; Helen M. Todd, "Why Children Work: The Children's Answer," *McClure's* 40 (April 1913): 74 (quotation); Hoffman, *Woman's "True" Profession*, 206; Cowan, *Our Parents' Lives*, 90–91; PF, JJ, JU, DN, JK, RW, HH, MW, OHC.

52. Cowan, *Our Parents' Lives*, 94 (quotation), 86; Gesell, *Normal Child*, 229 (quotation).

53. Fuller, *Old Country School*, 13–19, 190; HT, IF, HM, LS, OHC.

54. Maude Elliott, "Pioneer School Teaching in the 20th Century," in *Model Ts, Pep Chapels, and a Wolf at the Door: Kansas Teenagers, 1900–1941,* ed. Marilyn Irvin Holt (Lawrence: Division of Continuing Education, University of Kansas, 1994), 69–70; William A. Owens, *This Stubborn Soil: A Frontier Boyhood* (New York: Vintage, 1986), 227 (quotation), 205–15.

55. Coleman, *American Indian Children,* 87 (quotation), 86–90; David Wallace Adams, *Education for Extinction: American Indians and the Boarding School Experience, 1875–1928* (Lawrence: University Press of Kansas, 1995), 117–23; Trennert, *Phoenix,* 119; CY, 1362.

56. Rice, *Public-School System,* 173; N. Ray Hiner, "Children's Rights, Corporal Punishment, and Child Abuse: Changing American Attitudes, 1870–1920," *Bulletin of the Menninger Clinic* 43 (1979): 243; Todd, "Why Children Work," 75–76.

57. Paul Theobald, *Call School: Rural Education in the Midwest to 1918* (Carbondale: Southern Illinois University Press, 1995), 139 (quotation), 135; David L. Carlton, *Mill and Town in South Carolina, 1880–1920* (Baton Rouge: Louisiana State University Press, 1982), 177 (quotation); Cordier, *Schoolwomen,* 258–59 (quotation); Link, *Hard Country,* 35–36; Tyack, *One Best System,* 70; Abbott and Breckinridge, *Truancy,* 149–52.

58. Cowan, *Our Parents' Lives,* 87; I. A. Newby, *Plain Folk in the New South: Social Change and Cultural Persistence, 1880–1915* (Baton Rouge: Louisiana State University Press, 1989), 439; OHC interviews.

59. Tyack, *One Best System,* 255 (quotation); JR, OHC (quotation).

60. Brumberg, *Going to America,* 126 (quotation); CD (quotation), DB, EP, OP, IH, OHC; Edward L. Ayers, *The Promise of the New South: Life after Reconstruction* (New York: Oxford University Press, 1992), 212 (quotation).

61. Henry Seidel Canby, *American Memoir* (New York: Greenwood Press, 1968), 55. On teaching, see Finkelstein, *Governing;* Cuban, *How Teachers Taught.*

62. HS, 365, 382; CY, 1104; Margo, *Race,* 7.

63. RJ (quotations), EE, OHC; Newby, *Plain Folk,* 438 (quotations).

64. Ibid., 418–19; Daniel P. and Lauren B. Resnik, "The Nature of Literacy: A Historical Explanation," in *Perspectives on Literacy,* ed. Eugene

R. Kintgen et al. (Carbondale: Southern Illinois University Press, 1988), 199 (quotation); Thorndike, "Reading," 323 (quotation), 323–32.

65. *Psychological Examining in the United States Army,* ed. Robert M. Yerkes, Memoirs of the National Academy of Sciences, volume 15 (GPO, 1921), 743 (quotation), 100, 156, 349–55, 742–57; Resnick, "Nature," 199.

66. Gray, "Silent Reading," 26; S. A. Courtis, "Standards in Rates of Reading," *NSSE* 14 (1915): 50–56; Rice, *Public-School System,* 137.

67. Kenneth Cmiel, *Democratic Eloquence: The Fight over Popular Speech in Nineteenth-Century America* (New York: William Morrow & Co., 1990), 240–44; O. F. Muson and J. F. Hoskinson, "Library and Supplementary Reading Books Recommended for Use in Elementary Schools," *NSSE* 16; 1 (1917): 33–59; J. F. Bobbitt at al., "Literature in the Elementary Curriculum," *Elementary School Teacher* 14 (December 1913): 158–66; Lewis Atherton, "Literary Selections Most Frequently Memorized in the Elementary School," ibid. (January 1914): 208–20.

68. Theobald, *Call School,* 115 (quotation); Cmiel, *Democratic Eloquence,* 240–42; James Fleming Hosic, "The Essentials of Composition and Grammar," *NSSE* 14 (1915): 90–115.

69. Rice, *Public-School Systems,* 72, 87, 89; Cowan, *Our Parents' Lives,* 88; W. W. Charters, "Minimal Essentials in Elementary Language and Grammar," *NSSE* 16 (1917): 103–4.

70. GG (quotation), BS, OHC; Thorndike, "Handwriting," 74 (quotation); Hugh Clark Pryor, "Spelling," *NSSE* 14 (1915): 78–89; Frank N. Freeman, "Handwriting," *NSSE* 14 (1915): 61–77; Tamara Plakins Thornton, *Handwriting in America: A Cultural History* (New Haven: Yale University Press, 1996), 66–68, 147–65; Monroe et al., *Educational Tests,* 175–82.

71. Antin, *Promised Land,* 210; Cowan, *Our Parents' Lives,* 102 (quotation).

72. Monroe, *Measuring,* 122 (quotation), 15–16, 123, 142, 148, 172, 271–72; Cordier, *Schoolwomen,* 127; MG, OHC.

73. Jessup, "Current Practices," 127 (quotation), 122–29; Finkelstein, *Governing,* 72–75; Norman Frost, *A Comparative Study of Achievement in Country and Town Schools* (New York: Teachers College, 1921), 10–12; Margaret S. Carter and Charles M. Carter, "The Value of an Education: Two 92-Year-Olds Reminisce," *Phylon* 49 (1992): 90; Monroe, *Measuring,* 98, 124–44, 173; *Psychological Examining,* ed. Yerkes, 202–34.

74. Link, *Hard Country,* 67 (quotation; Maury's italics); Theobald, *Call School,* 115–17.

75. Rice's italics, *Public-School System,* 175; RB, OHC (quotation); Adele Marie Shaw, "First-Hand Education in Sensible Schools," *World's Work* 8 (July 1904): 4996–5000; W. C. Bagley, "The Determination of Mini-

mum Essentials in Elementary Geography and History," *NSSE* 14 (1915): 132–34; Monroe, *Measuring*, 255–61.

76. Muzzey quoted in Frances Fitzgerald, *America Revised: History School-books in the Twentieth Century* (Boston: Little, Brown, 1979), 64; MY, OHC (quotation); W. C. Bagley and H. O. Rugg, *The Content of American History as Taught in the Seventh and Eighth Grades* (Urbana: University of Illinois, 1916), 15–16, 45–49; Bagley, "Determination," 143–45; Brumberg, *Going to America*, 126–27.

77. Because many children repeated first grade, second-grade enrollments more closely approximate the numbers entering school annually. *Report of the Commissioner of Education for the Year 1903* (GPO, 1905), 1176; Bureau of Education, *Statistics*, 7; Fuller, *Old Country School*, 213–14; EE, OHC.

78. RB (quotation), MC, OHC; Brumberg, *Going to America*, 125 (quotation), 130; Leonard Covello, *The Heart Is the Teacher* (New York: McGraw-Hill, 1958), 42.

79. Grossman, *Land of Hope*, 256; Ayres, *Laggards*, 37; Trennert, *Phoenix*, 111.

Chapter 4

1. Clifford Merrill Drury, "Growing Up on an Iowa Farm, 1897–1915," *Annals of Iowa* 42 (1974): 181; Mary Neth, *Preserving the Family Farm: Women, Community, and the Foundations of Agribusiness in the Midwest, 1900–1940* (Baltimore: Johns Hopkins University Press, 1995), 20–21; Jane Adams, *The Transformation of Rural Life: Southern Illinois, 1880–1990* (Chapel Hill: University of North Carolina Press, 1994), 92, 102; BB, JV, VS, HM, OHC. On nineteenth-century children's farm labor, see Elliott West, *Growing Up with the Country: Childhood on the Far Western Frontier* (Albuquerque: University of New Mexico Press, 1989), 72–90.

2. Jacquelyn Dowd Hall et al., *Like a Family: The Making of a Southern Cotton Mill World* (New York: W. W. Norton and Co., 1987), 16 (quotation); Walter W. Armentrout, "Child Labor on Farms," in *Rural Child Welfare*, ed. Edward N. Clopper (New York: Macmillan, 1922), 73 (quotation); Drury, "Growing Up," 181; Neth, *Preserving*, 21, 158.

3. MH (quotation), LS, BW, MS, OHC; William A. McKeever, *Farm Boys and Girls* (New York: Macmillan, 1912), 188 (quotations); Neth, *Preserving*, 21, 24, 158; Susan H. Armitage, "Household Work and Child-rearing on the Frontier: The Oral History Record," *Sociology and Social Research* 63 (1979): 471–72; Adams, *Transformation*, 97.

4. Era Bell Thompson, *American Daughter* (1946; reprint, Chicago: University of Chicago Press, 1974), 103; Elizabeth Clark-Lewis, *Living In, Living Out: African American Domestics in Washington, D.C., 1910–*

1940 (Washington: Smithsonian Institution Press, 1994), 41; Elizabeth Hampsten, *Settlers' Children: Growing Up on the Great Plains* (Norman: University of Oklahoma Press, 1991), 55; Adams, *Transformation,* 92–93; Elliott West, *Growing Up in Twentieth-Century America: A History and Reference Guide* (Westport, Conn.: Greenwood Press, 1996), 34–35; VP, OHC.

5. Clark-Lewis, *Living In,* 27 (quotation); Hall, *Like a Family,* 17 (quotation); JJ (quotation), HW, VS, OHC.

6. EB, HM, EF (quotations), LH, LH, DN, OHC.

7. Clark-Lewis, *Living In,* 42, 31–32 (quotations); Armentrout, "Child Labor," 71; Hampsten, *Settlers' Children,* 20.

8. PH (quotation), OHC; McKeever, *Farm Boys and Girls,* 175; Adams, *Transformation,* 103 (quotation), 102; RJ (quotation), MH, OM, OHC; Clark-Lewis, *Living In,* 25; Thompson, *American Daughter,* 47; Hampsten, *Settlers' Children,* 15; Deborah Fink, *Agrarian Women: Wives and Mothers in Rural Nebraska, 1880–1940* (Chapel Hill: University of North Carolina Press, 1992), 150–52.

9. JK, EP (quotations), OHC; Armentrout, "Child Labor," 85 (quotation).

10. EC, HW, VS (quotations), LS, OHC.

11. OP (quotation), OHC; McKeever, *Farm Boys and Girls,* 180, 193, 177, 181 (quotations); Armentrout, "Child Labor," 61 (quotation).

12. ML, AM, LS, MH, OHC; Adams, *Transformation,* 102–3; Frances Sage Bradley and Margaretta A. Williamson, *Rural Children in Selected Counties of North Carolina* (GPO, 1918), 51, 85, 88; Armentrout, "Child Labor," 56–57.

13. Peter Gottlieb, *Making Their Own Way: Southern Blacks' Migration to Pittsburgh, 1916–30* (Urbana: University of Illinois Press, 1987), 17–18; William A. Owens, *This Stubborn Soil: A Frontier Boyhood* (New York: Vintage, 1989), 13; Bradley and Williamson, *Rural Children,* 50–52.

14. U.S. Children's Bureau, *Child Labor and the Work of Mothers in the Beet Fields of Colorado and Michigan* (GPO, 1923), 1–31, 92.

15. Edward N. Clopper and Lewis W. Hine, "Child Labor in the Sugar-Beet Fields of Colorado," in *Children in the Fields,* ed Dan C. McMurry (New York: Arno Press, 1975), 178; Drury, "Growing Up," 192; HB, SP, EC, LS, OHC.

16. Armentrout, "Child Labor," 71–72; *HS,* 375–76.

17. Clark-Lewis, *Living In,* 44–46; Walter I. Trattner, *Crusade for the Children: A History of the National Child Labor Committee and Child Labor Reform in America* (Chicago: Quadrangle Books, 1970), 107–9; Virginia Yans McLaughlin, *Family and Community: Italian Immigrants in Buffalo, 1880–1930* (Urbana: University of Illinois Press, 1982), 189–93; CY, 622–23.

18. Nettie P. McGill, *The Welfare of Children in Bituminous Mining Coal Communities in West Virginia* (GPO, 1923); Trattner, *Crusade*, 72–75.

19. Hall, *Like a Family*, 49, 62, 72; Cathy L. McHugh, *Mill Family: The Labor System in the Southern Cotton Textile Industry, 1880–1915* (New York: Oxford University Press, 1988), 38–49; Trattner, *Crusade*, 240n.; CY, 638–40; I. A. Newby, *Plain Folk in the New South: Social Change and Cultural Persistence, 1880–1915* (Baton Rouge: Louisiana State University Press, 1989), 501.

20. David L. Carlton, *Mill and Town in South Carolina, 1880–1920* (Baton Rouge: Louisiana State University Press, 1982), 176, 195–96; William A. Link, *The Paradox of Southern Progressivism, 1880–1930* (Chapel Hill: University of North Carolina Press, 1992), 170–73; CY, 614–15, 659; Trattner, *Crusade*, 80–86.

21. Newby, *Plain Folk*, 138; Valerie Quinney, "Childhood in a Southern Mill Village," *International Journal of Oral History* 3 (1982): 182; Hall, *Like a Family*, 60–61.

22. Newby, *Plain Folk*, 422, 134 (quotations), 135–37, 436–37, 502; Hall, *Like a Family*, 65 (quotation), 63–64, 376n; Carlton, *Mill and Town*, 177 (quotation), 182.

23. Hall, *Like a Family*, 95, 93, 94 (quotations); McHugh, *Mill Family*, 39, 53.

24. Hall, *Like a Family*, 160, 162 (quotations), 149; Quinney, "Childhood," 168, 179.

25. IF, GG, OHC.

26. Bruce Catton, *Waiting for the Morning Train: An American Boyhood* (Garden City, N.Y.: Doubleday and Co., 1972), 181–82; Harriette Simpson Arnow, *Old Burnside* (Lexington: University of Kentucky Press, 1977), 90, 102, 112; OHC interviews.

27. Viviana Zelizer, *Pricing the Priceless Child: The Changing Social Value of Children* (New York: Basic Books, 1985), 61–62.

28. Ibid., 60; U.S. Bureau of the Census, *Sixteenth Census of the United States: 1940. Population: Comparative Occupational Statistics for the United States, 1870 to 1940* (GPO, 1943), 97; id., *Thirteenth Census*, volume 4, *Population, 1910: Occupation Statistics* (GPO, 1914), 71, 73.

29. Id., *Thirteenth Census*, volume 4, 29 (quotations); Trattner, *Crusade*, 241n; Census Bureau, *Comparative Occupational Statistics*, 89, 97; Clopper and Hine, "Child Labor," 177–78; CY, 605.

30. See West, *Growing Up with the Country*, 72–100.

31. Bureau of the Census, *Occupations at the Twelfth Census* (GPO, 1904), cli; John Spargo, *The Bitter Cry of the Children* (New York: Macmillan, 1906), 158 (quotation), 157–59, 175–79; CY, 619, 643–49.

32. Helen M. Todd, "Why Children Work: The Children's Answer," *McClure's* 40 (April 1913): 74 (quotation), 69–79.

33. Jeremy P. Felt, *Hostages of Fortune: Child Labor Reform in New York State* (Syracuse, N.Y.: Syracuse University Press, 1965), 130–33; IK, OHC.

34. David Nasaw, *Children of the City: At Work and at Play* (New York: Oxford University Press, 1986), 88–100; Elizabeth Ewen, *Immigrant Women in the Land of Dollars: Life and Culture on the Lower East Side, 1890–1925* (New York: Monthly Review Press, 1985), 152–53.

35. Nasaw, *Children,* 74 (quotation), 53, 63, 82–86, 137, 152–59, 192; CY, 627, 629; Felt, *Hostages,* 41–42, 61; LeRoy Ashby, *Saving the Waifs: Reformers and Dependent Children, 1890–1917* (Philadelphia: Temple University Press, 1984), 106–12.

36. Ashby, *Saving,* 108, 118; IK, OHC.

37. Nasaw, *Children,* 101–13; Ewen, *Immigrant Women,* 123–25; Judith E. Smith, *Family Connections: A History of Italian and Jewish Immigrant Lives in Providence, Rhode Island, 1900–1940* (Albany: State University of New York Press, 1985), 58; JA, OHC.

38. Eileen Boris, *Home to Work: Motherhood and the Politics of Industrial Homework in the United States* (Cambridge: Cambridge University Press, 1994), 108–9 (quotation), 94–110; id., "Reconstructing the 'Family': Women, Progressive Reform, and the Problem of Social Control," in *Gender, Class, Race, and Reform in the Progressive Era,* ed. Noralee Frankel and Nancy S. Dye (Lexington: University Press of Kentucky, 1991), 76; U.S. Children's Bureau, *Industrial Home Work of Children: A Study Made in Providence, Pawtucket, and Central Falls, R.I.* (GPO, 1922), 11–12, 21–30, 39–45; Nasaw, *Children,* 109–10.

39. S. J. Kleinberg, *The Shadow of the Mills: Working-Class Families in Pittsburgh, 1870–1907* (Pittsburgh: University of Pittsburgh Press, 1989), 117 (quotation); Edith Abbott and Sophonisba P. Breckinridge, *Truancy and Non-Attendance in the Chicago Schools* (Chicago: University of Chicago Press, 1917), 129, 135–43.

40. Catharine Brody, "A New York Childhood," *American Mercury* 14 (1928): 60, 61 (quotations); LF, MS, TB, MC, GG, AH, HT, LC, MG, RK, JT, OHC.

41. Ethel Spencer, *The Spencers of Amberson Avenue: A Turn-of-the-Century Memoir,* ed. Michael P. Weber and Peter N. Stearns (Pittsburgh: University of Pittsburgh Press, 1984), xxi (quotation), 42–43; Tamara K. Hareven and Randolph Langenbach, *Amoskeag: Life and Work in an American Factory-City* (New York: Pantheon Books, 1978), 246 (quotation); Zelizer, *Pricing,* 84–85, 98–99.

42. WA, RK, OHC; Daniel Horowitz, *The Morality of Spending: Attitudes toward the Consumer Society in America, 1875–1940* (Baltimore: Johns Hopkins University Press, 1985), 55, 118; Anna Koehler, "Children's Sense of Money," *Studies in Education* 1 (1897): 327–28; Zelizer, *Pric-*

ing, 98, 102; Benjamin Spock and Mary Morgan, *Spock on Spock: A Memoir of Growing Up with the Century* (Franklin Center, Pa.: Franklin Library, 1989), 9; David I. Macleod, *Building Character in the American Boy: The Boy Scouts, YMCA, and Their Forerunners, 1870–1920* (Madison: University of Wisconsin Press, 1983), 51.

43. Jacob A. Riis, *The Children of the Poor* (1892; reprint, New York: Charles Scribner's Sons, 1923; first pub. 1892), 93; Kleinberg, *Shadow,* 178; Trattner, *Crusade,* 33–41, 240n. On growing NCLC and Children's Bureau awareness of rural problems, see Lindenmeyer, *"A Right to Childhood: The U.S. Children's Bureau and Child Welfare, 1912–46"* (Urbana: University of Illinois Press, 1997), 135–36.

44. Trattner, *Crusade,* 52–73, 100, 107–9, 149–53; Carlton, *Mill and Town,* 174–95; *CY,* 650–57, following 718; Boris, *Home,* 110–15; Jane Addams, *Twenty Years at Hull House* (1910; reprint, New York: Signet Classics, 1981), 149–53.

45. Link, *Paradox,* 305 (quotation); Ardis Cameron, "Landscapes of Subterfuge: Working-Class Neighborhoods and Immigrant Women," in *Gender,* ed. Frankel and Dye, 67 (quotation); *CY,* 603; Trattner, *Crusade,* 115.

46. Trattner, *Crusade,* 82–83, 99, 120–32; Stephen B. Wood, *Constitutional Politics in the Progressive Era: Child Labor and the Law* (Chicago: University of Chicago Press, 1968), 66–154, 193–277; *CY,* 703–6.

47. Wood, *Constitutional Politics,* 82–83, 108–9, 171–72, 251–54, 260; Carlton, *Mill and Town,* 212–13; Newby, *Plain Folk,* 504, 513.

48. Trattner, *Crusade,* 148 (quotation), 112, 116; Nasaw, *Children,* 145–52. Philip M. Holleran, "Explaining the Decline of Child Labor in Pennsylvania Silk Mills, 1899–1919," *Pennsylvania History* 63 (1996): 78–95, concludes, however, that none of the common explanations, including technological change, accounts convincingly for the decline.

49. Nasaw, *Children,* 182–92; McHugh, *Mill Family,* 48–54; Hall, *Like a Family,* 60; Selwyn K. Troen, "The Discovery of the Adolescent by American Educational Reformers, 1900–1920: An Economic Perspective," in *Growing Up in America: Historical Experiences,* ed. Harvey Graff (Detroit: Wayne State University Press, 1987), 416–18.

50. Thomas Wessel and Marilyn Wessel, *4-H: An American Idea, 1900–1980* (Chevy Chase, Md.: National 4-H Council, 1982), 3–25.

51. Ibid., 22–24; E. C. Lindemann, "Boys' and Girls' Clubs as Community Builders," National Conference of Social Welfare, *Proceedings* 44 (1917): 636; Franklin M. Reck, *The 4-H Story: A History of 4-H Club Work* (Ames: Iowa State College Press, 1951), 23–132; "Boys' and Girls' Club Work in the United States," *Bulletin of the Pan American Union* 50 (1920): 305–7.

52. "Boys' and Girls' Club Work," 303 (quotation); Neth, *Preserving,* 130; Wessel, *4-H,* 32; Armentrout, "Child Labor," 64–65.

53. Raymond G. Fuller, "Rural Recreation," in *Rural Child Welfare,* ed. Clopper, 149 (quotations); JW, ML, LC, IF, EC, IP, VK, MW, AM, OHC; Ernest Burnham, *Two Types of Rural Schools* (New York: Teachers College, 1912), 28–31; Ted Ownby, *Subduing Satan: Religion, Recreation, and Manhood in the Rural South, 1865–1920* (Chapel Hill: University of North Carolina Press, 1990), 107.

54. Fuller, "Rural Recreation," 158, 159 (quotations); *Model Ts,* ed. Holt, 54; LH, MB, LD, BW, EF, VS, DN, OHC; Bradley and Williamson, *Rural Children,* 53; James Wilder and Robyn Hansen, comps., "A Glossary of Outdoor Games," in *Hard at Play: Leisure in America, 1840–1940,* ed. Kathryn Grover (Amherst: University of Massachusetts Press, 1992), 227–43.

55. E. Anthony Rotundo, *American Manhood: Transformations in Masculinity from the Revolution to the Modern Era* (New York: Basic Books, 1993), 31 (quotations), 34–47; Anne Trensky, "The Bad Boy in Nineteenth-Century American Fiction," *Georgia Review* 27 (1973): 503–17; Theodore Roosevelt, "What We Can Expect of the American Boy," *St. Nicholas* 27 (1900): 573; Macleod, *Building Character,* 52–53, 152–53.

56. BB, RF, GG, RJ, HW, OHC; B. F. Skinner, *Particulars of My Life* (New York: Alfred Knopf, 1976), 83–84, 116–23; Amanda Dargan and Steven Zeitlin, *City Play* (New Brunswick, N.J.: Rutgers University Press, 1990), 93, 186; Nasaw, *Children,* 22–33.

57. George E. Johnson, *Education through Recreation* (Cleveland, O.: Cleveland Foundation, 1916), 51–74; T. R. Croswell, "Amusements of Worcester School Children," *Pedagogical Seminary* 6 (1899): 326, 335, 344; Zach McGhee, "A Study in the Play Life of Some South Carolina Children," ibid. 7 (1900): 464–65; HT, LS, OHC; Harold Seymour, *Baseball: The People's Game* (New York: Oxford University Press, 1990), 9–10.

58. Roosevelt, "What We Can Expect," 574; Croswell, "Amusements," 326, 340; McGhee, "Play Life," 464–65; Johnson, *Education,* 57–59; J. Hammond Moore, "Football's Ugly Decades, 1893–1913," in *The American Sporting Experience: A Historical Anthology of Sport in America,* ed. Steven A. Riess (Champaign, Ill.: Leisure Press, 1984), 174–87.

59. David Macleod, "Socializing American Youth to Be Citizen-Soldiers," in *Anticipating Total War,* ed. Manfred Boemeke et al. (forthcoming).

60. Robert L. Griswold, *Fatherhood in America: A History* (New York: Basic Books, 1993), 73 (quotation); Michael C. Coleman, *American Indian Children at School, 1850–1930* (Jackson: University Press of Mississippi, 1993), 22; Robert A. Trennert Jr. *The Phoenix Indian School: Forced Assimilation in Arizona, 1891–1935* (Norman: University of Oklahoma Press, 1988), 131.

61. F. G. Bonser, "Chums: A Study in Youthful Friendships," *Pedagogical Seminary* 9 (1902): 229 (quotations), 223; A. Caswell Ellis and G. Stan-

ley Hall, "A Study of Dolls," ibid. 1 (1896): 143; LS, EK, OHC; Brody, "New York Childhood," 60.

62. Craig H. Roell, *The Piano in America, 1890–1940* (Chapel Hill: University of North Carolina Press, 1989), 8 (quotation), 17, 26, 38, 159, 186–87; id., "The Piano in the American Home," in *The Arts and the American Home, 1890–1930,* ed. Jessica H. Foy and Karal Ann Marling (Knoxville: University of Tennessee Press, 1994), 87, 92–93; Foy, "The Home Set to Music," in ibid., 63–76; Johnson, *Education,* 79–80; Spencer, *Spencers,* 89.

63. Victoria Bissell Brown, "Golden Girls: Female Socialization in Los Angeles, 1880 to 1910" (Ph.D. diss., University of California, San Diego, 1985), 227 (quotations), 134, 211; Henry D. Sheldon, "The Institutional Activities of American Children," *American Journal of Psychology* 9 (1898): 427–29; Croswell, "Amusements," 320, 330; Will S. Monroe, "Play Interests of Children," National Education Association, *Addresses and Proceedings* 38 (1899): 1085; Johnson, *Education,* 22, 64; Lee F. Hanmer and Clarence Arthur Perry, *Recreation in Springfield, Illinois* (Springfield: Springfield Survey Committee, 1914), 24; HH, MG, LC, MW, OHC.

64. LH, MH (quotations), JP, VH, MG, OHC; Rowland Haynes, "Recreation Survey, Milwaukee, Wisconsin," *Playground* 6 (April 1912): 53; Nasaw, *Children,* 29.

65. Allen Guttmann, *Women's Sports: A History* (New York: Columbia University Press, 1991), 115–25; Susan K. Cahn, *Coming on Strong: Gender and Sexuality in Twentieth-Century Women's Sport* (New York: Free Press, 1994), 15–16; J. Thomas Jable, "The Public Schools Athletic League of New York City," in *American Sporting Experience,* ed. Riess, 219–33; Brown, "Golden Girls," 269–73, 443, 455, 473; Clarence E. Rainwater, *The Play Movement in the United States* (Chicago: University of Chicago Press, 1922), 108; B. Sutton-Smith and B. G. Rosenberg, "Sixty Years of Historical Change in the Game Preferences of American Children," *Journal of American Folklore* 74 (1961): 19–20; Monroe, "Play Interests," 1085; McGhee, "Play Life," 465.

66. Johnson, *Recreation,* 49–50; Hanmer and Perry, *Recreation,* 26–28.

67. Rainwater, *Play Movement,* 242 (quotation), 8–10, 282; David Glassberg, "Restoring a 'Forgotten Childhood': American Play and the Progressive Era's Elizabethan Past," *American Quarterly* 32 (1980): 360 (quotation), 351–68.

68. Seymour, *Baseball,* 120–23; Johnson, *Education,* 52; Macleod, *Building Character.*

69. Macleod, *Building Character* (quotation), 68; Steven A. Riess, *Sport in Industrial America, 1850–1920* (Wheeling, Ill.: Harlan Davidson, 1995), 101, 142–43.

70. Jerry Griswold, *Audacious Kids: Coming of Age in America's Classic Children's Books* (New York: Oxford University Press, 1992), vii–viii; LH, HM, BD, OHC; Anne Scott MacLeod, *American Childhood: Essays on Children's Literature of the Nineteenth and Twentieth Centuries* (Athens: University of Georgia Press, 1994), 114–20.

71. Griswold, *Audacious Kids,* 20–23; MacLeod, *American Childhood,* 75–76; Daniel T. Rodgers, *The Work Ethic in Industrial America, 1850–1920* (Chicago: University of Chicago Press, 1978), 132–44.

72. Peck quoted in Gillian Avery, *Behold the Child: American Children and Their Books, 1621–1922* (Baltimore: Johns Hopkins University Press, 1994), 200; Rodgers, *Work Ethic,* 144 (quotations); Mark Twain, *The Adventures of Tom Sawyer* (1876; reprint, Toronto: Bantam Books, 1981); Booth Tarkington, *Penrod* (1914; reprint, Bloomington: Indiana University Press, 1985); MacLeod, *American Childhood,* 74–75.

73. Arthur Melville Jordan, *Children's Interests in Reading,* rev. ed. (Chapel Hill: University of North Carolina Press, 1926), 10, 18; Louisa May Alcott, *Little Women* (New York: Grosset & Dunlap, 1947), esp. chaps. 8, 41–47; MacLeod, *American Childhood,* 14–26.

74. Jacob A. Riis, *How the Other Half Lives* (1890; reprint, New York: Hill and Wang, 1957), 166; Hanmer and Perry, *Recreation,* 13.

75. Franklin K. Mathiews, "Blowing Out the Boy's Brains," *Outlook* 108 (1914): 652; *Eight Dime Novels,* ed. E. F. Bleiler (New York: Dover Publications, 1974), ix; *American Boys' Series Books,* comp. Barbara A. Bishop (Tampa, Fla.: typescript). Thanks to Francis Molson.

76. Jane S. Smith, "Plucky Little Ladies and Stout-Hearted Chums: Serial Novels for Girls, 1900–1920," *Prospects* 3 (1977): 163 (quotation), 155–74.

77. Abigail A. Van Slyck, *Free to All: Carnegie Libraries and American Culture, 1890–1920* (Chicago: University of Chicago Press, 1995), 25–26, 106–9, 174–215; David I. Macleod, *Carnegie Libraries in Wisconsin* (Madison: State Historical Society of Wisconsin, 1968), 40–41, 82–84, 98.

78. MacLeod, *American Childhood,* 123–26; Macleod, *Carnegie Libraries,* 99; Sally Allen McNall, "American Children's Literature, 1880–Present," in *American Childhood: A Research Guide and Historical Handbook,* ed. Joseph M. Hawes and N. Ray Hiner (Westport, Conn.: Greenwoood Press, 1985), 380.

79. Croswell, "Amusements," 318; Bonser, "Chums," 227.

80. Nasaw, *Children,* 124 (quotation), 116–23; Alan Havig, "The Commercial Amusement Audience in Early 20th-Century American Cities," *Journal of American Culture* 5 (Spring 1982): 8–13; David Nasaw, *Going Out: The Rise and Fall of Public Amusements* (New York: Basic Books, 1993), 27, 168–73; Johnson, *Education,* 76; Robert Sklar,

Movie-Made America, rev. ed. (New York: Vintage, 1994), 41–46; McGill, *Welfare*, 58; Haynes, "Recreation Survey," 47.

81. Jane Addams, *The Spirit of Youth and the City Streets* (1909; reprint, Urbana: University of Illinois Press, 1972), 6, 75 (quotations), 93; Nasaw, *Going Out*, 184; Sklar, *Movie-Made America*, 92, 126.

82. David Nasaw, "Children and Commercial Culture: Moving Pictures in the Early Twentieth Century," in *Small Worlds: Children and Adolescents in America, 1850–1950,* ed. Elliott West and Paula Petrik (Lawrence: University Press of Kansas, 1992), 25 (quotation), 23–25; Sklar, *Movie-Made America*, 126–33; Johnson, *Education*, 47.

83. Robert W. Lynn and Elliott Wright, *The Big Little School: Sunday Child of American Protestantism* (New York: Harper & Row, 1971), 47–54; Ownby, *Subduing Satan*, 108, 150; Thompson, *American Daughter*, 87–88; Eileen Mary Brewer, *Nuns and the Education of American Catholic Women, 1860–1920* (Chicago: Loyola University Press, 1987), 84.

84. Henry Seidel Canby, *American Memoir* (New York: Greenwoood Press, 1968), 68; Amy E. Tanner, "Contributions from the Child-Study Department of Wilson College," *Pedagogical Seminary* 13 (1906): 511–13 (quotation); Lynn and Wright, *Big Little School*, 64–65, 81; JS, JJ, LH, EE, OHC; Walter S. Athearn et al., *The Religious Education of Protestants in an American Commonwealth* (New York: George H. Doran Co., 1923), 359, 365, 419.

85. Stephen A. Schmidt, *A History of the Religious Education Association* (Birmingham, Ala.: Religious Education Press, 1983), 18 (quotations), 14–47.

86. Colleen McDannell, "Parlor Piety," in *American Home Life, 1880–1930: A Social History of Spaces and Services,* ed. Jessica H. Foy and Thomas J. Schlereth (Knoxville: University of Tennessee Press, 1992), 178, 180; AW, MH, OHC.

87. Clark-Lewis, *Living In* (quotation), 36; OHC; Burnham, *Two Types*, 35–43.

88. "Loss in Sunday-School Attendance," in John T. McFarland et al., *The Encyclopedia of Sunday Schools and Religious Education* (New York: Thomas Nelson and Sons, 1915), volume 2, 641; Athearn, *Religious Education*, 289.

89. Henry Cabot Lodge, *Early Memories* (New York: C. Scribner's Sons, 1913), 72; Ownby, *Subduing Satan*, 152; Macleod, *Building Character*, 42–44.

90. Scot M. Guenter, *The American Flag, 1777–1924: Cultural Shifts from Creation to Codification* (Rutherford, N.J.: Farleigh Dickinson University Press, 1990), 130–31 (quotation); Estelle M. Darrah, "A Study of Children's Ideals," *Popular Science Monthly* 53 (1898): 88–99; Will

Grant Chambers, "The Evolution of Ideals," *Pedagogical Seminary* 10 (1903): 101–43; David Spence Hill, "Comparative Study of Children's Ideals," ibid. 18 (1911): 219–31; Earl Barnes, "Children's Ideals," ibid. 7 (1900): 3–12; Henry H. Goddard, "Ideals of a Group of German Children," ibid. 13 (1906): 208–20.

91. Darrah, "Study," 96.

92. Sheldon, "Institutional Activities," 436.

93. Ibid., 435, 436 (quotations); Kenneth Teitelbaum, *Schooling for "Good Rebels": Socialist Education for Children in the United States, 1900–1920* (Philadelphia: Temple University Press, 1993), 4, 134.

94. Edward L. Ayers, *The Promise of the New South: Life after Reconstruction* (New York: Oxford University Press, 1992), 58 (quotation); AB, OHC (quotation).

95. VP, JK (quotations), OHC; Harry Golden, *The Right Time: An Autobiography* (New York: G. P. Putnam's Sons, 1968), 49.

96. Nasaw, *Going Out,* 167, 171–73.

97. Kenneth Porter, "Racism in Children's Rhymes and Sayings, Central Kansas, 1910–1918," *Western Folklore* 24 (1965): 191–96; Monroe, "Play Interests," 1089; Thompson, *American Daughter,* 86, 113.

98. Sarah and A. Elizabeth Delany, *Having Our Say: The Delany Sisters' First 100 Years* (New York: Kodansha International, 1993), 66–67 (quotations), 43, 53, 70–71, 78.

99. Nasaw, *Children,* 155 (quotation); James Grossman, *Land of Hope: Chicago, Black Southerners, and the Great Migration* (Chicago: University of Chicago Press, 1989), 179.

100. Mary White Ovington, *Half a Man: The Status of the Negro in New York City* (1911; reprint, New York: Hill and Wang, 1969), 40; Richard Wright, *Black Boy* (New York: Harper & Row, 1966), 30–31; JU, OHC.

101. Grossman, *Land of Hope,* 253 (quotation); Quinney, "Childhood," 170 (quotation); Sheldon, "Institutional Activities," 436 (quotation).

102. Barnes, "Children's Ideals," 10 (quotation); Chambers, "Evolution," 119–20; Brown, "Golden Girls," 7–9.

103. Brown, "Golden Girls," 195 (quotation); Kate Douglas Wiggin, *Rebecca of Sunnybrook Farm* (1903; reprint, New York: Signet Classic, 1991), 14; Macleod, *Building Character,* 51.

104. Norman Triplett, "A Study of the Faults of Children," *Pedagogical Seminary* 10 (1903): 228 (quotation), 225–28.

105. Brody, "New York Childhood," 58.

106. Bonser, "Chums," 223–24; Macleod, *Building Character,* 282; Marquis James, *The Cherokee Strip* (New York: Viking Press, 1965), 50; Nasaw, *Children,* 29–32.

107. JJ, VS, OHC; Sears Roebuck and Co., *Catalog* 118 (1909): 954–57; 134 (1917): 419, 428–29.
108. Leonard Covello, *The Heart Is the Teacher* (New York: McGraw-Hill, 1958), 44–45.

Chapter 5

1. N. Ray Hiner, "Adolescence in Eighteenth-Century America," *History of Childhood Quarterly* 3 (1975): 271 (quotation), 253–80; Alice Schlegel and Herbert Barry III, *Adolescence: An Anthropological Inquiry* (New York: Free Press, 1991), 2–3, 33–34; Harvey J. Graff, *Conflicting Paths: Growing Up in America* (Cambridge, Mass.: Harvard University Press, 1995), 253 and passim.
2. G. Stanley Hall, *Youth: Its Education, Regimen, and Hygiene* (New York: D. Appleton, 1907), 135 (quotation); id., *Adolescence: Its Psychology and Its Relations to Physiology, Anthropology, Sociology, Sex, Crime, Religion, and Education* (New York: D. Appleton, 1904), volume 2, 71 (quotation), 145–231, 292–301; volume 1, 432–71; Joseph F. Kett, *Rites of Passage: Adolescence in America, 1790 to the Present* (New York: Basic Books, 1977), 237.
3. David I. Macleod, *Building Character in the American Boy: The Boy Scouts, YMCA, and Their Forerunners, 1870–1920* (Madison: University of Wisconsin Press, 1983), 20; J. M. Tanner, *Growth at Adolescence,* 2nd ed. (Oxford: Oxford University Press, 1962), 152; Howard V. Meredith, "Change in the Stature and Body Weight of North American Boys During the Last 80 Years," *Advances in Child Development and Behavior* 1 (1963): 70–114.
4. Robert A. Woods and Albert J. Kennedy, *The Settlement Horizon: A National Estimate* (New York: Russell Sage Foundation, 1922), 77 (quotation); CY, 651 (quotation); Joseph F. Kett, "Curing the Disease of Precocity," in *Turning Points: Historical and Sociological Essays on the Family,* ed. John Demos and Sarane Spence Boocock (Chicago: University of Chicago Press, 1978), 183–211.
5. Eric C. Schneider, *In the Web of Class: Delinquents and Reformers in Boston, 1810s–1930s* (New York: New York University Press, 1992), 166 (quotation); Ellen Ryerson, *The Best-Laid Plans: America's Juvenile Court Experiment* (New York: Hill and Wang, 1978), 36–43.
6. Ryerson, *Best-Laid Plans,* 31–33, 45–46; Robert M. Mennel, *Thorns and Thistles: Juvenile Delinquents in the United States, 1825–1940* (Hanover, N.H.: University Press of New England, 1973), 107–9, 114; Steven L. Schlossman, *Love and the American Delinquent: The Theory and Practice of "Progressive" Juvenile Justice, 1825–1920* (Chicago: University of Chicago Press, 1977), 62–66, 127–30.

7. Joseph M. Hawes, *Children in Urban Society: Juvenile Delinquency in Nineteenth-Century America* (New York: Oxford University Press, 1971), 158–70, 223–46.

8. Ibid., 186 (quotation), 168; Mary E. Odem, *Delinquent Daughters: Protecting and Policing Adolescent Female Sexuality in the United States, 1885–1920* (Chapel Hill: University of North Carolina Press, 1995), 135 (quotation); David J. Rothman, *Conscience and Convenience: The Asylum and Its Alternatives in Progressive America* (New York: Harper-Collins, 1980), 233–35; Ryerson, *Best-Laid Plans*, 40–43, 77.

9. David Nasaw, *Children of the City: At Work and At Play* (New York: Oxford University Press, 1985), 23.

10. Sophonisba P. Breckinridge and Edith Abbott, *The Delinquent Child and the Home* (New York: Charities Publication Committee, 1912), 29–30 (quotation), 39; Schlossman, *Love*, 147; Rothman, *Conscience*, 250–54.

11. Peter C. Holloran, *Boston's Wayward Children: Social Services for Homeless Children, 1830–1930* (Rutherford, N.J.: Fairleigh Dickinson University Press, 1989), 246 (quotation); Schlossman, *Love*, 169–87; John R. Sutton, *Stubborn Children: Controlling Delinquency in the United States, 1640–1981* (Berkeley: University of California Press, 1988), 166–67; Elizabeth Pleck, *Domestic Tyranny: The Making of American Social Policy against Family Violence from Colonial Times to the Present* (New York: Oxford University Press, 1987), 129–32.

12. Rothman, *Conscience*, 241; Holloran, *Boston's Wayward Children*, 209–10; Schlossman, *Love*, 159–60, 177–78; Steven Schlossman and Stephanie Wallach, "The Crime of Precocious Sexuality: Female Juvenile Delinquency in the Progressive Era," *Harvard Educational Review* 48 (1978): 73–75.

13. Schneider, *Web*, 159; Rothman, *Conscience*, 254; Ryerson, *Best-Laid Plans*, 89–90; Sutton, *Stubborn Children*, 199; Evelina Belden, *Courts in the United States Hearing Children's Cases* (GPO, 1920), 41.

14. Ryerson, *Best-Laid Plans*, 92 (quotation); Schneider, *Web*, 184.

15. Odem, *Delinquent Daughters*, 8–18, 39–68, 95–102, 158–72; Ruth Rosen, *The Lost Sisterhood: Prostitution in America, 1900–1918* (Baltimore: Johns Hopkins University Press, 1982), 144; Linda Gordon, *Heroes of Their Own Lives: The Politics and History of Family Violence, Boston, 1880–1960* (New York: Penguin Books, 1988), 218–19.

16. Odem, *Delinquent Daughters*, 115, 136, 145; Schlossman and Wallach, "Crime," 68–72.

17. Odem, *Delinquent Daughters*, 177 (quotation), 176–78; Abbott and Breckinridge, *Delinquent Child*, 26, 204.

18. Belden, *Courts*, 11; U.S. Bureau of the Census, *Benevolent Institutions, 1910* (GPO, 1912), 28–29; *HS*, 15.

19. Sara A. Brown, "Delinquency and Neglect," in *Rural Child Welfare: An Inquiry by the National Child Labor Committee Based upon Conditions in West Virginia*, comp. Edward N. Clopper (New York: Macmillan, 1922), 231, 225, 226; Kate Holladay Claghorn, *Juvenile Delinquency in Rural New York* (GPO, 1918), 16, 46, 42–43.

20. George W. Fiske quoted in Macleod, *Building Character*, 100; ibid., 63–69, 114.

21. Kett, *Rites*, 173 (quotation), 194–95; Macleod, *Building Character*, 23–24, 44, 153, 261–62.

22. Macleod, *Building Character*, 48, 50, 49.

23. Ibid., 74–82, 105–6, 117–29, 259–89.

24. Ibid., 108, 284 (quotations), 154, 189–91, 282–85.

25. Ibid., 51.

26. *A Handbook for Leaders of Younger Girls* (New York: Young Women's Christian Associations, 1919), 8–9, 27.

27. Helen Buckler et al., *WO-HE-LO: The Story of Camp Fire Girls, 1910–1960* (New York: Holt, Rinehart and Winston, 1961), 22; Luther Halsey Gulick, "The Camp Fire Girls and the New Relation of Women to the World," National Education Association, *Addresses and Proceedings* 50 (1912): 325, 327; Hartley Davis with Mrs. Luther Halsey Gulick, "The Camp-Fire Girls," *Outlook* 101 (1912): 189, 182.

28. Buckler, *WO-HE-LO*, 44, 53, 139, 41, 147; MC, OHC.

29. Mary Aickin Rothschild, "To Scout or to Guide? The Girl Scout-Boy Scout Controversy," *Frontiers* 6 (1981): 115–21; Juliette Low, *Girl Scouts as an Educational Force* (GPO, 1919), 3–8; Macleod, *Building Character*, 50–51, 183–84.

30. Buckler, *WO-HE-LO*, 53; Macleod, *Building Character*, 291–300.

31. David Tyack and Elisabeth Hansot, *Learning Together: A History of Coeducation in American Public Schools* (New Haven: Yale University Press, 1990), 143 (quotation); *Report of the Commissioner of Education for the Year 1893–94* (GPO, 1896), volume 1, 33–4; Bureau of Education, *Biennial Survey of Education, 1918–20* (GPO, 1923), 7; Howard P. Chudacoff, *How Old Are You? Age Consciousness in American Culture* (Princeton: Princeton University Press, 1989), 98; HS, 374.

32. Bureau of Education, *Biennial Survey*, 507; AB, TB, MG, HH, LH, OHC; David F. Labaree, *The Making of an American High School: The Credentials Market and the Central High School of Philadelphia, 1838–1939* (New Haven: Yale University Press, 1988), 42, 45; Reed Ueda, *Avenues to Adulthood: The Origins of the High School and Social Mobility in an American Suburb* (Cambridge: Cambridge University Press, 1987), 116.

33. Kett, *Rites*, 235–36; Ueda, *Avenues*, 144–46.

34. William J. Reese, *The Origins of the American High School* (New Haven: Yale University Press, 1995), 260; Thomas W. Gutowski, "Student Initiative and the Origins of the High School Extracurriculum: Chicago, 1880–1915," *History of Education Quarterly* 28 (1988): 54 (quotation), 53–55; John E. Miller, "End of an Era: De Smet High School Class of 1912," *South Dakota History* 20 (1990): 185–206.

35. Edward A. Krug, *The Shaping of the American High School, 1880–1920* (Madison: University of Wisconsin Press, 1969), 58–65, 84–88; *Cardinal Principles of Secondary Education: A Report of the Commission on the Reorganization of Secondary Education Appointed by the National Education Association* (GPO, 1918), 10–11.

36. *HS*, 377; Tyack and Hansot, *Learning Together*, 183–220.

37. James McLachlan, *American Boarding Schools: A Historical Study* (New York: Charles Scribner's Sons, 1970) 285 (quotation); *Model Ts, Pep Chapels, and a Wolf at the Door: Kansas Teenagers, 1900–1941*, ed. Marilyn Irvin Holt ([Lawrence]: University of Kansas, Continuing Education Division, 1994), 52 (quotation); IP, OHC; Jesse Buttrick Davis, *The Saga of a Schoolmaster* (Boston: Boston University Press, 1956), 40–46.

38. Gutowski, "Student Initiative," 50–51, 60–72; Jeffrey Mirel, "From Student Control to Institutional Control of High School Athletics: Three Michigan Cities, 1883–1905," *Journal of Social History* 16 (1982): 83–100; Benjamin G. Rader, *American Sports: From the Age of Folk Games to the Age of Televised Sports*, 3rd ed. (Englewood Cliffs, N.J.: Prentice Hall, 1996), 109–11; Galen Jones, *Extra-Curricular Activities in Relation to the Curriculum* (New York: Teachers College, 1935), 17.

39. Jones, *Extra-Curricular Activities*, 20–21; Macleod, *Building Character*, 41; George F. Johnson, *Education through Recreation* (Cleveland: Cleveland Foundation, 1916), 40–41, 76; Lee F. Hanmer and Clarence Arthur Perry, *Recreation in Springfield, Illinois* (Springfield: Springfield Survey Comm., 1914), 40–42.

40. Davis, *Saga*, 128–33; Gutowski, "Student Initiative," 56–59; William Graebner, "Outlawing Teenage Populism: The Campaign against Secret Societies in the American High School, 1900–1960," *Journal of American History* 74 (1987): 411–17.

41. CY, 1308–10; H. T. Steeper, "The Extra-Curriculum Activities of the High School," *Education* 39 (1919): 369–71.

42. Aubrey Augustus Douglas, "The Junior High School," *NSSE* 15; 3 (1916): 13–43; Krug, *Shaping*, 327–35; Bureau of Education, *Biennial Survey*, 505, 516.

Bibliographic Essay

$\mathbf{S}$ince so many aspects of life impinge on the history of childhood, the literature on childhood in the late nineteenth and early twentieth centuries is somewhat scattered. Contemporary concepts of childhood prove rather elusive, though several authors trace important changes in thinking about the young. Viviana A. Zelizer, *Pricing the Priceless Child: The Changing Social Value of Children* (New York: Basic Books, 1985), posits a shift from viewing children in economic terms as only modestly valuable to seeing them in emotional terms as almost limitlessly precious. Howard P. Chudacoff traces sharpening age distinctions in *How Old Are You? Age Consciousness in American Culture* (Princeton: Princeton University Press, 1989). The ideas of child study pioneer G. Stanley Hall receive exemplary treatment in Dorothy Ross, *G. Stanley Hall: The Psychologist as Prophet* (Chicago: University of Chicago Press, 1972). Joseph F. Kett traces changing ideas of adolescence in *Rites of Passage: Adolescence in America, 1790 to the Present* (New York: Basic Books, 1977).

Since children seldom leave extensive firsthand accounts before their teens, efforts to reconstruct their experiences draw heavily on reminiscent accounts. More immediate, though stilted, testimony derives from child study questionnaires administered to children. *Pedagogical Seminary* and other journals sometimes furnish relatively unprocessed reports. An anthology re-creating children's experiences from varied sources is *Small Worlds: Children and Adolescents in America, 1850–1950,* ed. Elliott West and Paula Petrick (Lawrence: University Press of Kansas, 1992). Focusing primarily on the eighteenth and nineteenth centuries, Harvey J. Graff draws firsthand accounts from teenage diaries and later memoirs in *Conflicting Paths: Growing Up in America* (Cambridge, Mass.: Harvard University Press, 1995).

Good autobiographies offer vivid recollections of childhood, but the imaginative reconstruction required to produce satisfying narrative precludes reading these as unfiltered reporting of childish experience. An extreme example is Richard Wright's only partially autobiographical *Black Boy: A*

Record of Childhood and Youth (1945; reprint, New York: Harper and Row, 1966). More conventional autobiographies valuable to this study include Sarah and A. Elizabeth Delany, *Having Our Say: The Delany Sisters' First 100 Years* (New York: Kodansha International, 1993); Benjamin Spock and Mary Morgan, *Spock on Spock: A Memoir of Growing Up with the Century* (Franklin Center, Pa.: The Franklin Library, 1989); Ethel Spencer, *The Spencers of Amberson Avenue: A Turn-of-the-Century Memoir,* ed. Michael P. Weber and Peter N. Stearns (Pittsburgh: University of Pittsburgh Press, 1984); William A. Owens, *This Stubborn Soil: A Frontier Boyhood* (New York: Vintage Books, 1986); and Catharine Brody's evocative sketch "A New York Girlhood," *American Mercury* 14 (1928): 57–66. Twenty-Two Navajo Men and Women, *Stories of Traditional Navajo Life and Culture* (Tsaile, Ariz.: Navajo Community College Press, 1977), combines memoir and oral history. David Nasaw, *Children of the City: At Work and at Play* (New York: Oxford University Press, 1986), draws from autobiographies and other sources a lively account of immigrant children's street life. Nasaw's generally positive assessment has troubled historians who echo progressive reformers, but autobiographers resist seeing themselves as defeated victims.

Historians have turned enthusiastically to oral history to reconstruct the lives of ordinary people. In a sobering essay, "When You Listen to the Winds of Childhood, How Much Can You Believe?" *Curriculum Inquiry* 22 (1992): 235–56, Neil Sutherland warns that ordinary memory, not just the autobiographer's art, necessarily transforms the past. Sutherland believes that memories of childhood are most reliable when informants reconstruct the scripts of daily life, telling of routines rather than unique events. On the whole, I have heeded Sutherland's caution in using one of this book's major sources: the oral history of childhood collection in the Clarke Historical Library at Central Michigan University includes transcripts of more than 200 interviews with Americans born between the late 1890s and 1915. Childhoods in Michigan and neighboring states predominate, though accounts of southern experiences are fairly common. Two useful books on early-twentieth-century childhood that draw on oral history are Stephan F. Brumberg, *Going to America, Going to School: The Jewish Immigrant Public School Encounter in Turn-of-the-Century New York City* (New York: Praeger, 1986), and Elizabeth Hampsten, *Settlers' Children: Growing Up on the Great Plains* (Norman: University of Oklahoma Press, 1991). Several other books, though not centered on childhood, include vivid accounts of children's experiences based on historical interviews: Jacquelyn Dowd Hall et al., *Like a Family: The Making of a Southern Cotton Mill World* (Chapel Hill: University of North Carolina Press, 1987); Neil M. Cowan and Ruth Schwartz Cowan, *Our Parents' Lives: The Americanization of Eastern European Jews* (New York: Basic Books, 1989); and Elizabeth Clark-Lewis, *Living In, Living Out: African American Domestics in Washington, D.C., 1910–1940* (Washington: Smithsonian Institution Press, 1994).

Historians of family life and material culture are filling in the setting of children's lives, although children themselves often appear only fleetingly. Concerning families, a good introduction is *American Families: A Research Guide and Historical Handbook,* ed. Joseph M. Hawes and Elizabeth Nybakken (New York: Greenwood Press, 1991). Writing on parenting is surprisingly scant, but see Robert L. Griswold, *Fatherhood in America: A History* (New York: Basic Books, 1993), and Molly Ladd-Taylor, *Raising a Baby the Government Way: Mothers' Letters to the Children's Bureau, 1915–1932* (New Brunswick, N.J.: Rutgers University Press, 1986). Julia Wrigley, "Do Young Children Need Intellectual Stimulation? Experts' Advice to Parents, 1900–1985," *History of Education Quarterly* 29 (1989): 41–75, is broader than its title suggests. Two classic manuals sum up advice to control and segregate early childhood: L. Emmett Holt, *The Care and Feeding of Children* (New York: D. Appleton and Co., 1894 [and many editions thereafter]); Mrs. Max [Mary] West, *Infant Care,* Children's Bureau Publication No. 8 (Washington: Government Printing Office, 1914). In *A Home-Concealed Woman: The Diaries of Magnolia Wynn Le Guin, 1901–1913,* ed. Charles A. Le Guin (Athens: University of Georgia Press, 1990), a white Georgian mother of nine reflects on motherhood in practice. Many publications of the Children's Bureau report parental practices and material conditions, although modern readers will question some contemporary judgments. Frances Sage Bradley and Margaretta A. Williamson, *Rural Children in Selected Counties of North Carolina,* Children's Bureau Publication No. 33 (Washington: Government Printing Office, 1918), is especially comprehensive.

The most basic material conditions were demographic. On birthrates, one must consult specialized articles such as those cited in my notes. On infant mortality, see Samuel H. Preston and Michael R. Haines, *Fatal Years: Child Mortality in Late-Nineteenth-Century America* (Princeton: Princeton University Press, 1991), and Robert Morse Woodbury, *Causal Factors in Infant Mortality: A Statistical Study Based on Investigations in Eight Cities,* Children's Bureau Publication No. 142 (Washington: Government Printing Office, 1925). Richard A. Meckel, *Save the Babies: American Public Health Reform and the Prevention of Infant Mortality, 1850–1929* (Baltimore: Johns Hopkins University Press, 1990), and Charles R. King, *Children's Health in America: A History* (New York: Twayne Publishers, 1993), describe the responses of physicians and urban reformers.

Cultural influences shaped children's activities. On clothing, see Jo B. Paoletti and Carol L. Kregloh, "The Children's Department," in *Men and Women: Dressing the Part,* ed. Claudia Bush Kidwell and Valerie Steele (Washington: Smithsonian Institution Press, 1989), 22–41. Most studies of play and toys mix folklore and antiquarianism, but Bernard Mergen, *Play and Playthings: A Reference Guide* (Westport, Conn.: Greenwood Press, 1982), is helpful. Surveys of children's literature are drearily encyclopedic. Instead, read Anne Scott MacLeod's splendid *American Childhood: Essays on Children's Literature of the Nineteenth and Twentieth Centuries* (Athens: University of Georgia Press, 1994), and classics such as Kate Douglas Wiggin, *Rebecca of Sunnybrook Farm* (1903; reprint, New York: Signet Classics, 1991).

Insightful introductions to progressive reform include Richard L. McCormick, "Public Life in Industrial America, 1877–1917," in *The New American History,* ed. Eric Foner (Philadelphia: Temple University Press, 1990), 93–117; Robert M. Crunden, *Ministers of Reform: The Progressives' Achievement in American Civilization, 1889–1920* (Urbana: University of Illinois Press, 1984); William A. Link, *The Paradox of Southern Progressivism, 1880–1930* (Chapel Hill: University of North Carolina Press, 1992); and for reference, *Historical Dictionary of the Progressive Era, 1890–1920,* ed. John D. Buenker and Edward R. Kantowicz (New York: Greenwood Press, 1988). On child welfare, Ronald D. Cohen, "Child-Saving and Progressivism, 1885–1915," in *American Childhood: A Research Guide and Historical Handbook,* ed. Joseph M. Hawes and N. Ray Hiner (Westport, Conn.: Greenwood Press, 1985), and Susan Tiffin, *In Whose Best Interest? Child Welfare Reform in the Progressive Era* (Westport, Conn.: Greenwood Press, 1982), survey historical writing. For an influential contemporary summary, see John Spargo, *The Bitter Cry of the Children* (New York: Macmillan, 1906). Two excellent studies of policy formation are Robyn Muncy, *Creating a Female Dominion in American Reform, 1890–1935* (New York: Oxford University Press, 1991); and Molly Ladd-Taylor, *Mother-Work: Women, Child Welfare, and the State, 1890–1930* (Urbana: University of Illinois Press, 1994). LeRoy Ashby, *Saving the Waifs: Reformers and Dependent Children, 1890–1917* (Philadelphia: Temple University Press, 1984), furnishes valuable case studies. Kriste Lindenmeyer, *"A Right to Childhood": The U.S. Children's Bureau and Child Welfare, 1912–46* (Urbana: University of Illinois Press, 1997), describes bureau programs. Linda Gordon, *Heroes of Their Own Lives: The Politics and History of Family Violence, Boston 1880–1960* (New York: Penguin Books, 1988), offers a trenchant critique of reform in practice. *Children and Youth in America: A Documentary History,* volume 2: *1866–1932,* ed. Robert H. Bremner et al. (Cambridge, Mass.: Harvard University Press, 1971), itself two volumes, reprints a wealth of documents centering on reform and public policy.

Historians of education have produced a large and disputatious literature since the 1960s, but the best goes much beyond polemic. Lawrence A. Cremin, *The Transformation of the School: Progressivism in American Education, 1876–1957* (New York: Vintage Books, 1961), is still fresh. Important progressive-era texts include J. M. Rice, *The Public-School System of the United States* (New York: The Century Co., 1893); John Dewey's readable *The School and Society* (Chicago: University of Chicago Press, 1907); and Leonard P. Ayres, *Laggards in Our Schools: A Study of Retardation and Elimination in City School Systems* (New York: Charities Publication Committee,

1909). On the limited influence of Cremin's reformers, see Herbert M. Kliebard, *The Struggle for the American Curriculum, 1893–1958* (Boston: Routledge and Kegan Paul, 1986), and Ellen Condliffe Lagemann, "The Plural Worlds of Educational Research," *History of Education Quarterly* 29 (1989): 185–214. David Tyack and his collaborators set progressive-era debates in a broad perspective. See especially David B. Tyack, *The One Best System: A History of American Urban Education* (Cambridge, Mass.: Harvard University Press, 1974), and David Tyack and Elisabeth Hansot, *Learning Together: A History of Coeducation in American Schools* (New Haven: Yale University Press, 1990). Studies of policy at the local level abound. Three of the best are Patricia Albjerg Graham, *Community and Class in American Education, 1865–1918* (New York: John Wiley and Sons, 1974); William J. Reese, *Power and the Promise of School Reform: Grassroots Movements during the Progressive Era* (Boston: Routledge and Kegan Paul, 1986); and Ronald D. Cohen, *Children of the Mill: Schooling and Society in Gary, Indiana, 1906–1960* (Bloomington: Indiana University Press, 1990).

Specialized studies have proliferated. On midwestern rural schools, see Wayne E. Fuller, *The Old Country School: The Story of Rural Education in the Middle West* (Chicago: University of Chicago Press, 1982), and Paul Theobald, *Call School: Rural Education in the Midwest to 1918* (Carbondale: Southern Illinois University Press, 1995). Studies of southern schooling include William A. Link, *A Hard Country and a Lonely Place: Schooling, Society, and Reform in Rural Virginia, 1870–1920* (Chapel Hill: University of North Carolina Press, 1986); James D. Anderson, *The Education of Blacks in the South, 1860–1935* (Chapel Hill: University of North Carolina Press, 1988); Robert A. Margo, *Race and Schooling in the South, 1880–1950: An Economic History* (Chicago: University of Chicago Press, 1990). The most comprehensive of many good studies of boarding schools for Native Americans is David Wallace Adams, *Education for Extinction: American Indians and the Boarding School Experience, 1875–1928* (Lawrence: University Press of Kansas, 1995). On kindergartens, see Barbara Beatty, *Preschool Education in America: The Culture of Young Children from the Colonial Era to the Present* (New Haven: Yale University Press, 1995). Edward A. Krug, *The Shaping of the American High School, 1880–1920* (Madison: University of Wisconsin Press, 1969), describes policy formation, and Thomas W. Gutowski, "Student Initiative and the Origins of the High School Extracurriculum: Chicago, 1880–1915," *History of Education Quarterly* 28 (1988): 49–72, questions the accepted narrative of adult imposition. Unfortunately, historians have rarely studied actual teaching or student learning. Although Barbara Finkelstein, *Governing the Young: Teacher Behavior in Popular Primary Schools in Nineteenth-Century United States* (New York: Falmer Press, 1989), discusses mainly the years before 1890 and Larry Cuban, *How Teachers Taught: Constancy and Change in American Classrooms, 1890–1980* (New York: Longman, 1984), emphasizes the years after 1920, both offer valuable perspectives.

Like historians of education, writers on juvenile justice have weighed the balance between uplift and control. Joseph M. Hawes, *Children in Urban Society: Juvenile Delinquency in Nineteenth-Century America* (New York: Oxford University Press, 1971), offers lively narrative and a generally positive assessment. David J. Rothman, *Conscience and Convenience: The Asylum and Its Alternatives in Progressive America* (New York: HarperCollins, 1980), judges juvenile justice more harshly, as on the whole does Steven L. Schlossman, *Love and the American Delinquent: The Theory and Practice of "Progressive" Juvenile Justice, 1825–1920* (Chicago: University of Chicago Press, 1977). Mary E. Odem, *Delinquent Daughters: Protecting and Policing Adolescent Female Sexuality in the United States, 1885–1920* (Chapel Hill: University of North Carolina Press, 1995), also finds most reforms unhelpful or worse.

Other progressive-era innovations to uplift and supervise the young have received limited coverage. Walter I. Trattner, *Crusade for the Children: A History of the National Child Labor Committee and Child Labor Reform in America* (Chicago: Quadrangle Books, 1970), sees the issue exclusively through reformers' eyes. Dominick Cavallo, *Muscles and Morals: Organized Playgrounds and Urban Reform, 1880–1920* (Philadelphia: University of Pennsylvania, 1981), centers on ideology. There is yet no counterpart to David I. Macleod, *Building Character in the American Boy: The Boy Scouts, YMCA, and Their Forerunners, 1870–1920* (Madison: University of Wisconsin Press, 1983), on organizations for girls.

For fine surveys of childhood in previous and subsequent decades and for good bibliographic advice, see Priscilla Ferguson Clement, *Growing Pains: Children in the Industrial Age, 1850–1890* (New York: Twayne Publishers, 1997); Joseph M. Hawes, *Children between the Wars: American Childhood, 1920–1940* (New York: Twayne Publishers, 1997); and Elliott West, *Growing Up in Twentieth-Century America: A History and Reference Guide* (Westport, Conn.: Greenwood Press, 1996).

Index

The Author

David Macleod is professor of history at Central Michigan University, where he teaches courses on American social history, the progressive era, and childhood and youth in the United States. His previous publications include *Building Character in the American Boy: The Boy Scouts, YMCA, and Their Forerunners, 1870–1920.*

The Editors

Joseph M. Hawes is a professor of history at the University of Memphis. His most recent book is *American Children between the Wars, 1920–1940* (Twayne, 1997).

N. Ray Hiner is Chancellors' Club Teaching Professor of History and Education at the University of Kansas. He has published widely on the history of children and education in the United States and is coeditor (with Joseph M. Hawes) of *Growing up in America* (1985), *American Childhood* (1985), and *Children in Historical Perspective* (1991). He is currently writing a book about children in the life and thought of Cotton Mather.